Praise for *Careers*

"*Careers By the People* should be on every guidance counselor's desk—and in every student's backpack. It's crisp, honest, informed, and wonderfully entertaining. At last, a practical, accessible guide for anyone seriously committed to finding that 'perfect' job!" **—Coit D. Blacker, professor emeritus, Stanford University**

"Don't have time to test-drive 101 career paths to uncover what each one is really like? Thanks to Mike Wysocki, you won't have to. Packed with thought-provoking and snackable wisdom, *Careers By the People* is like eavesdropping on others' coffee chats, 101 times over." **—Gorick Ng, Harvard University career and first-gen student adviser;** *Wall Street Journal*–**bestselling author of** *The Unspoken Rules*

"*Careers By the People* is an invaluable resource for anyone pursuing the skills and educational credentials necessary for a rewarding career. Capitalizing on the wisdom and experience of professionals in a wide range of disciplines, this engaging and accessible guide is a must for students and graduates seeking a pathway toward professional fulfillment." **—John Kennedy, vice chancellor for University Relations, University of Massachusetts Amherst**

"I love this book! If you're exploring career paths or hoping to manage or start a business, here's the road map of how real people think and feel about what they do all day. *Careers By the People* goes beyond facts and statistics and reveals with scintillating candor: How does this job feel? How can my work create meaning and value? How can I have a good life?" **—John Bowe, co-editor of** *Gig: Americans Talk About Their Jobs*

"While many books are interesting, and others make you think about your life, Mike Wysocki has written something that combines both these traits but also adds a helpful message about what one should do in life. Every young person should read this book before they decide on their career choice; older people, like myself, should read this book before they change jobs. One could also read *Careers By the People* just to get a sense of what people are doing in America today." **—Carl Rogers Ackerman, PhD, author of** *A Success Story in Public Education: The Clarence T. C. Ching PUEO Program at Punahou and its Partnership-Marriage Methodology*

"This is an outstanding book on navigating your way through job transitions. Wysocki and the plethora of professionals who provide their stories really help the reader understand the difference between jobs and careers and how to navigate this space. I wish I had read this book several years ago when I exited from the military into corporate America." **—Jay Garcia, senior manager, Fortinet Veterans Program & Community Engagement**

"*Careers By The People* is a must-read for anyone entering the workforce or someone looking to challenge themselves and their career. This book is about that life-changing journey that can help anyone become successful in their career and lead a happy work/life balance." **—Roy G. Burr, MBA, career services, Alcorn State University**

"*Careers By the People* provides students with perspective into a vast array of career paths that cannot be learned in a classroom. As a college senior, this insight by professionals from various fields provides students with crucial insight to explore different careers that may be suitable for them." **—Kyle Murphy, Suffolk University, class of 2022**

"*Careers By the People* catalogs 101 careers and lets the reader explore them through the voices and experiences of the folks who live them. Author Mike Wysocki uses a personal and authentic tone to help the next generation avoid getting stuck in a career they dislike; or worse, potentially missing out on the perfect career because they never even know about it. I can't wait to use this resource with my own students as they explore their own post–high school paths and opportunities." **—Tara Lindsey, high school academic dean and junior advisor and internship coordinator, Kihei Charter School, Hawaii**

"*Careers By the People* helps to bring clarity to the messiness of career development by personalizing stories that offer unique perspective and valuable insight." **—JAKE Small, assistant director, Boston University College of Communication Career Services**

"This book is the perfect starting point for anyone seeking to explore new professional opportunities. As a career counselor with interest in hearing others' career stories, this is a collection of mini biographies written in a conversational way that makes it easy and enjoyable to read. As someone who works with job seekers who want to learn about different roles, organizations and industries, this book makes this step much easier. Each person's story provides candid answers to questions job seekers would be asking in informational interviews. This is an incredibly valuable resource that offers job seekers a glimpse of so many different jobs and careers while also providing them with both information and context that they can use as a starting point for further research." **—Anne Grieves, associate director, Career Design, Northeastern University**

"Students thrive when provided with straightforward, honest advice, and *Careers By the People* is like having candid conversations with dozens of experienced professionals about what works (and doesn't) when making important career decisions. An excellent resource for anyone getting started in the workforce or diving deeper into their goals." **—Julie Morikawa, president, ClimbHI**

"*Careers By the People* is a must-have for high school and college students unsure what to do with their careers. It should also be a must-read for those in their early careers who want to find more meaningful options to consider." **—Byron C. Scott, MD, MBA, adjunct faculty, Isenberg School of Management, University of Massachusetts Amherst**

"*Careers By the People* offers interesting answers to questions about career choices from a variety of different professions. When it comes to the details of day-to-day work life, this book holds jobs from customer service to CEOs in the same esteem. This is an essential resource of honest input to guide any young person's career path." **—Juli Patao, associate professor of cooperative education and CareerLink director, University of Hawaii Maui College**

"Reading *Careers By the People* is like speed-networking with 101 different careers at a time. You'll come away from this book with a strong understanding of the entire landscape of careers available to you, as well as the peaks and pitfalls hidden within each and every field." **—Montgomery Thomas, associate director for alumni and graduate career strategy, Suffolk University**

"*Careers By The People: Candid Career Advice from 101 Experienced Professionals* is exactly the kind of book I wish I had when I was first thinking about what to do with my life a few decades ago. It would have saved me a lot of time and effort in sorting out the various options available to me—many of which I had no idea even existed. Mike Wysocki has assembled an invaluable resource that anyone at any point in their work life can consult when considering pursuing a particular line of work—or moving into a completely new occupational arena. Finally, we get to hear sound advice and recommendations from those who are actually in the careers they are describing. This kind of first-hand insights are hard to come by these days as most of the books written in this genre involve second-hand perspectives and interpretations. But Wysocki takes you directly to the source. In fact, I plan to use *Careers By the People* in my graduate class on career development. I highly recommend this exquisite little primer for anyone who has ever wondered if they are in the 'right' field for them—and what alternatives might be possible." **—Aaron Hughey, university distinguished professor in the department of counseling and student affairs at Western Kentucky University**

"At CareerSpring, we recognize that information and advice from real-world professionals are critical components of career access and success. *Careers By the People* presents an array of first-person accounts of career experiences grouped by personality type, making it easy for the reader to navigate toward the careers they're interested in—as well as ones they'd never before considered." **—Paul Posoli, founder, CareerSpring**

"While profoundly unveiling the curtain, *Careers By the People* does more than exemplify what it means to join the workforce but furthermore introduces scenarios and ideologies of which prove to be conducive to understanding realities and fiction within differentiating industries." **—Rainier Gracial, senior at California Baptist University**

"The world of work is changing fast. Information about work in the digital age is plentiful yet hard to assess for accuracy. *Careers By the People* is a guidebook through some of the obstacles workers face as they navigate the twenty-first-century world of work. The information comes straight from the source via interviews with 101 workers representing 101 different career experiences. The types of work represented span all social classes and geographies. The questions asked, and answered, are the kinds career-seekers wish they could ask employers outside the job interview setting. This book is an essential resource for teachers, counselors, academic advisors, coaches, and more. It is also an excellent tool to put in the hands of career-seekers young and mature as they embark on a journey of exploration and success." **—Dr. Brian Hutchison, a.k.a. Global Career Guy, core faculty, Walden University**

"We all have our own strengths and challenges, and finding a 'good fit' career takes exploration, experimentation, and sometimes time to find our way. Wysocki's collection of interviews can provide a good step to expanding one's view of potential careers through the voices of others." **—Cathy Kim, PhD, National Board–certified teacher, technology integration & learning sciences, math & science education, Pacific Lutheran University**

"*Careers By the People* is a valuable resource for job-seekers of all ages that uses relatable language and diverse perspectives to explore the realities of a wide range of career fields. As a nonprofit focused on ensuring K–12 students are prepared to succeed in the careers of their dreams, HawaiiKidsCAN believes this book is a great complementary piece to efforts like Hawaii Career Pathways, where students can take assessments, view compensation data, and see the specific credentials needed to enter the field. We hope this book will be widely available to students as they consider their post–high school opportunities." **—David Sun-Miyashiro, founding executive director, HawaiiKidsCAN**

"*Careers By the People* is a valuable resource for people who are considering their career options and want to get a glimpse into a wide range of occupations. Before you commit to a particular path, gain insight and save time by learning from people who have come before you." **—Erica Mattison, certified career coach, founder and CEO, Erica Mattison Coaching & Consulting, LLC**

"I really enjoy the personal insights from varying careers in this book. All too often, people over-glorify and under-stress certain aspects of their career transition, and this serves as a good resource to dispel that." **—Peter M. Cline, founder and director of Boots to Books, Army Infantry veteran**

"In *Careers By the People*, Mike Wysocki does a wonderful job of showing all the possibilities out there to create a great life for yourself! I highly recommend this book to anyone who is charting a new path for their future." **—Ken Rusk, construction entrepreneur and author of the bestselling book *Blue Collar Cash***

"*Careers By the People* provides an accessible way for job seekers, new and returning, to gain valuable insight on 101 careers. Wysocki's collection of interviews will change the way universities advise students on career planning, by allowing students to match their level of education with possible career paths. This text will allow job seekers to see the best and the worst of job options, so they can make informed decisions regarding their career planning." **—Jared W. Miller, MA, student support advisor, DeVry University; adjunct instructor, Bellevue University**

"Having hope for the future is a key characteristic a young person can have to help them persevere through adversity. *Careers By the People* is a practical, insightful tool that can help teens and young adults create a vision for the future and believe they can achieve it. This book should be required reading in high schools, career centers, and college orientations." **—Ashley King Nittle, director of communications, PRO Youth & Families**

"For some of us, a job is just a means to an end; for others, a job is the crux of our lives. No matter which one you are, *Careers By the People* is a valuable resource for anyone questioning where to place their professional skill and worth. As author Mike Wysocki reminds us, our careers fill up at least forty years of our lives—this book will help you determine how to spend that time wisely so you don't look back on it with regret." **—Philip Wilkerson, host of the *Positive Philter* podcast and Positive Philter LLC; higher education and career development professional**

"This is a fun book because you get to hear what real people think about their jobs and what it took to get there." **—Dr. Janet Wall, founder, Career Planning Academy**

CAREERS BY THE PEOPLE

Candid Career Advice
from 101 Experienced Professionals

Mike Wysocki

ISBN 13: 978-1-63489-574-3

Library of Congress Catalog Number has been applied for.
Printed in the United States of America
First Printing: 2022

26 25 24 23 22   5 4 3 2 1

Cover by Mayfly Design

Wise Ink Creative Publishing
807 Broadway St. NE
Suite 46
Minneapolis, MN 55413

For my parents, Edward and Gloria. Even though you have passed, your guidance and persistence that I rebelled against as a youth are now understood.

AUTHOR'S NOTE

The best way to approach *Careers By the People* is to read the introduction, then the occupations that most interest you, and then the conclusion. Also, make sure to review the "Talking Points" section. You can review the professions that are less compelling to you at your leisure.

CONTENTS

CHAPTER TWO: THE HUSTLERS

CHAPTER THREE: THE EINSTEINS

CHAPTER FOUR: THE ROCK STARS

CHAPTER FIVE: THE GOOD KIDS

CHAPTER SIX: THE PERFECTIONISTS

INTRODUCTION

"I'll Figure It Out"

I've been selling technology solutions for years, and I'm decent at it. But that's all: just decent. After all this time, I'm still not stellar at it because, ultimately, it doesn't interest me. Sure, I've met nice people and made some lifelong friends along the way, but I never look forward to Mondays or have any passion for what I do. Working in sales in the technology field is considered a solid and stable profession because the media and employment guides emphasize how lucrative it can be. This assumes that money leads to happiness, success, and/or career satisfaction. Sure, money helps, but there's more to a profession than a fat commission check. After thirty-plus years in the trenches, I don't know many in sales who actually enjoy it. It's a daily grind.

I'm not alone. According to recent research, almost half of all Americans are dissatisfied with their jobs. With a workforce of 157 million people, that is an astronomical statistic. It also offers a compelling motivating factor for the current rise in both graduate school applications and prescription drug sales.

So, why are so many people unhappy? A significant reason for many workers' discontent is the fact that most did not actively choose their careers. Instead, they allowed the market to dictate their decisions. This may have been based on factors like population trends, economic bubbles, and even marketing hype. There should be little surprise, then, that people feel alienated and disgruntled with something that takes up so much of their waking life.

I compiled this book to help you make a wise, informed choice when choosing a profession. The 101 interviews assembled in this book are just the tip of the iceberg when it comes to your options in the job market, but rarely do you ever find such candid insights about how real-world workers feel about their jobs. *Careers By the People* exists as an antidote to the haphazard approach to crucial career decisions that is sadly so widely accepted and perpetuated in our society. Choosing a career may be one of the most difficult and important decisions in life, but its importance is very often neglected.

One reason people approach their job hunt like they're playing a game of darts is that the search is time consuming and filled with frustration. With time constraints and limited resources, many people find it impossible to adequately research careers and/or industries to determine the best fit for their interests, aspirations, and talents. With no career focus or foundation in place, in time the search for money, happiness, or stability prompts them to drift from one job to the next without any professional game plan beyond leaving their current position for another. They only know they have to make a change. What's more—and unfortunately for the job seeker— professional headhunters tend to have the employer's best interests in mind rather than the employee's. In my day, career counseling was usually delegated to the teacher who drew the short straw in the principal's office. Most career offices have stepped up their game since then, so the advancement of opportunity has shifted in your favor, increasing the chances of you acquiring the profession you truly desire.

But sometimes that gets you only so far. Once you've landed in the right place, it isn't always clear how to ascend in your chosen profession. Some jobs, like sales, have similar responsibilities across industries, while others, like electrical engineering, are highly specialized. As a result, what may be the next logical step for one person might not make sense for another.

What it really comes down to is finding a field that holds your interest and continually challenges you. After that has been decided, the question becomes: What can you do that will make you an expert in that area? What literature exists that will teach you more about a subject? What will inspire you to learn more? Maybe it's finance. How does the market work? What are the hottest companies to invest in? What's the next growth market? Perhaps it's the field of real estate, medicine, law, technology, entertainment, environment, government—or the myriad unexplored careers related to space exploration. The goal is to find that one field and remain in it so you can pole vault your career to the moon.

> *"I coulda been a contender. I coulda been somebody."*
> —Marlon Brando as Terry Malloy in *On the Waterfront*

Don't Just Watch the Game. Be *in* the Game.

Careers By the People is a guidebook for anyone out there who isn't satisfied with being a cog in the machine and wants to be intrigued and challenged by their profession. This book will tell you if the grass really is greener on the other side—but if that side isn't greener, maybe there's an entirely different field.

The concept for this book came about during a brisk walk in New York's Upper East Side. A childhood chum noted to me that, after being an officer in the navy and a corporate attorney at a prestigious firm, he knew two careers he shouldn't have chosen. Then again, where could he have received career advice forty years ago—the office of a guidance counselor? Most guidance counselors have been in academia for the majority of their lives and have no idea what it's like to be an archaeologist; they only know what an archaeologist does. "Career" books? Most are vague and focus on "best jobs," "hot jobs," or "safe jobs," but don't feature real day-to-day data from industry veterans.

There is a lot of bad advice out there, and I've received my fair share of it. Here are a few stories from my life that motivated me to write *Careers By the People*:

- As a kid, I was told I would never get hired at the post office. I was advised, "Don't set your goals so high. You will never make it into the post office."

- My high school counselor was a waste of time. No matter how much I told him I wanted to go to college, he always said to go into the military or a trade. Finally, the guy told me to apply to Boston State—and it didn't exist.

- In college, I was at the career center when I spotted a magazine cover that read, "What's a Demographer?" I picked up the magazine right before getting called in to speak with the career counselor. I have no idea what we talked about. A week passed. When I went back to get the magazine, it wasn't there. Damn! I should have "borrowed" it. The cover still haunts me. Might have been a solid career choice.

- I attended a wedding where a man talked to me about careers. He said, "No matter what, don't be an insurance adjuster; it sucks. The client and your manager will always hate you. I did it for forty years." So, this guy not only hated his job but had also been doing it for forty years. Years later, I learned that the best sales reps are former insurance adjusters. They get treated so poorly that being in sales is like heaven. That's saying something—working in sales sucks.

- My first job out of college was with Fidelity Investments, which was known as one of the best places to work in Boston. The hiring manager went to the University of

Massachusetts; we hit it off, the interview went well, and I made the cut. I was eager to figure out how to make it up the ladder, but I kept hitting roadblocks. I didn't see a future there. I even talked to a few fund managers and they said to leave and get more experience in banking. So, I left to sell insurance and make the big bucks . . . and lasted all of six months. Years later, I was investing with Fidelity and I asked my representative about his career. He loved it. I wish I hadn't given up so easily, but I had no focus and had been listening to the wrong people. Bottom line: Before you leave a position hastily, triple-check with associates in other departments. Get feedback. Talk with human resources and try to find a career path if you happen to make it into an awesome organization. When you go for cash over passion, be wary. I could tell you stories of working for less-than-honorable men and shady deals and scenarios that would call anyone's ethics into question. I think it's best summed up by another former Weymouth resident, Hal Holbrook, as Lou Mannheim in Oliver Stone's *Wall Street*: "Man looks in the abyss, there's nothing staring back at him. At that moment, man finds his character. And that is what keeps him out of the abyss."

- In my first week in distribution sales, one of the hotshot sales reps told me about an associate he had just spoken with. The associate had the "prime" job: product manager. The hotshot rep said that being a product manager opened doors to bigger and better things—power and money. Three years later, I became a product manager. Six months after that, I quit. Why? It was the worst job I'd ever had.

Due to such low expectations in life, I truly thought I was going to end up pumping gas at the station up the street from my house. It's shocking how many people think you can't make it or fear failure so much that they project their trepidations onto you and treat you like a child.

Every Path Leads to Retirement. Which One Are You On?

As you move through this book, note that no career is perfect. With the good comes the bad. When I'm having a bad day in sales, I remind myself that it's better than being a roofer in the summer in Phoenix, Arizona.

To make the best use of *Careers By the People*, readers are encouraged to approach it like a restaurant guide, browsing a range of options to see what sparks their curiosity. Read the stories of others through your own unique lens. Use the information provided here to help you understand yourself. Do you need to be the center of attention (think of a VP of sales) or are you more of a behind-the-scenes type (think director of operations)? Do you like puzzles? Maybe engineering is a decent choice for you. Are you all right with gridlock? Perhaps you should pursue a position in government. Can you handle constant failure? If so, you would be a natural at sales. Again, your career is likely to last forty years. What can get you motivated over and over, day after day, hour by hour, week after week, month after month, year over year, decade upon decade? In one of the final scenes in *Good Will Hunting*, Robin Williams's character drills Matt Damon's character with the question, "What do you want to do?" Damon's character avoids the question with sarcasm. But your life isn't a movie. So, what is it? What do you want to do?

The objective of *Careers By the People* is to help you narrow your search so that you don't exhaust yourself trying to find the profession that resonates with you. Your first goal should be to determine a few career choices that most interest you. This might take a month or a year, but the amount of time it requires is not nearly as important as finding a profession that has the potential to keep you motivated, challenged, engaged, and fulfilled long term. From there, conduct research on the best occupations for you. Perhaps find an internship or volunteer, both of which I'll cover more in the final pages. The idea is to help you clarify what calls to you. That time spent will save you from years of grief and grinding.

Here's another eye-opening reason that the surveys in this book are so powerful. Ask someone in their forties about their career satisfaction, and usually they're more confused by the question than the newly graduated, or embarrassed by their choices and rarely positive about them. Maybe they chose well, or maybe they will just lie to you and themselves. Sure, they might have some assets, but are they in any way fulfilled or expecting to be?

Many are not, and just as many hold out hope. Although they may have been through terrible gigs and failed jobs, they still have faith in finding one that clicks. The type of job where you want to wake up earlier and be the first one in the office or on the phone; where Monday morning doesn't begin with the blues; where you actually feel that you're accomplishing something and not wasting time; where you feel that you're part of something, contributing to the betterment of society and receiving some measure of gratification; where you are mentally stimulated; where you are respected; where your decisions count. A job that empowers you to be good at something, or even great.

This is the whole justification for *Careers By the People*. The hope is that this book offers you ideas and angles to get what you want, so you can determine what is the occupation for you instead of taking that "safe job" and being a cog in the machine. Think of the Brando quote. It's one of the most iconic scenes in film because it resonates with everyone. All Brando's character wanted to do was to make it in life. He just wanted to "be somebody."

Keep in mind that rarely does someone say, "Wow, ballsy move! Go for it!" But I believe they should—at least in an informed way. Get some insight on being in "X" career before you put ten years into trying to get that prestigious job only to discover that you hate it and yourself for making poor choices. Why waste precious time?

"I became an archaeologist. Before long, my career was in ruins."
—unknown

Forge Your Own Path, but Learn from Others

The designations of these chapters were modeled after psychologist John Holland's six personality types, the Holland Occupational Themes. Holland published these traits in the late 1950s, along with the theory that people generally fell into one of six categories based on what types of careers suited their personalities. To this day, the Holland Occupational Themes are still a popular tool career counselors use to help people with their career placement. Under the following titles, *Careers By the People* is reissuing them for the modern world:

- Enterprise: The Ballers (the leaders)

- Realistic: The Hustlers (the people who get things done)

- Investigative: The Einsteins (the thinkers)

- Artistic: The Rock Stars (the creators)

- Social: The Good Kids (the helpers)

- Conventional: The Perfectionists (the organizers)

The goal of these surveys is to help you determine the smartest career choice through the decisions others have made. I hope the candid interviews in the following pages will help you gain a clearer picture of what different professions entail.

You'll find that *Careers By the People* is focused on and dedicated to those who haven't figured out what they want to do. I skipped "glamorous" jobs because there is enough info on "the good life" on TV. Many books offer career advice or info on "hot careers" and are typically written by people with their own agendas, yielding profiles of a given field that are more sociopolitical descriptions of a type of worker than useful snapshots of the field itself. This is the only book that actually talks to people who have been in their fields for roughly five or more years and offers an unvarnished view of what it is to be, say, an actuary or a merchant marine.

Think of it this way: *Careers By the People* has done all the legwork for you so you don't make the same mistakes I did. Selling isn't bad. My clients and partners are respectable folks. But technology doesn't interest me much, and, as I said, I wish I had found my passion—or at least half of it. I wish I could wake up on Monday to what I should be doing or what I should have done.

As I compiled this book, my goal was to seek out experts in a range of professions. I wanted them to tell their stories and provide an honest, inside look at their careers. I researched and determined a detailed list of questions to understand their professions and what they thought about their choices after spending years in their chosen careers. I asked them more than twenty questions so readers could compare responses across industries. Inquiries ranged from "What issues have prevented your advancement?" to "How much fulfillment do you get out of your career?" I not only concentrated on "big-ticket" careers such as professors, executives, and lawyers, but also included manual labor jobs like farmers and beekeepers. The aim was to cover the whole gamut of careers. What are the pros and cons of each profession, and why? What is a day in the life of a chief executive officer (CEO) like, or that of a registered nurse? What do these people say about their careers when no one is around, and what do they really want to do? (Their last names have been withheld so that they could truthfully tell their stories without backlash.)

Over the course of five-plus years, I collected hundreds of responses. The most enlightening replies are included here.

The majority of responders you'll find in the following pages are located throughout the United States. I grouped the questionnaires into six chapters based on Holland's six personality types so that you can easily find the surveys that strike you as the most interesting, original, and helpful. You might find some responses funny. Others may be depressing. Others still might be thought provoking. All are authentic and eye opening.

Go for the Gusto!

> *"All our dreams can come true, if we have the courage to pursue them."* —Walt Disney

My theory is that anyone can be good at something. I'm good at technology sales, but I really wanted to be great at something. Life might have been easier if I had determined the best career path early on and crushed it in that profession. Being the expert, the go-to, the leader in any field offers self-worth, and when your occupation is something you enjoy and keeps you yearning for more . . . well, that equals genuine success plus a beach house in Maui.

True, being an expert isn't for everyone. Perhaps you only want to find something that you abide by for forty hours per week. So, you really have to think it through. What drives you? If you're a couch potato, maybe it's selling couches or building the best couch to watch sports on?

Also true: You can apply the principles outlined on pages 535–538 to acquire a forty-hour-a-week profession. Jobs without grueling hours are typically in government, insurance, operations, remote work, retail, and a few others. These opportunities will be less profitable but, if chosen properly, may be more enjoyable—and come with less stress—than other careers. Believe it or not, some government and federal positions offer pensions, which are as archaic as it gets; it's like seeing a Connecticut Yankee in King Arthur's Court riding on a unicorn.

An interesting example of these types of professions can be found in chapter 3. Lisa, a database developer from Detroit, loves her vocation and never works overtime, and all of her training was performed on the job—a point that she asserts may be stunning to some, whereas in reality, the technology industry is more informal about your educational background as long as you are willing to be trained and certified on aspects of your job. Since I spent thirty years in IT, I know that it's not uncommon to work with associates who forgo college for technical certifications so they can enter the technology world. Moreover, if you are open to living in an affordable location, like Lisa, you can have more control over your choice of professions than if you lived on the coasts.

One example I always think of is a sales friend in Milwaukee. He informed me that he was quite happy being in technology sales. "Wysocki, I don't deal with the big-city stress. We don't make LA money, but also my bills are less. My company treats us well and the management is nice. My house cost is a third of yours and the wife and I live a simple life."

Also, don't overlook blue-collar jobs, as they can be quite satisfying. Being outdoors, engaging in physical labor, learning different aspects of a vocation—all can be the perfect fit for some people. Ken Rusk offers insight into this in his book *Blue Collar Cash*. You still have to do your career homework, though; breaking rocks in the hot sun will not be as enjoyable as designing a mid-century modern house. My buddy toiled at a post office job for over three decades and noted its pros and cons. It's a union gig, so getting fired is almost impossible. Roughly 60 percent of the time—or twenty years of your career—your supervisor is fair. And, if you live frugally, you can cope. One major selling point to a forty-hour-a-week occupation is once you're off the clock, you're done for the day. Many other fields, like sales, never end. When your client calls, you take the call or risk losing the client. So, through some examples we can see that getting what you want is the easy part. Figuring out what that is—now that's the hard part. Is the grass greener?

When putting together *Careers By the People*, I came across some amazing success stories. A few professionals who loved their jobs said that the best part of their career was the freedom they found. "I make all the choices," one said. "I love it. I can play on a recording session for twelve hours straight, then come home and have the desire to play even more. I am highly paid and get to travel everywhere." There are several who genuinely look forward to the start of their workweek.

Not everyone does, though—think of those statistics I mentioned earlier—and those stories are included in this book as well.

People spend hours determining what TV to buy, months on what car to purchase, and years on what house to procure, but how much time do they spend on what career to choose? It's a decision that will wrap up thirty to forty years of people's lives, but they don't research or test these jobs out; they simply hear "good career," "it makes money," "you will always have food and stability," "it's the future"—and other such pragmatic things—and go for it. In sports, you have a ten-year career—if you're lucky. In corporate America, you may be in your profession for forty-plus years. Graduate college at twenty-two and retire at sixty-two—forty years. So why not make those forty years enjoyable?

Don't blow it. Focus on what you can do and want to do—and do it well.

> *"If you think you got what it takes, shove it out, run it up the flagpole, and see who salutes it."* —Lemmy Kilmister

Forty Years Is a Long Time. Slow Down and Focus Up!

During my career in technology, I've watched in amazement as people jump to other fields for a few years, such as mortgage brokerage, then bounce back to tech. It screams instability.

Sure, everyone deserves a mulligan here and there, but with no consistency, one usually loses in both professions.

One career survey noted that 30 percent of people change career paths every year. Bouncing careers may not be a sound option if it makes you a jack-of-all-trades and a master of none. Lack of dedication to a field limits your potential—and that usually shoots you in the foot. In fact, by retirement, the average worker has floated through sixteen different jobs. With the help of *Careers By the People*, readers could cut that number in half and find professional satisfaction much earlier in their careers.

After all, in thirty years, do you want to be writing about what you should have done, or do you want to do it now? I'm a grinder. Thirty years of grinding. Seeking, digging, and finding business. Closing a deal and having to find another one over and over again, quarter after quarter, year after year. If you want "stable" work, the world always needs grinders. C'mon, it's a blast!

But there's an alternative. Let's start with the ideas in this book, the occupations and questions that will give you enough ammunition to help you nail down your choices. Read through the 101 career questionnaires. Choose what interests you, then read about a few others to learn a little more. Absorb these experts' thoughts like I did when I spoke to the insurance adjuster who worked for forty years in a profession he despised. This is your chance to network with 101 people you have just met. Take in the wisdom of why they did what they did and how they perceived their professions. Read about their successes and failures, their opinions and ideas. This is your shot to hear the truth about the working world. Hopefully, you can pick up a nugget or two that can save you from years of anguish, boredom, and malaise. Let's start this journey. Or, as Axl Rose once said, "Welcome to the jungle."

CHAPTER ONE
The Ballers

PRESIDENT AND CHAIRMAN OF THE BOARD

Name

Eric F.

Location

Portland, Oregon

Education

Master of Business Administration

Total years in profession

28

Brief occupation description/goal of occupation

Managing high-tech businesses in Europe and North America. Building businesses; restructuring business start-ups and large Fortune 500 companies.

Why did you choose this career path?

In 1983, I decided to become the top boss and got an MBA (master of business administration), as I felt I had been passed over in a reorganization due to changes in management. Ever since then, I have been the managing director, CEO (chief executive officer), or chairman of the ventures I have been in.

What do you like about your occupation?

I like building businesses, defining customer needs and delivering on them, and managing people. It is very exciting to see the fruit of a lot of planning and work. The speed of innovation in high tech is addicting.

What do you dislike about your occupation?

I hate down cycles when the whole industry contracts and you have to lay off people to cope with the downturn. I hate dealing with people who are dishonest—and there are a lot of them around.

What are the misconceptions about your profession?

The biggest misconception is that a business trip is a vacation. The second one is that TV has made the general public believe that business leaders live a sweet life with lots of parties and lots of assistants to do the work while they play golf. I do not know of any high-tech start-ups that were built by people playing golf—on the contrary, it is a lot of hard work with many periods of fourteen-plus working hours, seven days a week.

On a scale of 1 to 10 (10 being great), how would you rate your occupation and why?

I would say 10. Being a president, CEO, and/or chairman is high on the self-realization pyramid and gives good reinforcement to one's ego on a daily basis. Being the top dog for more than twenty years now, it would be difficult for me to do anything else.

What factors or former positions led to this occupation?

Product development, followed by a sales job in the period of 1978–1983, with an MBA completed in 1984 that led to becoming a business leader.

What career choices were most helpful?

During high school and college, I already knew that I wanted to become a business leader, but I didn't know how to get there. My first job as a product developer was handed to me the day I graduated from engineering school, but I was not the typical lab-oriented person, so I looked for a job in sales just two years after graduation. After four very successful years in sales, I quit my job, sold my house, and went to business school, where I got my MBA. That was the move that put me on the shelf I wanted to be on. Everyone I knew thought I was crazy, because they wanted me to stay in the job I had—no one supported this, so I had to make the decision against all odds.

What career choices were least helpful/detrimental?

I can't point to any one detrimental decision, as I have gotten out on the other end in a better career situation every time. However, there are some: biting off larger challenges than I was really ready for. It is very, very risky—and looking back, I am not sure I would have given myself the same job opportunities had I been the one hiring. Acquiring the wrong companies at the wrong time. During a few of my jobs I have been in charge of acquisitions that went up to $2 billion in size and prices; some of these have not worked out, and when you are using other people's money in such large amounts, they get a bit upset when the payback does not happen.

Did you have a mentor? If so, how did you find them? Did they help?

I did not have a mentor. Through business school, I picked up one very close friend, and we have supported each other along the way. But no, I have not been able to have or use a mentor. I am actually a mentor for a number of younger people today and wish I'd had the wisdom to listen to experience when I was younger.

What type of education was needed for your position?
Engineering plus MBA.

Was your formal education necessary for this position?
In the beginning, yes, but now it is based on track record and experience.

Do you have to update your career with ongoing training and certificates?
Yes, I go to some brush-up business courses once every second or third year, which is more to get inspired and maintain a network.

Is your work environment "hectic," "all work and no play," "serene," "laid back," or other? Briefly explain.
Hectic. A few years back, I played golf once a week; last year, I played one round. I do get to do other things—like go on vacations with the family, etc. Right now we are in a build-up phase, and that requires a lot of overtime.

What types of conflicts do you deal with?
Mainly business related in terms of what people expect to get out of using our product. Some human resource issues; they come and go.

Do you interface with coworkers, groups, or vendors, or do you work alone?
Yes, I interface with thousands of people.

What is management like?
My BOD (board of directors) is very, very competent and one of the best I have ever worked with, an extremely good working climate—a chemistry among all of us.

Is input accepted, or do you fare better as a "yes man"?

Input is accepted; that is how we build the enterprise.

Is your position secure, or are you frequently looking for the next opportunity?

It is secure at this time—the company is doing very well. If we start not to do so well, my job will be on the line.

How important is/was networking or connections in finding your current or other positions? Is it a factor in advancement once you're on the job?

It was my network that put me in this job.

What would be your next career move?

A similar CEO, president job.

Do you relocate often? Are there travel requirements?

I relocated a lot in my early career; today we stay put where we are.

If you could choose again, how much would money be a factor?

Money is a big factor when you don't make a lot of it. As you start making more money, it becomes less of a factor, but I would not take a job today for a lower salary than what I have today.

Would you choose the same career path?

Yes, but in a more controlled manner.

Any comments or words of advice for someone entering your field?

Yes: Be patient, be realistic, and use your tools to map out the strategy. Don't believe in other individuals until they have proven they are worth believing in.

CHIEF EXECUTIVE OFFICER (CEO)

Name

Richard K.

Location

Los Angeles, California

Education

Bachelor of Science in Mechanical Engineering; coursework in Engineering Management and Master of Business Administration

Total years in profession

28

Brief occupation description/goal of occupation

I am cofounder/CEO/president of a software company in information security. This is the second software company I have started. My goal is to grow this company and sell it. Over my career, I have worked with eight start-up or early-stage companies. Of those, I was involved with three acquisitions and one IPO (initial public offering).

Why did you choose this career path?

I had always aimed to be in upper management since the beginning of my career at a large auto manufacturer. I was told that I had to gain experience in multiple areas to grow into a position of upper management.

What do you like about your occupation?

I love the ability to start something from scratch. This provides a lot of freedom and responsibility for my own success. In start-ups and smaller companies, there are no real politics like those that exist in larger companies.

What do you dislike about your occupation?

It is actually a lot of work and effort, and very "lonely at the top." When working for a company or person, you are able to talk openly to associates. As CEO, you have to look for support from outside people, rather than internal.

What are the misconceptions about your profession?

CEOs are constantly in the news for making millions, getting golden parachutes, etc. In a start-up, none of that exists. As you get a great reputation, that can come in handy at larger companies. But the reward here is the stock options.

On a scale of 1 to 10 (10 being great), how would you rate your occupation and why?

I would say 9 (no such thing as a 10)—I love what I do and the ability to help run a company.

What factors or former positions led to this occupation?

I was always intrigued by being in management. I would rather work smart, not hard. Somehow, I saw that as the end goal here. Along the way, I worked with and managed a number of different types of groups in engineering, computer networks, software, programming, and, ultimately, sales. Having worked and managed in each of these areas helps in an overall management role. After that, I have worked at a number of other start-ups, starting sales and marketing efforts. Then I founded the company I am at now.

What career choices were most helpful?

Early on, I moved across the country three times for career opportunities. First, I moved to get out of the automotive industry during the industry's downturn; then I moved back to the Midwest to run CAD (computer-aided design), then back to California for the sales opportunity (especially since I had fallen in love . . .).

What career choices were least helpful/detrimental?

I really did not have any career choices that were not helpful or detrimental. I have always moved up and progressed in my career with each position.

Did you have a mentor? If so, how did you find them? Did they help?

I have had a few. I found them at companies that I worked with, and sometimes through associations of mine. They were very helpful in providing education, direction, and strategy for me at various positions along the way.

What type of education was needed for your position?

I learned to program at the age of fourteen, so I started my relationship with computers then. That probably helps the most. Then my MBA is the other part of my education that was essential in terms of running the business.

Was your formal education necessary for this position?

I use a lot of different areas of my education, as well as experience from my past careers, on a daily basis. But for the most part, I find that degrees are good for teaching you how to organize and do research. Those two skills are probably the most important for me.

Do you have to update your career with ongoing training and certificates?

Ongoing training has occurred in the areas of sales, negotiations, time management, personality resource management, etc.

When you were hired, did you receive professional training or was it basically "on-the-job training"?

On-the-job training. Since I started the company, I would have had to train myself.

In a typical week, are your hours fixed or flexible? On what days do you tend to work overtime?

My workweek is a very long one. I am based in California and have a development center in Raleigh, NC, so I usually get on email at 6:30 a.m. and work through to 6:00 p.m. Then, after dinner, I will get back on the computer. I also need to spend time working on the weekend as well.

Is your work environment "hectic," "all work and no play," "serene," "laid back," or other? Briefly explain.

I am presently working from home, and I work hard and smart. There isn't a lot of time to play, but my dogs do like to stop in and say hi from time to time, so it's not quite all work and no play . . . they won't let me!

What types of conflicts do you deal with?

Someone once told me, you know your company is becoming successful when you start to have personnel problems. Since people are the core of the business, the biggest conflicts are with the people, both internally and externally.

Do you interface with coworkers, groups, or vendors, or do you work alone?

I interface with everyone—employees, our outsourced sales, and the resellers we have throughout the country.

Is input accepted, or do you fare better as a "yes man"?

I love input of all types. Our company policy is that saying something is wrong without a solution is whining. And we serve cheese with wine.

Is your position secure, or are you frequently looking for the next opportunity?

Very secure. I am the major stockholder in the company, so . . . unless someone wants to buy us.

How important is/was networking or connections in finding your current or other positions? Is it a factor in advancement once you're on the job?

Networking and connections are extremely important in all aspects of life.

How much fulfillment do you get out of your career?

I love my job and get a lot of fulfillment from it. I truly appreciate the opportunity to start companies and love what I am doing with the technology.

If you could choose again, how much would money be a factor?

A lot of money for a job with a miserable working environment is not good, and too little money in the same environment is also not good. At the same time, money plays a part of the total package.

Would you choose the same career path?

Absolutely. But I am not done . . .

Any comments or words of advice for someone entering your field?

Doing a start-up these days is a lot different than it was in the past. Funding is a lot more difficult in some sectors and takes a lot longer. Work out the business plan and figure out a doable plan. Then take the timeline you calculated and double it. Then take the funding you need and double that.

INDEPENDENT INVESTOR

Name

William R.

Location

Rapid City, South Dakota

Education

Doctor of Philosophy—ABD Doctor of Philosophy; "all but dissertation"

Total years in profession

37

Brief occupation description/goal of occupation

After getting a good education, I became an assistant to the chancellor of a national university. After less than two years (managing research money for the university), a partner and I started our own money management firm.

Why did you choose this career path?

Because at age twenty-seven I decided to retire. Not in the sense that I would stop working, but in the sense that I wanted to be my own man. I decided that I would never work for anyone else, that I would live where I wanted to live, and that I would do whatever I wanted to do.

What do you like about your occupation?

Freedom. I have lived on the seashore of Southern California, high in the mountains (beside Mt. Shasta), and for the past twenty-two years at the foot of a mountain near a very rural small town of about four hundred people.

What do you dislike about your occupation?

Nothing. I have loved every minute of it. It has been over ten years since I have been to my office to work. I sold the office building last year, but my business is still operating. I manage my personal accounts from my home office and my laptop.

What are the misconceptions about your profession?

Biggest misconception: it is easier to work for someone else than it is to run your own show. It takes brains, drive, and desire—in reverse order—to be an independent entrepreneur. Many forget the reverse order part.

On a scale of 1 to 10 (10 being great), how would you rate your occupation and why?

I rate my chosen path as a 10 because it gave me everything I ever wanted from life. It provided freedom, a great life for my family, the satisfaction of helping others, and wealth beyond the dreams of avarice.

What factors or former positions led to this occupation?

My work at a major university led me to quickly realize that life at the top of a big organization is very comfortable, but confining. I wanted independence and the ability to go wherever my desire, drive, and brains could take me.

What career choices were most helpful?

The start of my career required several difficult choices: stop working on my PhD, take a job in California, resign my comfortable chosen position, and set out on my own. After those decisions were made, it was all smooth sailing.

What career choices were least helpful/detrimental?

Whenever I let others make decisions for me, I was sorry thereafter.

Did you have a mentor? If so, how did you find them? Did they help?

I had several people whom I learned a lot from, like professors and vice chancellors, but no one who eased my way through the ins and outs of my career choices. By definition, an independent investor relies on himself.

If you didn't have a mentor, would you have liked one?

Things have turned out so well for me that I can say no. During my active days, I did learn a lot from those I dealt with . . . a group of very successful people.

What type of education was needed for your position?

My profession was part art (the part no one could teach you, but you had to be able to do) and part knowledge-based. I would say that the abilities to think, write, and communicate clearly were needed but were not sufficient.

Was your formal education necessary for this position?

No, but I feel my education helped me an awful lot.

**In a typical week, are your hours fixed or flexible?
On what days do you tend to work overtime?**

I did not/do not consider my chosen path to be work. Early on, I put
in lots of time (I slept on the floor next to my desk when I had to), but
something I enjoyed so much could not possibly be work. By age
fifty, I was cutting back, and by age fifty-five I stopped going to my
office so I could spend all my time managing my personal affairs.

**Is your work environment "hectic," "all work and no
play," "serene," "laid back," or other? Briefly explain.**

I would say busy, enjoyable, rewarding. I made all the rules . . . and
one was that I would never wear a watch . . . because I did not care
what time it was.

What types of conflicts do you deal with?

Problems were solved quickly; conflicts never really existed. This all
gets back to the fact that I was making all the rules I lived by.

**Do you interface with coworkers, groups,
or vendors, or do you work alone?**

A partner and I worked together for almost thirty years with our
clients, a few vendors, and a small staff.

**Is your position secure, or are you frequently
looking for the next opportunity?**

Right now I spend my days trading a few of my own accounts, and
living the life I have lived since my late twenties . . . doing whatever I
feel like doing.

**How important is/was networking or connections
in finding your current or other positions? Is it a
factor in advancement once you're on the job?**

Not for me, because I ran my own show. I started with very little
and ended up with lots. When you run your own show, you can
give yourself whatever title and whatever position you want in your

organization . . . as long as you are successful. I designed my own reality, and in that reality failure was never an option.

What would be your next career move?

I am slowly cutting back and will soon begin to transfer the fruits of my life to my children and grandchildren. It is very difficult to transfer assets to others who do not have the education you gained while accumulating them.

Do you relocate often? Are there travel requirements?

I moved twenty times in the eight years I spent in college. Since then I have moved only five times, and the last move was twenty-two years ago. My travel requirements were always minimal.

Do you prefer going to work or leaving? Why?

I did not work. I spent my time sharing knowledge and helping others become successful investors, and in the process I helped myself. I went to my office at dawn and came home when I felt like it . . . usually as darkness approached.

How much fulfillment do you get out of your career?

A great deal. As I have said, my career put me in a position to help clients, family, and myself. And I never had to "work" to do it.

Do you feel that you are fairly compensated?

My salary was limited only by what I could earn in my consulting and trading activities. I was a multimillionaire by my late thirties, and I have never looked back.

If you could choose again, how much would money be a factor?

Money was never the prime objective, in my view. It is secondary to a lot of other things. But as an old gal I knew once told me, money cannot buy happiness, but it sure can buy convenience. It is nice if you can get happiness and money in the same package.

Would you choose the same career path?

Yes, without hesitation.

Any comments or words of advice for someone entering your field?

Following an independent path is not for everyone. Independence requires a particular mindset and the ability to prosper on your own. If you can meet the requirements, I believe you can live the good life. I am still enjoying every minute of my adventure.

MORTGAGE BANKER

Name

Robert L.

Location

San Francisco, California

Education

Bachelor of Arts

Total years in profession

13

Brief occupation description/goal of occupation

Secure the lowest mortgage rates with the best customer service to build a big book of referral business.

Why did you choose this career path?

Real estate has always been my passion. When I had a chance right out of college to work on the financing end of real estate, I jumped on it immediately, and I am still doing it with passion.

What do you like about your occupation?

I deal with people from all walks of life (from CEOs of major corporations to the average person who is just trying to make it).

What do you dislike about your occupation?

It has become so overcrowded with people who want to jump in to make a quick buck, then leave the industry. These inexperienced agents have given a bad name to our industry.

What are the misconceptions about your profession?

Easy and fast money. This industry carries the 80/20 rule. Twenty percent of the top agents make 80 percent of the money.

On a scale of 1 to 10 (10 being great), how would you rate your occupation and why?

I would say an 8. It is a challenging and exciting industry; however, the long hours do take their toll on the family life.

What factors or former positions led to this occupation?

Real estate, finance, and sales.

Do you have to update your career with ongoing training and certificates?

Yes, the DRE (Department of Real Estate) requires continuing education every few years.

When you were hired, did you receive professional training or was it basically "on-the-job training"?

I had to first get my DRE license, and then I took a bunch of professional training courses.

In a typical week, are your hours fixed or flexible? On what days do you tend to work overtime?

Flexible, but I work many weekends and evenings when realtors call me to quote their clients.

Is your work environment "hectic," "all work and no play," "serene," "laid back," or other? Briefly explain.

Hectic. There is never a dull moment at work.

What types of conflicts do you deal with?

Nervous first-time homebuyers who get cold feet at the very end of the transaction.

Do you interface with coworkers, groups, or vendors, or do you work alone?

I interact with vendors all day (escrow, appraisers, realtors).

What are your coworkers like?

A great group of people.

What is management like?

Efficient and no-nonsense.

Is input accepted, or do you fare better as a "yes man"?

Input is accepted.

Is your position secure, or are you frequently looking for the next opportunity?

I have a very secure job.

How important is/was networking or connections in finding your current or other positions? Is it a factor in advancement once you're on the job?

Networking is very important.

Do you relocate often? Are there travel requirements?

No relocation and no traveling required.

Do you prefer going to work or leaving? Why?

Going to work; a new day and another buck.

How much fulfillment do you get out of your career?

My career is extremely challenging, and it pays well; thus, I am completely fulfilled.

If you could choose again, how much would money be a factor?

A lot.

Would you choose the same career path?

Yes.

Any comments or words of advice for someone entering your field?

You have to be a self-motivator in order to succeed in this industry.

VICE PRESIDENT OF ADMINISTRATION

Name

Michelle W.

Location

Houston, Texas

Education

Master of Science

Total years in profession

16

Brief occupation description/goal of occupation

Oversee all accounting, human resources, information technology, office management, and mailroom functions of the company.

Why did you choose this career path?

Career advancement opportunity, availability of positions regardless of location, prior on-the-job training, ability to work in an ever-changing position and wear many hats.

What do you like about your occupation?

I like the fact that my position allows me to wear different hats while becoming involved in various aspects of the company. If one department is slow, another one will certainly be picking up. Being involved in most of the company's day-to-day functions ensures that I can see the "bigger picture," and (therefore) position myself as a viable strategic planner.

What do you dislike about your occupation?

Dealing with areas that do not allow for creativity—especially accounting. I prefer being allowed to develop out-of-the-box solutions to various company problems, so I tend to excel in the strategic areas where guidelines are not so black and white.

What are the misconceptions about your profession?

That I get paid a lot of money! Also, I run into issues where people in departments that I do not manage believe I fully comprehend each detail of the business. Ideally, I will be able to become well versed in every service-oriented arena; however, until that time, my focus remains on the back-end business operations. I also tend to be nominated as the "point person" for numerous tasks, and this can sometimes become overwhelming.

On a scale of 1 to 10 (10 being great), how would you rate your occupation and why?

I would say 7. Because I work for a small company, it can be difficult to properly delegate tasks to direct reports. While I don't want to personally become overworked, I also don't want to overwork my employees. This can result in my taking on additional roles that I don't really have time for, and that takes away from the time I wish to spend on strategic planning and problem solving.

What factors or former positions led to this occupation?

I started off as an administrative file clerk and was allowed the opportunity to grow and learn additional tasks by various employers. Gradually, my accounting tasks were increased and, once I reached the point of negotiation with other clients and vendors, the HR tasks were added. The VP of administration seemed like a natural progression.

What career choices were most helpful?

Admin Professional to HR Administrator/Interfranchise Collections Specialist functions; Business and Financial Operations Manager.

What career choices were least helpful/detrimental?

Commissions Support Analyst via Superior Technical Resources— only because this reinforced my least favorite task: accounting.

Did you have a mentor? If so, how did you find them? Did they help?

Yes, past supervisors who may have no idea how their guidance and suggestions helped me along the way.

What type of education was needed for your position?

A high school diploma (or GED) was required for my first position; however, applied knowledge was the main factor in my reaching my current position. Truly, my education has been a non-issue and was pursued for strictly personal reasons. Despite graduate education, what has helped me has been supervisors who recognized my ability to grasp new ideas and, ultimately, had faith in me.

Was your formal education necessary for this position?

Not outside of high school. My résumé and experience were utilized in order to progress to various positions. In order to achieve my ultimate goal, simply learning the industry and related laws is most of what is required.

Do you have to update your career with ongoing training and certificates?

I choose to. The only certification I've obtained is the PHR (Professional in Human Resources), and I do maintain that status via ongoing training.

When you were hired, did you receive professional training or was it basically "on-the-job training"?

On-the-job training.

In a typical week, are your hours fixed or flexible? On what days do you tend to work overtime?

They are fixed for the most part, though I am pretty free with time off, etc. I do work a lot of overtime, as I enjoy working in the office when most others aren't there. The days I choose to devote to overtime are Tuesdays and Fridays.

Is your work environment "hectic," "all work and no play," "serene," "laid back," or other? Briefly explain.

The work environment is a mixture that I call "hectic but fun." I work with the other employees in an attempt to relax the atmosphere and keep everyone talking, venting, and sane. Sometimes, the mere act of having someone who understands your situation listen and offer advice can make all the difference. We take monthly group lunches and are developing a list of other group tasks that we can do for fun—out of the office.

What types of conflicts do you deal with?

Personnel conflicts: personalities of employees and other managers that don't click, insecure managers who tend to bark orders, insecure employees who are too afraid to take on a new task or ask for help, and individual employee issues involving self-esteem and/or tardiness.

Do you interface with coworkers, groups, or vendors, or do you work alone?

I interface with other coworkers, vendors, and clients.

What are your coworkers like?

Fun-loving, dedicated, willing to put in extra time to accomplish tasks; burned out, afraid of the future, overwhelmed.

What is management like?

Most are sympathetic, willing to listen and do what's best for the company, determined to create and maintain a happy/healthy environment; a few are insecure in their own abilities and tend to lash out at other employees—particularly those employees who clearly have lower self-esteem.

Is input accepted, or do you fare better as a "yes man"?

Input is accepted whether solicited or not.

What issues have prevented your advancement?

The area I currently live in is not known for its booming job market. The town is an industry town that focuses on the refining business, so anything outside of that is viewed as secondary. I also, personally, waver on how much responsibility I wish to take on. This can cause self-inflicted limits.

Is your position secure, or are you frequently looking for the next opportunity?

Though I do consider my position as secure as the owners', I am also always looking for opportunities. I believe that you reap what you sow, which means it's important to keep my "feelers" out there in an effort to accomplish my personal goals.

How important is/was networking or connections in finding your current or other positions? Is it a factor in advancement once you're on the job?

Networking has not (yet) made a difference; however, I regularly maintain and communicate with my network in the event that I need to call on anyone for any reason. In my current job, I focus on maintaining respectful relationships with all employees. While I consider this the right thing to do, I also know that you never know when you might need to utilize an extra set of hands to complete a task. Willing participants do a much better job than those involuntarily selected.

What would be your next career move?

I want to be the VP or director of operations for my company (or a similar company).

Do you relocate often? Are there travel requirements?

No—though I do want to return to Austin, TX. Travel requirements are less than 25 percent; however, there are random occasions where travel is needed.

Do you prefer going to work or leaving? Why?

I prefer leaving because I am not a morning person. I feel accomplished at the end of my day, and I like to relish that feeling.

How much fulfillment do you get out of your career?

This job is not as fulfilling as my last, but I do enjoy the fact that constant learning is a necessity. My undergraduate degree is in music, and I would probably feel more fulfilled if my job was in a performing arts arena and/or more creative.

If you could choose again, how much would money be a factor?

If I had another job to consider, I probably would not have chosen this one due to salary. I felt and still feel that I was supposed to select this position, despite the pay cut, and I therefore believe this position will ultimately pay off.

Would you choose the same career path?

Probably.

Any comments or words of advice for someone entering your field?

Pay attention to the ever-changing laws and to court cases. Read up on what it takes to maintain a company, and focus on how those standard tasks relate to the business at hand. Remember to stay in touch with field experts and be willing to think outside the box.

VICE PRESIDENT
OF INFORMATION
TECHNOLOGY

Name

Michael S.

Location

Nashville, Tennessee

Education

Some college and military

Total years in profession

45

Brief occupation description/goal of occupation

It began as a programmer and elevated through all the various IT (information technology) paths (e.g., analyst, manager, director, and finally to VP).

Why did you choose this career path?

It was my job in the navy, and computers were relatively unheard of when I got out of the service. IT types were hard to find, so job opportunities were plentiful, and most in the field job-hopped, which made them tremendous pay increases each time.

What do you like about your occupation?

Independence, creativity, and challenge.

What do you dislike about your occupation?

Over time, once folks got used to computers they expected things to be done yesterday, and as a result a lot of sloppy un-debugged programs entered the marketplace.

What are the misconceptions about your profession?

That we could perform miracles and automate anything without taking the required time to analyze the manual tasks. The more we researched, we found many doing their jobs without actually knowing how to do them. In other words, many did their jobs by rote or found comfort zones and never paid attention to details. As a result, many systems had to be scrapped.

On a scale of 1 to 10 (10 being great), how would you rate your occupation and why?

I would say 10. Seeing various tasks come to fruition and productivity increase for the company is gratifying. Once we gained workers' trust, they began cooperating more, which led to us being able to create systems that made their jobs easier.

What factors or former positions led to this occupation?

The US Navy—I never heard of a computer until I joined and they sent me to many IBM schools for training. From there, I simply had what it took to understand how they worked and why they worked. Like they say, the rest was history.

What career choices were most helpful?

Having this background enabled me to do consulting and help others as well as my own company.

What type of education was needed for your position?

Logic, business acumen, and a will to learn with a desire to face challenges head-on.

Was your formal education necessary for this position?

Nowadays most colleges offer IT courses and degrees. When I came out of the navy, I had the equivalent of today's PhD; besides, all one had to say was that they worked on computers in the service and they were hired on the spot.

Do you have to update your career with ongoing training and certificates?

In the early stages, yes, but it reached a point where it wasn't necessary unless a new computer was being introduced.

When you were hired, did you receive professional training or was it basically "on-the-job training"?

Very professional, by IBM's best teachers; after all, the government was paying IBM to train their service personnel, and we worked on many top-secret projects, so it had to be done right the first time around.

In a typical week, are your hours fixed or flexible? On what days do you tend to work overtime?

Anywhere from sixty to ninety hours, and during installations there were times we worked right through holidays.

Is your work environment "hectic," "all work and no play," "serene," "laid back," or other? Briefly explain.

Early on it could get hectic, but as you grow into more management roles, it gets calmer. This type of career path is always laden with a certain amount of pressure, mainly due to the fact that some software isn't fully debugged.

What types of conflicts do you deal with?

Mostly people afraid of losing their job to some machine.

Do you interface with coworkers, groups, or vendors, or do you work alone?

We always worked with a variety of folks depending on what the need was; for example, a new application, a new system, etc.

What are your coworkers like?

For the most part extremely creative and studious. There were many along the way who couldn't take the pressure and caved in.

What is management like?

There are many who don't belong in these positions and got them mainly from longevity, not ability.

Is input accepted, or do you fare better as a "yes man"?

Being a yes man is a killer in the IT world; we always had to dig deep to get facts.

How important is/was networking or connections in finding your current or other positions? Is it a factor in advancement once you're on the job?

It's extremely important . . . in the beginning it was the old IBM programmers versus other computer makers, but over time we learned that to truly gain knowledge and advance, networking was key.

Do you relocate often? Are there travel requirements?

The only time I had to travel was in those cases where a new system was being introduced company wide; then we'd travel to all locations to ensure personnel were trained.

How much fulfillment do you get out of your career?

Plenty.

Would you choose the same career path?

Yes.

Any comments or words of advice for someone entering your field?

Stay in school, complete college, earn the degree in whatever field you like, and don't be afraid to reach higher . . . too many are too anxious to graduate when with a little more effort and time, they too can attain their doctorates or possibly get into the medical field.

VICE PRESIDENT OF SALES

Name

William C.

Location

Chicago, Illinois

Education

Master of Arts

Total years in profession

12

Brief occupation description/goal of occupation

I'm VP of sales in the software industry. I have started to get into smaller companies where I can build the sales and the teams that make the technology take off. The goal of the occupation is to make some money so that I can start my own gig—no matter what the widget is— and get the heck out of this ultra-competitive industry. I want to ultimately work for myself. There is nothing worse than dealing with the politics of organizations— especially large ones.

Why did you choose this career path?

It kind of chose me. I was preparing to go to law school and went down to Atlanta to live with a buddy several months before I was scheduled to begin classes. I went to a temp agency, and the next day they placed me at a successful modem company. I worked there for a bit, and they asked me to stay on until I went to school. Around July, the federal government and I had an argument over my payments on my existing loans, and they won the argument by calling me in default of all my loans. This quickly made me ineligible for any new loans, thus ending my law school hopes, at least for that time frame. I was offered a job by the VP of sales there. He mentored me for about ten months and then sent me off to be an outside account manager in Chicago. The rest is history.

What do you like about your occupation?

Competition—sales is a risk/reward career. Some people do not have the capability of handling the risk part. They freak out, especially in this industry where things change on a daily basis. I never had that problem, so I like the challenge. I also like the money. I don't particularly like money itself—it is a means to an end, not an end in itself. It will afford me the ability to make my own thing and watch my kids grow up, and give at least some of my time to helping folks build a better life.

What do you dislike about your occupation?

The internal politics. The people who lie. The people who would do anything to get ahead. The stubbornness of leaders.

What are the misconceptions about your profession?

That it is all gravy. This industry quickly became one of the most competitive industries the world has ever seen.

On a scale of 1 to 10 (10 being great), how would you rate your occupation and why?

I would say 8. It is hard for me to complain because I have done well, but I do not do anything to help people except for helping the people who work for me to be better professionals and support their families.

What career choices were most helpful?

To not jump into what's new and exciting. I have been good at waiting for the best and right thing to come along.

Do you have to update your career with ongoing training and certificates?

Not necessarily, but it helps. Even though I shunned them early in my career, I think the sales process trainings are useful, especially to make sure that a salesforce has one common language when discussing their sales. TAS and Sandler have been the most effective in my career, depending on what type of sale we need to do.

In a typical week, are your hours fixed or flexible? On what days do you tend to work overtime?

Flexible—weekdays. Not weekends if I can help it.

What types of conflicts do you deal with?

All types. Business and personal. Compensation issues, personality issues . . . from executive political conflicts to complaints that someone's perfume is too strong.

Do you interface with coworkers, groups, or vendors, or do you work alone?

Interface with all the above—quite a bit.

What are your coworkers like?

Pretty solid. I have been here long enough that I have been able to build a solid team. For the folks outside of sales, as a whole they are good, but if you are not contributing to executing the strategy, then I will not have a solid opinion of you.

What is management like?

I am leaving the company—on to my next gig—so maybe that is a comment on the latest change in management.

Is input accepted, or do you fare better as a "yes man"?

For this one—a yes man would be preferable. I simply find that to be completely intolerable.

What issues have prevented your advancement?

Working the channel can pigeonhole you a bit. That is why I made sure I ran direct sales groups and inside sales.

Is your position secure, or are you frequently looking for the next opportunity?

Typically, very secure. I have not moved around very much in my career.

How important is/was networking or connections in finding your current or other positions? Is it a factor in advancement once you're on the job?

Always. You are only as good as people perceive you to be.

What would be your next career move?

I am making it. Another small company with a solid technology that has some money and the willingness to make a strong play via the channel.

Do you relocate often? Are there travel requirements?

I have relocated twice, from Atlanta to Chicago for my first outside position and then to California for this last company. I am moving back to Chicago for my wife and baby girl in the next few days.

Do you prefer going to work or leaving? Why?

Depends on the day, but as a whole it is leaving. I have stated this is not my ultimate goal, so that should lend a hint as to why. Also, my life is about my wife and kid. They are my first and most important job.

How much fulfillment do you get out of your career?

About 68 percent out of 100—for the reasons I have discussed.

Do you feel that you are fairly compensated?

Yes—but I need more.

If you could choose again, how much would money be a factor?

It has to play some part, because I want some freedoms in my life and I have not been given a dime in my life by anybody. I have paid my way since I was twelve . . . no kidding. So I have to make money so that I can stretch my wings a bit . . . means to an end . . .

Any comments or words of advice for someone entering your field?

Know your product—use your CRM (customer relationship management) system—always do right by your customer and your partner—don't lie—make a commitment and achieve it.

INDUSTRIAL CHEMICAL SALES

Name

Gabriela R.

Location

Annapolis, Maryland

Education

Bachelor of Science

Total years in profession

13

Brief occupation description/goal of occupation

Industrial sales to new and existing customers, to include bid contracts for local and state government.

Why did you choose this career path?

Flexibility, independence, and a challenging opportunity as a second income earner with family responsibilities.

What do you like about your occupation?

I run my own territory.

What do you dislike about your occupation?

Stress—self-imposed, albeit.

What are the misconceptions about your profession?

The fact that it is a "sales" position and doesn't offer a true service.

On a scale of 1 to 10 (10 being great), how would you rate your occupation and why?

I would say 8. When presented well, customers see the need for your service/product and it becomes a win-win scenario. If not presented well/unprofessionally, you are seen as an annoying pest.

What factors or former positions led to this occupation?

Experience in my college newspaper led to a local newspaper and sales, which led to other sales positions. I like competition.

What career choices were most helpful?

Work and connections during college.

What career choices were least helpful/detrimental?

Having to tie up free time in dead-end jobs to make ends meet during high school and college—quality time not spent at its best.

Did you have a mentor? If so, how did you find them? Did they help?

I had people who noticed me—one high school teacher who changed my focus, one college professor with real-life experience who only taught once he reached retirement (not an elitist), and friends who had connections in various companies.

What type of education was needed for your position?

A BS in business administration/marketing–management.

Was your formal education necessary for this position?

Yes, only to open the door; the rest was based on performance. Before my application was accepted, a formal test for proficiency in analytical and mathematical skills was given.

Do you have to update your career with ongoing training and certificates?

Yes: specialized training in presentations, product knowledge, and safety.

In a typical week, are your hours fixed or flexible? On what days do you tend to work overtime?

Fixed and flexible hours were required, yet I could juggle the schedule. I worked a forty-hour in-the-field workweek and used additional time for phone and paperwork.

Is your work environment "hectic," "all work and no play," "serene," "laid back," or other? Briefly explain.

I was efficient, so I was able to juggle a "hectic" schedule, meet my quotas, and still have time for children's activities. I did not have day care children; I worked strictly within their school parameters.

What types of conflicts do you deal with?

In sales, objections are commonplace. Overcoming specific objections was the key to results. Otherwise, as a female in industrial chemicals, I sometimes wasn't taken seriously until I began offering solutions, not sales pitches.

Do you interface with coworkers, groups, or vendors, or do you work alone?

I interacted with everyone, from the guy changing the tire to the guy who had to sign the contract that was going to monetarily impact his budget, and from a five-man business to Fortune 500+ businesses. It depended on the extensiveness of the sale and program and cost.

What are your coworkers like?

Varied. Only the serious lasted; goof-offs came and went. You could always read the writing on the wall. The beauty in it is that they really don't impact your work.

What is management like?

If I produce, I am left alone. Otherwise, there are suggestions, ride-alongs, etc.

Is input accepted, or do you fare better as a "yes man"?

Input is always accepted because the sales director is always interested in everyone doing well.

What issues have prevented your advancement?

My husband's career. Mine, as agreed when we had kids, would be secondary, and we moved a lot.

Is your position secure, or are you frequently looking for the next opportunity?

My position was secure because I proved myself through accomplishing/exceeding my goals. I was offered other positions (sales, trainer, facilitator, assistant manager) within the company in new locations, but due to family obligations, I declined.

How important is/was networking or connections in finding your current or other positions? Is it a factor in advancement once you're on the job?

I found positions on my own because I produced results. Networking is important to meet people to find out if you want to work for them. Some sales directors were anal and had to ride with you every day, which is contradictory to my style. In other words, if you were good, you picked your positions and where you wanted to go.

What would be your next career move?

If I returned to the industry, I would remain in outside sales, where I would be autonomous.

Do you relocate often? Are there travel requirements?

I was offered a position when we moved and turned it down. Travel overnight was a quarterly requirement; daily travel was about 120 miles.

Do you prefer going to work or leaving? Why?

I enjoyed getting up and going to work with a planned, organized day. Leaving was important only when I had a contract in hand—a sale.

How much fulfillment do you get out of your career?

I love to compete and succeed. I am my own worst critic.

Do you feel that you are fairly compensated?

My pay is a direct reflection on my results. So yes, I am paid fairly; I make as much as I am able.

Are the benefits and vacation schedule fair?

Yes. I have never called in sick. I am able to fit in doctor/dentist appointments in my schedule without taking a vacation day or affecting my sales results.

If you could choose again, how much would money be a factor?

If I were the primary income earner, it would play a larger role. Because I had to start over several times due to moves, I did not earn what is expected and very reasonable for sales.

Would you choose the same career path?

Yes, if you consider the career path "sales." I would lean more toward real estate if my commitments allowed. Because I had three small children, those hours did not work. I did, however, invest in property that I fixed up, and it paid off. I wouldn't do my career path over, but now I would go back to school or intern to achieve my second career in life. My best college professor did just that. He used his real-life experiences to teach.

Any comments or words of advice for someone entering your field?

To be good in sales, you have to be empathetic, analytical, organized, efficient, focused, and professional with everyone, even if it's the guy changing the tire. Know your product as well as everyone else's product better than they know it; know your competition, know what you do best, and offer solutions. Do what you say, and never be late.

SPORTING GOODS MANUFACTURER REPRESENTATIVE

Name

Don L.

Location

Charlotte, North Carolina

Education

Bachelor of Science

Total years in profession

30

Brief occupation description/goal of occupation

Manufacturer's representative selling sporting goods to the retail and team segments of the market.

Why did you choose this career path?

Meeting people, travel, and having a commission-based position.

What do you like about your occupation?

People, products, and travel sometimes.

What do you dislike about your occupation?

Misinformation regarding product shipments. Weekend work sometimes and being away from family when traveling.

What are the misconceptions about your profession?

Sporting goods is an easy sales job.

On a scale of 1 to 10 (10 being great), how would you rate your occupation and why?

I give it a 9. Most days, my work is enjoyable, but some days, it is just a job.

What factors or former positions led to this occupation?

Interest in athletics, college major.

What career choices were most helpful?

Starting in a retail sporting goods store to learn the product and suppliers.

Did you have a mentor? If so, how did you find them? Did they help?

Yes, I worked with several people who helped me learn the team business, and several other sales agents were helpful in detailing the expectations of a sales agent.

What type of education was needed for your position?

Sales and marketing—I would have studied this more if I had known what I planned to do for a career.

Was your formal education necessary for this position?

No, but it helped.

Do you have to update your career with ongoing training and certificates?

No, just sales meetings and seminars.

When you were hired, did you receive professional training or was it basically "on-the-job training"?

Basically, it was on-the-job training.

In a typical week, are your hours fixed or flexible? On what days do you tend to work overtime?

My hours are flexible. That is a perk of the job, but I need to be accessible to my customers almost anytime.

Is your work environment "hectic," "all work and no play," "serene," "laid back," or other? Briefly explain.

Sometimes hectic, especially when the customer needs product. Sometimes, however, it is laid back.

What types of conflicts do you deal with?

Sales distribution is the most difficult. Some accounts do not want other accounts to sell the lines that I represent, and I have to determine the distribution in my territory.

Do you interface with coworkers, groups, or vendors, or do you work alone?

We have a sales agency with five independent agents in nine states.

What are your coworkers like?

All are independent agents. If they sell it, they get commissions, and if they don't, they don't get commissions. All are hard workers.

Is input accepted, or do you fare better as a "yes man"?

Input is definitely accepted.

Is your position secure, or are you frequently looking for the next opportunity?

My position is secure, and our position as a sales agency is secure with most of our lines; however, that can change rapidly. Consolidation of companies always puts the sales agent at risk.

How important is/was networking or connections in finding your current or other positions? Is it a factor in advancement once you're on the job?

Networking is very important with our accounts and the companies we represent.

Do you relocate often? Are there travel requirements?

I do not have to relocate and can live just about anywhere within my territory. There are travel requirements, but I set my own schedule, so I can usually determine the travel.

How much fulfillment do you get out of your career?

I enjoy supplying teams with their equipment.

Do you feel that you are fairly compensated?

Yes—with commissions, income is only limited by how much I can sell.

Are the benefits and vacation schedule fair?

I actually have no benefits, being an independent agent. I set my vacation schedule; so, yes, it is fair.

If you could choose again, how much would money be a factor?

I chose this career because it is what I wanted to do, not just because of the money.

Would you choose the same career path?

Yes.

Any comments or words of advice for someone entering your field?

Do that for which you have a passion and would enjoy doing. Sales can be fun and stressful and also very rewarding. If you are good at what you choose to do, the money will take care of itself.

REAL ESTATE AGENT

Name

Jone A.

Location

Louisville, Kentucky

Education

High school

Total years in profession

2

Brief occupation description/goal of occupation

I sell primarily residential real estate in a small community in Kentucky. The real estate market is extremely slow compared to most. Average time on the market for homes is 120–180 days. There is currently a six-month supply of homes for sale.

Why did you choose this career path?

To be able to set my own hours and continue to be a stay-at-home mom.

What do you like about your occupation?

When it pays, it pays well. The hours are great.

What do you dislike about your occupation?

There are no guarantees as to when and how much you will get paid. There are also very high fees associated with it. Realtors' dues and continuing education are expensive.

What are the misconceptions about your profession?

That all real estate agents are crooks who are out to cheat you out of money. That there is no knowledge required for the profession, and that we are all rich.

On a scale of 1 to 10 (10 being great), how would you rate your occupation and why?

I would say 7; I love the job, just not the uncertainty of the paycheck.

What factors or former positions led to this occupation?

Divorce.

What career choices were most helpful?

That I am very connected in the community, because of charitable volunteer work that I did while married and functioning as a stay-at-home mom.

What career choices were least helpful/detrimental?

That my ex is not very well liked or trusted, and it takes a while to get past that stigma.

Did you have a mentor? If so, how did you find them? Did they help?

Yes. My broker is a gentleman that I attended church with who had some rental property listed for me during the divorce. He is actually the one who suggested that I go into real estate.

What type of education was needed for your position?

Real estate school. It's required that you pass a state real estate exam.

Do you have to update your career with ongoing training and certificates?

Yes, education is required yearly, with a core content class being required once every four years.

When you were hired, did you receive professional training or was it basically "on-the-job training"?

I worked in my real estate office as I was going to school.

In a typical week, are your hours fixed or flexible? On what days do you tend to work overtime?

Flexible; evenings and weekends are peak hours.

Is your work environment "hectic," "all work and no play," "serene," "laid back," or other? Briefly explain.

Varied. Usually very laid back until after the contracts are written. Then the work begins. Closings are the most hectic times.

What types of conflicts do you deal with?

Buyer/seller resolution. Seller thinks the house is worth too much, buyer thinks not enough. Usual conflict.

Do you interface with coworkers, groups, or vendors, or do you work alone?

I network with a group of local realtors. Realtors in my office share leads. Real estate is all about relationships.

What are your coworkers like?

A varied group of people. Both brokers are older gentlemen who enjoy commercial real estate or auctions most. One agent deals mainly with relocations, and one deals in foreclosed properties. The other two agents are women with children as well.

Is input accepted, or do you fare better as a "yes man"?

Input is highly accepted in my office. Everyone will take all the help they can get. Sharing information is also a large part of real estate.

What issues have prevented your advancement?

The market is saturated with real estate agents.

Is your position secure, or are you frequently looking for the next opportunity?

My position is secure; the market is not.

How important is/was networking or connections in finding your current or other positions? Is it a factor in advancement once you're on the job?

Real estate is, once again, all about relationships. Networking is essential.

What would be your next career move?

Possibly something in the local school system—something that would keep the same hours as my daughter's schedule.

Do you prefer going to work or leaving? Why?

I enjoy going to work. It is never the same from one day to the next. My scenery changes constantly.

How much fulfillment do you get out of your career?

It's extremely gratifying when you find a home for someone, something that they love—especially first-time homeowners.

Do you feel that you are fairly compensated?

When the sale actually goes through, absolutely. The hours that you spend on clients who never buy, it doesn't even out yet. But I am still fairly new and unestablished. The real estate market is tough, and it takes some time to develop a trustworthy reputation.

If you could choose again, how much would money be a factor?

The money versus the hours . . . there is no comparison.

Would you choose the same career path?

The only other choice I would have made would have been early childhood elementary education, which is still an option to pursue while still keeping my real estate license.

Any comments or words of advice for someone entering your field?

Have at least a year's worth of savings to fall back on or don't quit your day job. Be fully capable of handling rejection, and expect it.

RETAIL MANAGER

Name

Heather D.

Location

Manchester, New Hampshire

Education

Some college

Total years in profession

10

Brief occupation description/goal of occupation

Basically, I ran a high-end retail store. I hired, fired, motivated a staff of up to thirty-two people, and did budget, payroll, heavy lifting, merchandising, training, and selling. And it goes on and on . . .

Why did you choose this career path?

My first job was in retail. I was just looking for some money back in high school. I didn't know any other options. You begin, and it is hard to stop.

What do you like about your occupation?

I like working with people, meeting new people all the time (including customers), helping someone "decorate" their home, and the challenge of it all.

What do you dislike about your occupation?

I don't like the hours—a lot of really long, hard, physical days. Then there's the pressure (e.g., always keeping sales increasing), not enough pay for the job required, and dealing with customer service issues.

What are the misconceptions about your profession?

That it would be always fun, that I would get paid well, thinking that customers would always be "nice," that you would work your scheduled shift (e.g., not always needing to be flexible), that it would be easy.

On a scale of 1 to 10 (10 being great), how would you rate your occupation and why?

I would say 7. It was always challenging, which was both good and bad. It keeps you busy ("on your toes," so to speak, all the time). Every day was always something different, whether good or bad.

What factors or former positions led to this occupation?

It was my first job out of high school. Not pursuing a college degree right away, it was easy to get a job in retail. No experience was needed to begin.

What career choices were most helpful?

I really am glad I had the retail experience, as it has given me experience in such a huge variety of projects, etc., so that I can relate to just about any other job. Although my most helpful choice was when I finally quit for good!

What career choices were least helpful/detrimental?

I think back to all the times I had been promoted and sometimes wish I had not accepted. Yes, I got the work experience, but for all the effort I put in, now it doesn't seem like it was worth it. Once you take that step into retail, it is hard to get out of it. You are so busy working and changing your life to revolve around work that you don't do what you need to do for yourself.

Did you have a mentor? If so, how did you find them? Did they help?

My manager at one of my jobs mentored me. She was an incredibly intelligent woman. One thing I will never forget about her is what she said when I was debating on starting college. Not knowing what career path I wanted to choose, the choice was difficult. She said simply and plainly, "You go to school to educate yourself, not to get a job." Right there, I decided to start the college process. It may seem like a simple concept, but it's one that I think is really overlooked.

What type of education was needed for your position?

None. I have always been a really quick learner and able to adapt, so I have been promoted rapidly over the years. A college degree did not play any part in it. Work experience is the key.

Do you have to update your career with ongoing training and certificates?

No. Occasionally training programs happen, but they are more geared toward the company rather than for the position.

In a typical week, are your hours fixed or flexible?
On what days do you tend to work overtime?

Schedule was usually up one to two weeks prior to the workweek. Weekends had the most overtime needed; also peak times during the workweek (between around 5:00 and 7:00 p.m.), or if any new ads were running and needed to be set up.

Is your work environment "hectic," "all work and no play," "serene," "laid back," or other? Briefly explain.

Hectic. I definitely tried to make the best of all situations, getting my staff involved in a "fun" way, but still always hectic.

What types of conflicts do you deal with?

What didn't I deal with! Customer issues daily (e.g., customers yelling over such small issues, and I had to defuse and fix the problem), employee issues (scheduling conflicts, fighting between two employees, HR issues), store issues (in one store, toilets overflowed just about every other week!), management pressures if sales were down daily, and the list keeps going.

Do you interface with coworkers, groups, or vendors, or do you work alone?

I interfaced with coworkers, vendors, and customers.

What are your coworkers like?

All different types. There was always a large number of personality types: some who you barely looked at before they called human resources, others who would work like crazy even if you didn't ask them to . . .

What is management like?

Firm, fair, yet friendly. At least that's what someone once told me.

Is input accepted, or do you fare better as a "yes man"?

Generally, input was accepted as long as it fell within the company guidelines.

What issues have prevented your advancement?

None. I have never had a problem advancing.

Is your position secure, or are you frequently looking for the next opportunity?

It was always secure as long as you did your job and kept sales up. Obviously, if you stop producing, well . . .

How important is/was networking or connections in finding your current or other positions? Is it a factor in advancement once you're on the job?

It's extremely important. The old saying stands: "It's not what you know, it's who you know." One job I found was because someone worked for the company and they put in a good word. Yes, I think it plays a key factor in my promotions as well.

Do you relocate often? Are there travel requirements?

No. Occasionally I traveled to help out in other stores or trainings/meetings.

Do you prefer going to work or leaving? Why?

Going to work. When you get there, you have a bit of time to think about what is going to happen before the store opens. By the time you leave, you still have things to do that didn't get done, so it comes home with you emotionally. It's hard to leave and leave work behind.

How much fulfillment do you get out of your career?

This is a hard question to answer. It's fulfilling when you feel like you accomplished your sales for the day, or you help that customer find what they have been searching three months for, or you solve the issue that no one else could solve. Did it really fulfill me? No.

If you could choose again, how much would money be a factor?

As long as I can live comfortably, money wouldn't be such an issue as having my time in life.

Would you choose the same career path?

Yes and no. Yes, because the experience is far better than any college class I have ever taken. No, because of the life that you end up living.

Any comments or words of advice for someone entering your field?

Don't give up your life's dreams. Retail makes it hard to manage your own time. You basically need to live your life for your company. As much as you think you have a choice in certain areas of schedules, etc., you don't. You need to be available when customers are going to be there.

PROGRAM MANAGER

Name

Don S.

Location

Northern Virginia

Education

Master of Business Administration with Bachelor of Science in Electrical Engineering

Total years in profession

8

Brief occupation description/goal of occupation

Responsible for the sale and implementation of electronic surveillance equipment to telecommunication providers in North America. Actively manage accounts and personnel from sales process through implementation and support.

Why did you choose this career path?

I previously worked for the FBI for five years and am familiar with electronic surveillance. My previous FBI supervisor was president of the company.

What do you like about your occupation?

Autonomy—I have always liked to make decisions and would rather be 80 percent correct and keep moving than wait months to be 100 percent correct. I have also learned a great deal about product positioning, the sales process, and customer relationships.

What do you dislike about your occupation?

I dislike the grind. Sales quotas are a never-ending burden. In addition, unreasonable customers can make work stressful. "The customer is always right" is not always right. Being a person who can get things done can be used against you by others who delegate and take credit.

What are the misconceptions about your profession?

Being on the business/sales side is very difficult, and there is no set process to make things better. To be successful, you need to work to provide increasing value to your customers.

On a scale of 1 to 10 (10 being great), how would you rate your occupation and why?

I give it a 7—I am well compensated and have autonomy. However, there is significant stress that seems unending at times.

What factors or former positions led to this occupation?

I have an electrical engineering degree and worked for the FBI's electronic surveillance group for five years.

What career choices were most helpful?

Getting an MBA was a good career choice, although it is not a panacea. Staying connected with former coworkers helps with later networking—never burn bridges and always stay professional.

What career choices were least helpful/detrimental?

Searching for compensation rather than a satisfying career is detrimental. Everyone should find out what they want to do and then do it—the money will follow.

Did you have a mentor? If so, how did you find them? Did they help?

I have never had a mentor, and it has hurt me.

What type of education was needed for your position?

My education (BS in electrical engineering and MBA) has provided me with an ability to learn both technical and business issues. It has been invaluable since learning is key to ongoing success. In addition, my education has allowed me to get interviews, which is more than half the battle.

Do you have to update your career with ongoing training and certificates?

Yes—I am constantly learning about new technologies, but it is much more informal. In my past technical positions, formal training for certification occurred.

When you were hired, did you receive professional training or was it basically "on-the-job training"?

My current job was all "on the job." I try to stay proactive with my industry and the skills to be successful. I consider this crucial to success in any profession. The desire to stay current is an indicator of an individual's job satisfaction.

In a typical week, are your hours fixed or flexible? On what days do you tend to work overtime?

Fifty to fifty-five hours—I find that it is much more efficient to be focused for fewer hours and get away from work to enjoy other aspects of life. I work flexible hours and do not understand employers who won't let people work that way.

Is your work environment "hectic," "all work and no play," "serene," "laid back," or other? Briefly explain.

I am in a small company. There is respect and fun, but we are constantly working for the customers. I would rate this aspect of my current job as a 9 out of 10.

What types of conflicts do you deal with?

Customer conflicts—trying to set expectations regarding implementations, sales, and support. In addition, there is some conflict internally working with scarce resources and trying to manage five people.

Do you interface with coworkers, groups, or vendors, or do you work alone?

I interoperate with several groups internally and externally.

What are your coworkers like?

My coworkers are all different types. However, they are all professional and take responsibility.

What is management like?

Management is good, but I wish they would listen to more of my input.

Is input accepted, or do you fare better as a "yes man"?

My input is accepted most of the time. Even if I agree with a decision, I often act as a "devil's advocate" in order to understand a particular employee's or customer's possible response.

What issues have prevented your advancement?

My company is currently growing, and I have given this question much thought. I believe I need to proactively work on my sales (customer interaction, technical presentations, etc.) skills and better delegate more day-to-day items. I want to develop a proactive portion to my work schedule to make this happen. Usually, these proactive items get pushed out due to reactive daily issues.

How important is/was networking or connections in finding your current or other positions? Is it a factor in advancement once you're on the job?

Networking is key, but I have never been good at it. My best networking has been my job performance.

What would be your next career move?

I want to become a better technical/business expert in the field of electronic surveillance.

Do you relocate often? Are there travel requirements?

I travel three to five days per month and can usually plan to meet my schedule. I have relocated cross country twice due to career changes and am glad I did.

How much fulfillment do you get out of your career?

I get some fulfillment out of my career but miss some of the tangible rewards of engineering and making a product. As I get older, I also appreciate that my compensation allows me to live a comfortable life and provide for my family.

If you could choose again, how much would money be a factor?

Money would still be a factor, but I would choose something more by how satisfying it was.

Would you choose the same career path?

Maybe—it is very easy to second-guess myself, but I am glad for the risks I have taken and my current life.

MANAGER OF RESIDENTIAL RENTAL PROPERTIES

Name

Susan D.

Location

Denver, Colorado

Education

Master of Arts

Total years in profession

15

Brief occupation description/goal of occupation

Recruit, screen, manage, and maintain/retain all prospective tenants within appropriate residential housing units. Coordinate all tenant services and contracts/leases. Collect monthly rental payments in the most expeditious manner. Minimize all expenses by carefully selecting best operational services for duration of tenant lease, as well as throughout landlord ownership.

Why did you choose this career path?

Flexibility of time with family commitments, the ability to develop permanent residual income, the opportunity to be my own boss, and tax advantages.

What do you dislike about your occupation?

Market demands and competition can vary considerably and may even be volatile, subject to changeable local and regional economics. When something must be accomplished now to satisfy tenant needs/requests, everything else in my life takes second priority. Hiring and trusting a knowledgeable manager in my absence can be tricky.

What are the misconceptions about your profession?

That one ideally must have a solid undergraduate training in business management or accounting.

On a scale of 1 to 10 (10 being great), how would you rate your occupation and why?

I'd give it an 8. It allows me to be "me" as I am accountable only to my spouse/co-owner, my CPA, and the Lord.

What factors or former positions led to this occupation?

After working within regular salaried managerial positions, my entrepreneurial spirit surfaced so that I could build an alternative retirement package for my husband and me.

What career choices were most helpful?

Being a tenant myself during the early and rather unsettled years of my college experience and marriage has been extremely helpful in understanding the prospective tenant mindset. Graduate training in counseling psychology has helped me better understand another's "big picture" of life and their specific agenda and driving priorities. Working with hundreds of clients in transition within state social services has shaped my ability to screen both prospective tenants and service providers effectively and quickly, and to tailor and deliver quality services/"product" within tight budgets.

What career choices were least helpful/detrimental?

Working as a contract employee for the federal government has confirmed that I need "my own operation/business" versus being caught in a bureaucratic cog.

Did you have a mentor? If so, how did you find them? Did they help?

Not really, except that as a child, I grew up and witnessed my parents' ability to develop a very healthy self-employed income while still tending to their own personal/marital/family commitments. This experience was extremely compelling.

What type of education was needed for your position?

Actually, basic common sense applied with good intelligence, an ability to learn from one's errors, and developing the realization that all choices have direct consequences. I can hire out any specific service in which I am not knowledgeable or skilled.

Was your formal education necessary for this position?

No, but it certainly has been and continues to be helpful.

In a typical week, are your hours fixed or flexible? On what days do you tend to work overtime?

Every day in this self-employment business is different. Some days I spend literally zero minutes working; other days I work more than twenty hours, but this is rare.

Is your work environment "hectic," "all work and no play," "serene," "laid back," or other? Briefly explain.

All of the above, depending upon the timing of contracts and circumstances out of my control.

Do you interface with coworkers, groups, or vendors, or do you work alone?

Primarily, I call the shots regarding all marketing and tenant matters. Otherwise, I work closely with my spouse in making overall final decisions. I do select various service providers/contractors to assist on specific projects as is needed.

What issues have prevented your advancement?

Lack of capital—both economic and time.

Is your position secure, or are you frequently looking for the next opportunity?

Extremely secure as I build stable projects, one by one.

How important is/was networking or connections in finding your current or other positions? Is it a factor in advancement once you're on the job?

Yes, being open to hiring specific talent and skills when mine/my partner's are deficient is essential. I am a born networker, so linking with others in a similar capacity and learning from them—providing they are willing to share of their experience—can be very rewarding both monetarily and emotionally.

Do you relocate often? Are there travel requirements?

No. Denver offers many rental opportunities with extreme equity advantages. It is both my self-determined "home" and my launching pad for future business opportunities.

How much fulfillment do you get out of your career?

As much as I had hoped. It allows me to blend my personal and professional lives together (typically nicely), which is very satisfying.

If you could choose again, how much would money be a factor?

Financing is necessary for ownership of property, so researching and selecting appropriate financial and lending/mortgage providers is essential.

Would you choose the same career path?

Yes. However, I would have begun this self-employment as a young adult, thus more than tripling my/our current net worth.

Any comments or words of advice for someone entering your field?

As the saying goes, "The good news is that you are your own boss. The bad news is that you are your own boss." Marry carefully. Partnerships both in life and in business are extremely complex and can be challenging.

PROJECT MANAGER

Name

Fred R.

Location

Los Angeles, California

Education

Bachelor of Science

Total years in profession

27

Brief occupation description/goal of occupation

Manage projects to meet cost, time, and quality (or quantity) requirements of the customer(s) and stakeholders.

Why did you choose this career path?

An outgrowth of mainframe configuration management and disappointment when performing other roles.

What do you like about your occupation?

The ability to manage people and processes and get involved with the newest technology while having to get into real details.

What do you dislike about your occupation?

The ability of any number of folks on the customer side, my employer's side, or our vendors' side to cause problems and disruption.

What are the misconceptions about your profession?

That project managers are technical experts in their field.

On a scale of 1 to 10 (10 being great), how would you rate your occupation and why?

I give it an 8—mostly good work, fun, usually with great folks.

What factors or former positions led to this occupation?

I started as a scientific programmer at a radar shop, then moved to mainframe systems programming, presales support for mainframe equipment, mainframe configuration management, "mini-computer" config management, systems architecture and management, PC sales, project management, and formal training, finally achieving a PMP (Project Management Professional) designation.

Did you have a mentor? If so, how did you find them? Did they help?

Yes—he was a project sponsor and was instrumental in getting my career going in a strong direction when it could have flip-flopped in various ways.

What type of education was needed for your position?

A bachelor's degree and Project Management Institute at Carnegie Mellon University–approved teacher-led classes.

Was your formal education necessary for this position?

Yes, as part of the requirements to achieve a PMP designation and for the systems architecture knowledge obtained.

Do you have to update your career with ongoing training and certificates?

Twenty hours a year is mandatory, with five allowed for a full-time position and eleven allowed for attending monthly PMI dinner meetings with lectures; the rest is made up of reading subject-matter books, taking self-study courses, and attending other lectures, classes, or symposiums.

When you were hired, did you receive professional training or was it basically "on-the-job training"?

When hired at Computer Science Corp, they sent me to a set of courses from UC Irvine taught at company facilities; much prior knowledge was gained by on-the-job training.

In a typical week, are your hours fixed or flexible? On what days do you tend to work overtime?

Generally, a fixed schedule, but some projects have required weekends and graveyard work (network installs and construction).

Is your work environment "hectic," "all work and no play," "serene," "laid back," or other? Briefly explain.

Usually "head down and stay busy," occasionally hectic, rarely laid back; but the day goes by quickly, and then the time to head home arrives "sooner."

What types of conflicts do you deal with?

Cost versus schedule versus quality/quantity of work—politics of doing a task by process A versus process B—not getting paid more than forty hours a week while needing to put in fifty hours to get it all done.

Do you interface with coworkers, groups, or vendors, or do you work alone?

This role acts as the communication hub for all involved: customers, my company highers and lowers, team members and their management, vendors, and some government authorities (permits, approvals, etc.).

What are your coworkers like?

Most are educated professionals with a good sense of work ethics.

What is management like?

Some are reminiscent of the pointy-haired dolt in *Dilbert* while some are caring, concerned friends who offer sound advice and guidance.

Is input accepted, or do you fare better as a "yes man"?

Usually, I make the calls for work, but when a decision is needed by a senior, my recommendation and alternate solutions must be presented along with analysis, pros, and cons on each.

What issues have prevented your advancement?

None—I was managing a group of fifteen project managers at a previous assignment and would take another such role, if found and offered.

Is your position secure, or are you frequently looking for the next opportunity?

At present I am frequently searching for a new source of employment, but previously I had three-and-a-half years at CSC.

How important is/was networking or connections in finding your current or other positions? Is it a factor in advancement once you're on the job?

Networking is very important in finding PM work, as a contractor or employee on the move; once in a permanent employee position, networking is almost mandatory for advancement. Early careers are often helped by "promotion through motion"—switching jobs (sometimes within the same company) every two to three years, each change bringing a promotion and pay raise.

What would be your next career move?

Back to managing a small or medium PM organization or permanent employee as a senior PM. Consulting pays well, but there is no security.

Do you relocate often? Are there travel requirements?

No; sometimes—at CSC I commuted to Tucson every week for nineteen months to manage a $10 million network install that came in early and under budget.

Do you prefer going to work or leaving? Why?

Leaving—home is where the heart is! Loving and toys await me at home. Stress and sweat await me at the office.

How much fulfillment do you get out of your career?

Great satisfaction arises from being a mentor to newly graduated and hired employees.

Do you feel that you are fairly compensated?

As a consultant, yes, despite no vacation, holiday pay, sick pay, or benefits; as an employee—underpaid, but better job security.

If you could choose again, how much would money be a factor?

Large—money doesn't buy happiness, but if you're going to be miserable anyway, you might as well live in a nice neighborhood.

Would you choose the same career path?

A few changes, but mostly yes!

Any comments or words of advice for someone entering your field?

Get that degree and start volunteering for project work; take the required teacher-led training early in your career; buy FasTrackPMP and cram hard for the PMP test.

ACCOUNT EXECUTIVE

Name

Ryan M.

Location

San Francisco, California

Education

Junior college, associate degree finishing Bachelor of Science

Total years in profession

1

Brief occupation description/goal of occupation

Mortgage lending (managing accounts up to funding). The goal of this occupation for me was to gain experience in the financial world. I have six years of sales experience and wanted some of that to be applicable in the financial world.

Why did you choose this career path?

To gain a balance between my home life and professional life. My current job respects personal time and gives employees ample time to spend with their families. This can be hard to find in sales positions that provide decent income.

What do you like about your occupation?

I work with fantastic, intelligent people. I spend a good portion of my day helping people who are sometimes in very difficult situations financially. At five o'clock I go home and forget about work until the next day, and the weekends are all mine.

What are the misconceptions about your profession?

That the positions require mortgage experience. Enough sales experience or talent can sometimes be enough. The unethical behavior of some brokers and their desire to be thought of as the same as a bank can cloud some borrowers' minds and make them wary. Banks are much more closely monitored than brokers and have more to lose through unethical practices.

On a scale of 1 to 10 (10 being great), how would you rate your occupation and why?

I would say 7 or 8. I don't get up excited to go to work, but I am treated well and the job is interesting.

What factors or former positions led to this occupation?

My experience as a sales manager for a high-end consumer retailer. The job sapped every ounce of spare time and cost me the last Christmas that I could have spent with my grandfather while he was alive. I decided family was more important than my job. That company has since gone bankrupt.

What career choices were least helpful/detrimental?

I wish I had taken school more seriously sooner. I would have saved a lot of the time I am spending now. Working full time and going to school is not easy, and it taxes your body and spirit. Leaving at six thirty in the morning and getting home at ten o'clock at night is tough.

Did you have a mentor? If so, how did you find them? Did they help?

I did not have a mentor. My father was very supportive and helped me in any decisions I made, which is as close as it comes for me.

If you didn't have a mentor, would you have liked one?

I think that as a young person, good judgment comes from bad experience, and a lot of that comes from bad judgment. People tell you what they learned in their youth, and it fails to sink in until you've learned firsthand why they told you what they did. Then you try to inform the next generation . . . a vicious cycle. The fortunate ones are those who either had the foresight to take advice to heart or had a mentor who was good enough to make an impact.

What type of education was needed for your position?

High school diploma or GED. College degree preferred, but not required. Sales experience required.

When you were hired, did you receive professional training or was it basically "on-the-job training"?

Three weeks of classroom training.

In a typical week, are your hours fixed or flexible? On what days do you tend to work overtime?

Fixed with optional overtime (forty hours weekly).

Is your work environment "hectic," "all work and no play," "serene," "laid back," or other? Briefly explain.

Hectic toward deadlines for funding and filing, laid back during the first half of the month.

What types of conflicts do you deal with?

The need to have things done quickly by people who are already busy. Also, dealing with customers who cannot be offered a loan by the bank but need us desperately.

Do you interface with coworkers, groups, or vendors, or do you work alone?

I interface with coworkers and customers (by phone).

What are your coworkers like?

Intelligent, funny, fun loving, and supportive.

What is management like?

I currently work for the best manager I have had in nine years. He is supportive, with a very open manner that allows his team to relax and do their job with as little stress as possible. Despite being new at his job, his team is the top performing.

Is input accepted, or do you fare better as a "yes man"?

Input is accepted, and in my opinion is required to make progress as a company.

What issues have prevented your advancement?

None. Advancement is not often desired in my position. The income potential can be massive if the person desires to put in the work. Even at the lower-income tiers, the job pays enough that most other positions seek to move to this one, and due to income, those who are here want to stay. The only real promotion is to sales management (which may pay less) or to another company with higher pay scales. If I chose to move to management (which I do not foresee), I would need to complete my BA or BS to be eligible.

Is your position secure, or are you frequently looking for the next opportunity?

Production positions tend to be secure due to the fact that they generate the company income. People in incentive/commission will often take a position with another company if the scale pays higher, but that is an optional move.

How important is/was networking or connections in finding your current or other positions? Is it a factor in advancement once you're on the job?

Networking can be very powerful in this industry. If you make good connections, you will always have a job.

What would be your next career move?

If I was to move, it would be to start my own business or make a serious lifestyle change. As far as work for work's sake, this job is good.

Do you relocate often? Are there travel requirements?

No relocation, no travel.

How much fulfillment do you get out of your career?

It feels good to help people in need financially.

Are the benefits and vacation schedule fair?

Very. Time off is set as personal time, so if you're the type of person who doesn't get sick, you have more vacation.

If you could choose again, how much would money be a factor?

Family is more important, but the bills have to be paid. The cost of housing in California demands that the position pay more and usually requires a two-income household.

Would you choose the same career path?

The issue for me is I'd prefer a position with the Forest Service, or something that would allow me to be outdoors and enjoy each hour at work. The problem there is that I could not have afforded my home (or any home here) on the starting salary.

Any comments or words of advice for someone entering your field?

Balance your life. Work is work. Your family will be by your side until the end—your job will not. You will not lie on your deathbed wishing you had put in those extra hours of overtime on Christmas. I have seen coworkers in sales positions burn through marriages. The banking industry can be financially rewarding if you work hard while you're there and have a healthy life on the outside. Also, define your goals. Working for a bank will be more balanced and secure than being a broker. Brokers and their companies can burn out and shut down, but you can earn more money while it's good.

MARKETING MANAGER

Name

Jeff B.

Location

Phoenix, Arizona

Education

Bachelor of Science

Total years in profession

8.5

Brief occupation description/goal of occupation

Channel, field, and strategic (vertical) marketing plans. These include sales and product promotions, solutions for internal sales associates, and indirect (reseller) sales associates. Demand/lead generation activities.

Why did you choose this career path?

I know someone at my first job who got me an interview.

What do you like about your occupation?

Freedom and creativity of position.

What do you dislike about your occupation?

Lack of direction. Bouncing around of goals by quarter.

What are the misconceptions about your profession?

Salespeople think you push trinkets!

On a scale of 1 to 10 (10 being great), how would you rate your occupation and why?

I would say 8. Hey, better than shucking shrimp in the bayou.

What factors or former positions led to this occupation?

Working for a computer distributor led to working for a software vendor. Getting the first position at the distributor? Taking a Club Med vacation, being myself, and meeting a group of people—one of whom was the contact to get me the interview.

What career choices were most helpful?

Sales job at a clothing store. Super Shuttle driver. Diverse experiences, dealing with people—and wanting the next job.

Did you have a mentor? If so, how did you find them? Did they help?

No, I wish I did. This question pertains to a direct work mentor, I assume. I do have a "life" friend who acts like a mentor.

What type of education was needed for your position?

My college degree helped. If I had the experiences, that would have gotten me the job, but chicken and the egg . . . need the degree to get the better job.

Was your formal education necessary for this position?

None. I leveraged up my experiences.

In a typical week, are your hours fixed or flexible? On what days do you tend to work overtime?

Flexible.

Is your work environment "hectic," "all work and no play," "serene," "laid back," or other? Briefly explain.

Hectic at times, laid back at others. Extremes, I would say.

What types of conflicts do you deal with?

My in-house customers (sales associates) have different ideals than my bosses or what I have been tasked with (budget and how to spend).

Do you interface with coworkers, groups, or vendors, or do you work alone?

I interface with coworkers—salespeople, marketing, strategic ops. Also with customers—resellers.

What are your coworkers like?

Pretty good. Educated for the most part, and polished.

What is management like?

Okay. Immediate management is good.

Is input accepted, or do you fare better as a "yes man"?

Input "gently" and agree at the end.

What issues have prevented your advancement?

I can be bullheaded. My last advancement was stopped in that my boss left, his boss left, and then my company got taken over. I lost my internal political cover. I worked externally to the new and old company's corporate offices.

Is your position secure, or are you frequently looking for the next opportunity?

Looking for next opportunity. Am "free" at the moment!

How important is/was networking or connections in finding your current or other positions? Is it a factor in advancement once you're on the job?

Very important in previous jobs to network, as is starting to network to land the next position. On the job? Networking kept me employed, though it did not raise me into other positions at the company.

What would be your next career move?

Sales, account management, marketing.

Do you relocate often? Are there travel requirements?

I do not want to relocate. I had quite a bit of travel, up to ten to fifteen days a month sometimes.

Do you prefer going to work or leaving? Why?

Going to work. I like the excitement and input.

Are the benefits and vacation schedule fair?

We need more vacation time in corporate America.

If you could choose again, how much would money be a factor?

Fifty percent.

Would you choose the same career path?

I would like to have been an owner of my own business. I'll still do that someday, though I will use the corporate gig to save up money for it.

Any comments or words of advice for someone entering your field?

Brush your teeth, don't eat spaghetti in an interview, and listen to the person talking to you!

CHAPTER TWO
The Hustlers

AUTOMOTIVE AND FARM MECHANIC

Name

Rick A.

Location

Western Wisconsin

Education

High school and two tech/trade diplomas

Total years in profession

21

Brief occupation description/goal of occupation

I repaired, rebuilt, and modified regular automobiles, race cars, farm machinery, heavy equipment, and military vehicles as well as different recreational vehicles over the years.

Why did you choose this career path?

I like doing something constructive with my hands and mind both. I wanted to be an automotive engineer. I couldn't afford the education, though.

What do you like about your occupation?

I like the satisfaction of repairing and modifying something common to most everyone in the industrialized world.

What do you dislike about your occupation?

I dislike the complex company-specific computers and testing equipment common in recent years making diagnostics brand specific and expensive.

What are the misconceptions about your profession?

The misconception that mechanics are all lower educated and dirty laborers with little or no pride in their profession.

On a scale of 1 to 10 (10 being great), how would you rate your occupation and why?

I would have to rate it as a 6 due to the complicated and specialized computers involved. Also, because I would prefer to be designing engines and driving trains instead of repairing and modifying them.

What factors or former positions led to this occupation?

My father was a part-time snowmobile mechanic and snowmobile racer while I was younger. I also spent a lot of my life growing up around farming, which of course means repairing and maintaining many kinds of equipment.

Did you have a mentor? If so, how did you find them? Did they help?

My step-grandfather spent over seven years teaching me most of what he knew.

What type of education was needed for your position?

Seven years learning under my step-grandfather's guidance and military technical training to prove that knowledge as legitimate.

Was your formal education necessary for this position?

Mostly yes, unless I only wanted to do the most menial forms of maintenance, such as oil changes, tires, exhaust, and brake systems.

When you were hired, did you receive professional training or was it basically "on-the-job" training?

I have had both kinds of training throughout my working years.

Do you interface with coworkers, groups, or vendors, or do you work alone?

I usually worked alone on most jobs. Some jobs required more than one person to complete the work.

What are your coworkers like?

My coworkers varied from very intelligent and fairly well educated to barely literate grease monkeys doing unskilled labor.

Is input accepted, or do you fare better as a "yes man"?

I can take orders when that is the best way to properly do my job, though I despise yes men and kiss-ups. I always provide input when I know a better or more efficient way of doing a job.

What issues have prevented your advancement?

Spinal and neck injuries prevent my doing the same work anymore, and a lack of finances prevents me from continuing my education goals of engineering.

Is your position secure, or are you frequently looking for the next opportunity?

I am currently looking for a new type of job within my limited abilities.

How important is/was networking or connections in finding your current or other positions? Is it a factor in advancement once you're on the job?

Not having connections rarely proved to be an obstacle since my skills spoke highly enough for me on their own.

What would be your next career move?

A new job/field fitting within my physical limitations.

How much fulfillment do you get out of your career?

I liked the fact I got an honest day's pay for an honest day's work.

Do you feel that you are fairly compensated?

At most times I felt satisfied. Other times, when dealing with cheapskates and penny-pinchers, I felt underpaid due to their complaining and expecting miracles in repairing their worn-out autos for little or next to no pay.

Any comments or words of advice for someone entering your field?

Either become an extremely skilled overall mechanic or specialize in one kind of repair or rebuilding in the job field.

COMMERCIAL FISHERMAN

Name

Roy G.

Location

Boston, Massachusetts

Education

Some college

Total years in profession

27

Brief occupation description/goal of occupation

We harvested shrimp from the Gulf of Mexico. The object was to catch as much shrimp as possible in the shortest time. This goal was often complicated by dangerous weather and sea conditions. We often stayed out fishing three to four weeks at a stretch.

Why did you choose this career path?

I love the sea and the freedom that this career offers. I had just gotten out of the navy and was comfortable on boats.

What do you like about your occupation?

It is always new. Each trip offers a new series of events. The payoff when you get "in the shrimp" is satisfying.

What do you dislike about your occupation?

The long time at sea, the stink, and the nasty and dangerous creatures we encounter.

What are the misconceptions about your profession?

That it is benign. Many a boat and crew went to sea never to return. Many accidents occur that maim fishermen. The shrimp sometimes disappear, and we make no money.

On a scale of 1 to 10 (10 being great), how would you rate your occupation and why?

I would rate it a 10. It is exciting and rewarding. It is always changing.

What factors or former positions led to this occupation?

I was hungry and asked the captain to put me to work just for meals.

What career choices were most helpful?

Deciding to become a captain on a boat.

Did you have a mentor? If so, how did you find them? Did they help?

My first captain was a mentor. I found him by chance.

In a typical week, are your hours fixed or flexible? On what days do you tend to work overtime?

In a typical week, we worked sunset to sunrise or longer.

Is your work environment "hectic," "all work and no play," "serene," "laid back," or other? Briefly explain.

It is both. At sea, with all the gear in the water in fifteen-foot seas, while standing on the end of a forty-foot outrigger at night, trying to untangle equipment is "hectic." The calm seas before sunrise, when the surface of the ocean is as smooth as glass and reflective as a mirror—when a dolphin leaps out of the water six feet into the air, making eye contact with you, and you see the intelligence therein—is "serene."

What types of conflicts do you deal with?

Personalities sometimes clash. Living on a boat is close quarters, and conflicts between people can be stressful. When the weather turns nasty, the sea conflicts with the floating of the boat, always seeking the opportunity to swallow it.

Do you interface with coworkers, groups, or vendors, or do you work alone?

I closely interface with the crew.

What are your coworkers like?

The best of times; we are like a family.

What is management like?

A good captain is a dream. A bad captain is a nightmare.

Do you relocate often? Are there travel requirements?

Yes, we go to Texas in the summer and Florida in the winter.

Do you prefer going to work or leaving? Why?

Both. When you are on shore, you soon get antsy to go out fishing. When you've been out fishing three weeks, you want to go to shore.

How much fulfillment do you get out of your career?

Immense.

If you could choose again, how much would money be a factor?

Not at all.

Would you choose the same career path?

Yes.

Any comments or words of advice for someone entering your field?

Be careful. Learn all you can. Save your money.

VEHICLE ASSEMBLY TECHNICIAN

Name

Owen H.

Location

Northeast Kentucky

Education

Some college

Total years in profession

11

Brief occupation description/goal of occupation

To assemble automobiles in a factory environment using correct and quality means. To build a quality vehicle.

What do you like about your occupation?
Salary, work schedule, and benefits.

What do you dislike about your occupation?
Repetitiveness, taxing to mental and physical self.

What are the misconceptions about your profession?
That all workers are unintelligent in this field, when actually it runs only about 90 percent.

On a scale of 1 to 10 (10 being great), how would you rate your occupation and why?
I would say 7. Benefits, salary, and schedule.

What factors or former positions led to this occupation?
I was formerly in middle management; however, it was long hours and a much smaller salary and benefits.

What type of education was needed for your position?
A high school diploma.

In a typical week, are your hours fixed or flexible? On what days do you tend to work overtime?
Fixed . . . overtime was just eliminated this week.

What types of conflicts do you deal with?
Coworkers get moody occasionally, and there are those supervisors with a "complex."

What are your coworkers like?
Unmotivated, complain a great deal, simpletons.

What is management like?

It varies between those who know how to psychologically squeeze everything out of employees (tactfully) and those who try to push and push—with good results over many, but the few it alienates causes more trouble than it is worth.

Is input accepted, or do you fare better as a "yes man"?

"Yes man." My company is in the shape it is because advice is not accepted from those workers who may have an education and work on the line.

What issues have prevented your advancement?

I have no desire to move to company management, and seniority rules all other advances.

Is your position secure, or are you frequently looking for the next opportunity?

It's a secure opportunity (due to seniority), but I am always looking for a better life.

How important is/was networking or connections in finding your current or other positions? Is it a factor in advancement once you're on the job?

I knew someone who opened the door for me on this position.

What would be your next career move?

The same sort of hours and salary, but I would very much like to be home more.

How much fulfillment do you get out of your career?

Financial fulfillment.

Do you feel that you are fairly compensated?

For the field, yes; for the permanent physical damage, no.

Any comments or words of advice for someone entering your field?

Don't do it unless you are very young (physical work) and have no other abilities, such as education. An education is wasted at this profession.

BEEKEEPER

Name

Sara W.

Location

Southern California

Education

Some college

Total years in profession

6

Brief occupation description/goal of occupation

Providing beehives for the bees to live, placing the beehives next to the intended agriculture, collecting the hives at the second and third stage of crop harvest, caring for bees during off-season, enjoying the honey and wax produced by the bees.

Why did you choose this career path?

A hive showed up one day and needed shelter. It was started more accidentally but became quite the investment, plus when there were no bees being kept within this district. I found a need and a resource of investors who were visionaries.

What do you like about your occupation?

I enjoy the calming effect that caring for the bees forces you to sustain.

What are the misconceptions about your profession?

That all bees are violent and killer bees. If I get stung once in a while, it is always an accident on the bee's part—it got pinched by my clothing and was startled.

On a scale of 1 to 10 (10 being great), how would you rate your occupation and why?

An 8, because though it is rewarding, it is very seasonal and some of the equipment is expensive ($10,000 for a collector. This machine separates the waxcomb, and the honey is collected for resale to distributors).

What career choices were most helpful?

My time as a librarian. I knew where to look for information on bees and the beekeeping industry, a billion-dollar industry expanding due to the fact that the wax is very special and royal jelly is used in diets.

What career choices were least helpful/detrimental?

My work as a kennel keeper. The dogs try to bite at the bees and often get the bees riled up by shoving their noses into the hive entrance. The bees feel threatened and will attack the offending dog.

**Do you have to update your career with
ongoing training and certificates?**

I had to register with the Department of Agriculture, and once a year
they come by and check on the hive.

**When you were hired, did you receive professional
training or was it basically "on-the-job training"?**

It was a self-hire and self-training. Bees are very forgiving when it
comes to mistakes. I found my bees were very patient since it was
on-the-job training.

**In a typical week, are your hours fixed or flexible?
On what days do you tend to work overtime?**

Flexible by the hours of the sun. During really hot summers, I found
the bees awake as long as they were warm.

What types of conflicts do you deal with?

Robber bees that will decimate a hive and over-predation by
squirrels eating too much of the hive. Bears are not a problem in the
desert.

**Do you interface with coworkers, groups,
or vendors, or do you work alone?**

Dealing with suppliers and resources is equivalent to any social
contact. With the hives, it is only me and one other employee for the
heavy removal of the boxes. Usually, it is very calming.

**Is your position secure, or are you frequently
looking for the next opportunity?**

I am always looking for an opportunity to cross my path. It is more
a sign of the times in an uncertain economy than being unsatisfied
with the type of work I have.

How important is/was networking or connections in finding your current or other positions? Is it a factor in advancement once you're on the job?

Prior to taking this position as beekeeper, I had no connections or networking contacts. Now, I cannot see keeping this position without them, since they are my source of livelihood and care of the bees.

What would be your next career move?

Internet marketing and resources. Seventy-five percent of all baby boomers are getting healthier and living longer, and retirement is not an option anymore. People demand more.

How much fulfillment do you get out of your career?

Since I realized that without bees to pollinate the alfalfa—and they are the only creature that pollinates the alfalfa—the livestock would starve within a year, and that all life would die in two years without the bee, I am very satisfied.

If you could choose again, how much would money be a factor?

In the beginning, it was simple costs for my time. It plays an important factor in the restraints of economy, six years later.

Any comments or words of advice for someone entering your field?

Fear of insects can be a problem, and if you expect money gain in the first week, get a real job. As a hobby, it is quite exciting to watch bees you have raised swarm to raise another brood.

VETERINARY TECHNICIAN

Name

Dawn T.

Location

Baton Rouge, Louisiana

Education

Associate's degree

Total years in profession

6

Brief occupation description/goal of occupation

A veterinary technician is to a veterinarian much like what a registered nurse is to a human physician. A vet tech is responsible for everything from assisting in surgical procedures to cleaning up after patients. The goal of a vet tech is to provide the veterinarian with skilled help while accomplishing surgical and medical tasks that in turn help to provide better care for patients and their owners.

Why did you choose this career path?

I have always loved animals and knew that I wanted to help them. After doing research on veterinary medicine, I felt that becoming a veterinary technician would allow me the most opportunity to help medically and also bond with them. While a veterinarian performs the procedures on a patient, a technician is the one who helps them recover and soothes them after the trauma.

What do you like about your occupation?

What I like best about my career is that I get to cuddle with puppies, kittens, and foals. This is a wonderful thing and very therapeutic. I can wake up in a foul mood, and the second I see a baby animal, my day is made.

What do you dislike about your occupation?

Though it is sometimes for the best, euthanasia is always hard. For those patients who are suffering, or have no chance at a healthy life, it is a necessary alternative.

What are the misconceptions about your profession?

Some misconceptions about my profession are that anyone with a high-school education can do it. This is very untrue given the fact that a registered veterinary technician has put in over eighty hours of college courses focusing on the veterinary profession and all the technical aspects of it. We learn in school to perform everything from complete blood counts and chemistry panels to sewing up patients after major surgeries.

On a scale of 1 to 10 (10 being great), how would you rate your occupation and why?

I would rate my occupation as a 7. If the pay for this career were better, it would definitely be a 10.

What factors or former positions led to this occupation?

I am a realist. I know that being a veterinarian would have been a dream for me, but by the time I was a sophomore in college, I had a child. I knew how much time and money it would take me to go to vet school, so I researched careers as a veterinary technician and knew it was perfect for my situation. I don't regret it.

What career choices were most helpful?

The choice to work at a clinic where clinical trials were a big part of company focus was helpful. This allowed me to stay current on present and future pharmaceuticals.

What career choices were least helpful/detrimental?

I do think that having a more diverse background (I have only worked in one clinic for my entire career) would have been much more helpful to me.

Did you have a mentor? If so, how did you find them? Did they help?

There were not a lot of registered veterinary technicians when I began my career, so I did not have a mentor. I do hope that I was a mentor to some of my coworkers.

What type of education was needed for your position?

There are no state or federal regulations and requirements, as of yet, for the education of veterinary technicians. Many veterinary clinics and hospitals require certifications, however.

Was your formal education necessary for this position?

For myself, education was necessary—I wanted to have a career that I felt knowledgeable and confident about—but the answer to this question is, no. No formal education is required.

Do you have to update your career with ongoing training and certificates?

There is some continuing education that is offered, but in the state of Louisiana, it is not required.

In a typical week, are your hours fixed or flexible? On what days do you tend to work overtime?

The hours are fixed, but it is a common occurrence for an emergency to come in at closing. In addition, there are a doctor and technician "on call" twenty-four hours a day.

Is your work environment "hectic," "all work and no play," "serene," "laid back," or other? Briefly explain.

Veterinary medicine is a lot like human medicine. It is very hectic, because we are taking care of many patients and also their "parents."

What types of conflicts do you deal with?

There are conflicts with owners over cost, and sometimes between staff.

Do you interface with coworkers, groups, or vendors, or do you work alone?

We are a medical team.

What is management like?

The management is the doctors. They are very straightforward and cannot be worried with trivial things.

What issues have prevented your advancement?

I have reached the "glass ceiling." As far as technicians go, I am as high as it goes.

Is your position secure, or are you frequently looking for the next opportunity?

My position is very secure.

How much fulfillment do you get out of your career?

My career is very fulfilling. I have the opportunity to help so many animals that do not have the ability to help themselves.

Would you choose the same career path?

Absolutely.

Any comments or words of advice for someone entering your field?

Before deciding on this career, volunteer at a number of clinics, hospitals, and zoos to make sure it is what you want to do.

PIZZA DELIVERY DRIVER

Name

Brandy B.

Location

Northern Texas

Education

Bachelor of Arts

Total years in profession

6

Brief occupation description/goal of occupation

Make as many deliveries as possible during open hours.

Why did you choose this career path?

Easy money and lots of personal time to study for college classes.

What do you like about your occupation?

Lots of time to do other things while driving.

What do you dislike about your occupation?

You receive no respect. People feel that you must be desperate to deliver pizza; if only they knew that I was probably making more per year than many of them.

What are the misconceptions about your profession?

There aren't that many. Actually, a lot of them are true. You get to see a lot of strange sights and get many unwanted offers.

On a scale of 1 to 10 (10 being great), how would you rate your occupation and why?

An 8. I always wanted more money with less work. That's why I am in college.

What factors or former positions led to this occupation?

I started college and needed a job where I could set my own hours and study while getting paid. I have to work full time and go to school full time.

What career choices were most helpful?

Becoming a driver instead of going into management.

What career choices were least helpful/detrimental?

Starting out in management. I was making about ten thousand less than the drivers.

**Did you have a mentor? If so, how did
you find them? Did they help?**

Yes, I was the only female and the youngest person in the store
for about four years. They were all mentors teaching me the ways
to get around all the bad work that nobody likes to do, but has to
be done (paperwork shortcuts, finding or correcting shortages or
overages, etc.).

What type of education was needed for your position?

None, but I was about the only one there who was not a felon. All
you need is a semi-clean driving record.

**In a typical week, are your hours fixed or flexible?
On what days do you tend to work overtime?**

Flexible. Overtime came on Fridays and Saturdays.

**Is your work environment "hectic," "all work and no
play," "serene," "laid back," or other? Briefly explain.**

My store was very laid back. We had loads of fun and got all our
work done.

What types of conflicts do you deal with?

Irate customers not liking their pizza.

**Do you interface with coworkers, groups,
or vendors, or do you work alone?**

Delivering is a lot of alone work.

What is management like?

Upper management are backstabbers. They would tell you one
thing and then do whatever they needed to do to get themselves
ahead: the usual for any business.

How important is/was networking or connections in finding your current or other positions? Is it a factor in advancement once you're on the job?

Networking within the company's other stores was the only way to get all that you needed to keep the one store running smoothly.

What would be your next career move?

Getting into grad school so that I can make more money.

Do you prefer going to work or leaving? Why?

I loved going into work. I had fun every day.

Do you feel that you are fairly compensated?

No, does anyone? We all want more money.

Would you choose the same career path?

Possibly, when I get accepted into grad school.

Any comments or words of advice for someone entering your field?

Do it for quick money, not for life. I started to feel like a lifer after six years.

FEDERAL CIVIL SERVICE

Name

Melissa C.

Location

Atlanta, Georgia

Education

Some college

Total years in profession

26

Brief occupation description/goal of occupation

Unit deployment manager—get military members ready to deploy to go to war.

Why did you choose this career path?

I like the excitement of the job.

What do you like about your occupation?

I like the fast pace of the job.

What do you dislike about your occupation?

I dislike having to send young people off to war.

On a scale of 1 to 10 (10 being great), how would you rate your occupation and why?

I give it a 9—I feel I am contributing something to my country.

What factors or former positions led to this occupation?

In the job before this one, I was a logistics person dealing with moving people and cargo in military aircraft to get them to the war zone.

What career choices were most helpful?

Accepting a job as a logistician helped me with the job I have now.

If you didn't have a mentor, would you have liked one?

Yes, I would have liked a mentor.

What type of education was needed for your position?

I had to have some college and had to go to a special school to be a logistician.

When you were hired, did you receive professional training or was it basically "on-the-job training"?

On-the-job training along with some professional training after starting the job.

**In a typical week, are your hours fixed or flexible?
On what days do you tend to work overtime?**

Flexible, and yes, most days I do work a lot of overtime.

**Is your work environment "hectic," "all work and no
play," "serene," "laid back," or other? Briefly explain.**

My work environment is all work and some play. It also gets very
hectic at times.

What types of conflicts do you deal with?

I deal a lot with people not wanting to deploy to fight the war. It
makes it hard to get them ready to go.

What are your coworkers like?

My coworkers are hardworking like me and take their job very
seriously.

What is management like?

Management is sometimes very hard on its people and not very
understanding of what their employees are having to deal with.

Is input accepted, or do you fare better as a "yes man"?

Input is accepted sometimes, but most times being a yes man gets
you what you want.

**How important is/was networking or connections
in finding your current or other positions? Is it a
factor in advancement once you're on the job?**

Having connections was very important when I decided I wanted
to work as a federal civil servant for the government. Connections
helped me get my foot in the door to get my job.

What would be your next career move?

I would like to move up the ladder to the next level of being a
logistician by moving into war plans.

Do you relocate often? Are there travel requirements?

No, I do not relocate. There are some travel requirements but not many.

How much fulfillment do you get out of your career?

I get some fulfillment out of my career because I feel I am contributing to my country.

Do you feel that you are fairly compensated?

No, I don't feel I am fairly compensated for the job that I do right now.

Are the benefits and vacation schedule fair?

The benefits are, but the vacation schedule is not fair. I can't take time off when I want to because I am deep in my position, and when I do take off, I worry all the time I am off that when I come back to the job it will be a mess.

If you could choose again, how much would money be a factor?

Money would be a factor if I could choose again.

Would you choose the same career path?

I believe I would choose the same career path because of the way I was raised. I was raised in a military family; the job I do is really with the military, and I understand what the people are going through.

Any comments or words of advice for someone entering your field?

The advice I would give to someone entering my field is to be ready to be under a lot of stress and have a lot of sleepless nights, and be ready to have to deal with people's emotions.

FARMER

Name

Carl L.

Location

Fargo, North Dakota

Education

Bachelor of Science

Total years in profession

6

Brief occupation description/goal of occupation

Owner/operator of a ten-thousand-acre grain farm.
My goal is to always be more profitable by selling my
products at a higher level and reducing my costs.

Why did you choose this career path?

This is a business my parents had started.

What do you like about your occupation?

I am in charge of what I do every day.

What do you dislike about your occupation?

The work is constant and I always feel guilty when I leave for even a couple of days.

What are the misconceptions about your profession?

People think all farmers carry pitchforks and wear straw hats and overalls when it is really getting to be a high-tech profession.

On a scale of 1 to 10 (10 being great), how would you rate your occupation and why?

An 8. I love the freedom and the feeling of being in control of my life.

What factors or former positions led to this occupation?

The door was always open for me to return to the family business. I spent eleven years away from it, but I got comfortable with the job I was doing and finally realized I couldn't keep doing it any longer. I needed a challenge and a job that offered some responsibility, so I gave it a try.

What career choices were most helpful?

I sold computers for six years, and those skills really have helped with my current job, especially in negotiating.

What career choices were least helpful/detrimental?

I spent too many years at that computer sales job doing the same thing year after year, which really set me back professionally.

**Did you have a mentor? If so, how did
you find them? Did they help?**

I kind of always did whatever I wanted and never had a mentor. I
probably should have been more serious when I was in my twenties
and a mentor would really have helped, but I don't know if I would
have been open to it then.

What type of education was needed for your position?

My BS in business administration has really helped in my farm
management position.

**Do you have to update your career with
ongoing training and certificates?**

Our company has always promoted ongoing training and education.

**In a typical week, are your hours fixed or flexible?
On what days do you tend to work overtime?**

In farming it all depends on the time of year. The only thing typical in
agriculture is that nothing is typical.

**Is your work environment "hectic," "all work and no
play," "serene," "laid back," or other? Briefly explain.**

Once again, it varies throughout the year, but I would describe it as
hectic. Organization is the key.

What types of conflicts do you deal with?

An ever-changing commodity market, employee issues, Mother
Nature, rising prices of real estate and steel.

**Do you interface with coworkers, groups,
or vendors, or do you work alone?**

We have a small staff including family and employees.

What are your coworkers like?

Very hardworking.

What is management like?

Strict, always watching the cash flow.

Is input accepted, or do you fare better as a "yes man"?

Input is demanded.

What issues have prevented your advancement?

In sales, the cash I was making was keeping me more interested in selling than moving up into management.

Is your position secure, or are you frequently looking for the next opportunity?

My position is secure but I must perform my role profitably over time in order to keep it.

What would be your next career move?

I think I will stay where I am now, but I will be doing some investing in local businesses that I am a part of.

How much fulfillment do you get out of your career?

I never thought I'd ever like farming, but there is huge responsibility with owning your own business, and that is very fulfilling.

If you could choose again, how much would money be a factor?

If I were to work for someone else, money and benefits would be a factor. But since I work for myself, I am more concerned with net worth and equity.

Would you choose the same career path?

Looking back, I guess I would, but I would have tried a few more jobs along the way that would have sharpened my skills. That's easy to say now.

Any comments or words of advice for someone entering your field?

Diversify. You don't have to have all your eggs in one basket. Invest in some other business to give you value add.

POLICE OFFICER (SERGEANT)

Name

Gary T.

Location

Los Angeles, California

Education

Master of Arts

Total years in profession

11

Brief occupation description/goal of occupation

Enforce federal, state, and local laws, keep the peace, and act as a deterrent against criminal activity.

Why did you choose this career path?

I was required to complete some internships as part of my undergraduate college degree. I interned at a Southern California police department and noticed that all the employees really seemed to enjoy their careers.

What do you like about your occupation?

The best part is working with people on a daily basis, never really knowing how your day is going to go, and actually getting to help somebody once in a great while.

What do you dislike about your occupation?

Monday morning quarterbacking—it seems like everyone else knows how to do the job of law enforcement better than law enforcement.

What are the misconceptions about your profession?

The main misconception is that the police are an "all-knowing" entity. Just because the Los Angeles Police Department (LAPD) knows something, it doesn't mean that neighboring law enforcement agencies are aware of it, and vice versa. On a more specific scale, just because an officer who works day shift is aware of an incident on his or her shift doesn't mean that the officers working nights know about it.

On a scale of 1 to 10 (10 being great), how would you rate your occupation and why?

I would say a 9. For certain personality types, this is simply a terrific career. The people I work with on a daily basis exemplify selflessness and determination.

What factors or former positions led to this occupation?

The college internship is what turned me on to law enforcement as a possible career choice. Research into other factors, such as benefits and variety of assignments within law enforcement, all only served to positively reinforce my inclination to this career.

What career choices were most helpful?

This is the only career I've known. I was hired immediately after graduating from college (undergraduate). I can say, emphatically, that a college education has definitely benefited my professional aspirations in law enforcement.

Did you have a mentor? If so, how did you find them? Did they help?

I didn't have a mentor prior to getting hired by my current employer. However, once hired, law enforcement has many "informal" mentors built into daily operations. For example, training officers, veterans, and supervisors all assist newly hired officers to learn their jobs.

What type of education was needed for your position?

For the agency I work with, a high school diploma or GED is the minimal requirement.

Was your formal education necessary for this position?

A formal education was not necessary, but it is an advantage in separating yourself from other candidates competing for a limited number of jobs or promotions.

Do you have to update your career with ongoing training and certificates?

The state of California does require ongoing training for all law enforcement officers. Officers can apply for and receive professional certifications from the state based on a combination of career length, type of formal education, and number of hours of training completed, if the officer is inclined to do so.

When you were hired, did you receive professional training or was it basically "on-the-job training"?

A newly hired police officer in California attends a police academy, which I would deem "professional training." Upon successful graduation from the academy, most officers must complete a formal field training program, which is along the lines of "on-the-job training."

In a typical week, are your hours fixed or flexible? On what days do you tend to work overtime?

As an officer, your hours are fixed. Overtime was determined by the needs of the organization based upon minimal manpower standards per shift and how busy it might have been that day. Since being promoted to sergeant, my hours have become much more flexible, with many "shift adjusts" and "hour adjusts" being done to accommodate departmental needs without being a drain on overtime funds.

Is your work environment "hectic," "all work and no play," "serene," "laid back," or other? Briefly explain.

By and large, my work environment is "serene." However, with one bad incident, we immediately shift into "chaos" mode until our priorities are achieved (keeping the peace).

What types of conflicts do you deal with?

We deal with people problems. As officers, we respond to calls where there has been a crime (committed by a person) or some sort of dispute (between people). As a supervisor, these principles haven't changed. Only now, as a sergeant, I deal with disputes between a citizen and officer, or between departmental employees.

Do you interface with coworkers, groups, or vendors, or do you work alone?

I work in a very small police department. As a result, "job titles" are not exclusive to assignments. When work needs to get done, everyone is expected to pitch in and help. Therefore, I interface with everybody.

What are your coworkers like?

My coworkers are people. They reflect the community in which they were raised. As a group, the values of law enforcement are likely more homogeneous than other career fields.

What is management like?

Management is interested in making sure the departmental goals are achieved. They keep their eye on the big picture and allow middle management to make the decisions on how to achieve them.

What issues have prevented your advancement?

I don't think my advancement has been prevented by any issues. I work in a highly competitive department. I compete for promotion against numerous officers with graduate degrees, military experience, extensive work knowledge, strong work ethic, and good moral values. When I compete and don't receive a position or promotion, it's because I'm not as good as the competition.

Is your position secure, or are you frequently looking for the next opportunity?

I'm a civil servant. My position with the department is very secure (within reason). However, internally, I'm always looking for additional responsibility, collateral duties, or new assignments, in order to be a more knowledgeable and versatile employee. As far as looking to leave my department for another, or pursue another career field, I have no interest whatsoever.

How important is/was networking or connections in finding your current or other positions? Is it a factor in advancement once you're on the job?

I believe that networking is very important in "getting one's foot in the door." When trying to get hired, I consistently ran into the same competitors testing for various law enforcement agencies. In making small talk, some phone numbers were exchanged and information about which agencies were hiring would flow. After getting hired, the networking and connections absolutely make an officer a more effective employee. It's much easier to call an officer from a neighboring agency to ask for information than to request the information through official channels. I suppose that, indirectly, this increased effectiveness through networking makes one candidate a little more attractive than another when advancement opportunities occur.

What would be your next career move?

I'm interested in promotion to the rank of lieutenant, but not at this point in my career. As a sergeant, I'm interested still in working in the detective bureau or internal affairs.

Do you feel that you are fairly compensated?

When I researched law enforcement as a potential career, I knew that I would never be "rich." This was acceptable in light of the fact that I knew I would be "comfortable." Law enforcement careers relegate people to a middle-class standard of living. If you want more than that, do something else. Do I think I'm fairly compensated? At times, yes (when things are routine), at other times, no (ever had a gun pointed at you?).

If you could choose again, how much would money be a factor?

For my lifestyle (unmarried, no children), money would not play any factor in an opportunity to choose again. Ask me again if I soon get married or have children, and my answer might change.

Would you choose the same career path?

Probably. I enjoy this job too much. If financial burdens forced me to look for a higher-paying career, I'd probably still try to be a reserve officer somewhere, simply because of the joy I get from work.

Any comments or words of advice for someone entering your field?

Do your homework. Look in a mirror and figure out what you want to do and what you believe in. Law enforcement is a challenging career with very real risks. Those in law enforcement must believe in the mission and responsibilities they take on. If you don't, you will not perform your duties adequately, or the work itself will make you a miserable person. It's challenging but rewarding at the same time.

TILE SETTER

Name

Mike H.

Location

Atlanta, Georgia

Education

Some college

Total years in profession

18

Brief occupation description/goal of occupation

I am a tile setter. I estimate jobs and give bids. I order materials. I have four employees.

Why did you choose this career path?

It was something I got into when I was eighteen, and I liked it very much.

What do you like about your occupation?

I like that every job is different. Each is like a puzzle I have to figure out.

What do you dislike about your occupation?

Scheduling is sometimes hard. It seems like people want everything right now.

What are the misconceptions about your profession?

They think that it is easy. You can't just learn how to set tile from a book or a quick class at Home Depot.

On a scale of 1 to 10 (10 being great), how would you rate your occupation and why?

I would say 7 . . . It does pay the bills, and it keeps my family fed. There are always worse jobs than mine. I remember picking tobacco on my grandparents' farm. Now that is hard work.

What factors or former positions led to this occupation?

I was working as a meat cutter and my friend needed some help on the weekends to install tile; I liked it a lot and eventually started full time.

What career choices were most helpful?

Deciding to start my own business installing tile.

What career choices were least helpful/detrimental?

Trying to get big too fast and being unable to control quality.

Did you have a mentor? If so, how did you find them? Did they help?

Yes. I was putting tile in one of his rental houses. He was an older man who had been in the Vietnam War, and he has always encouraged me to take risks and to think things through.

What type of education was needed for your position?

None, just common sense.

Do you have to update your career with ongoing training and certificates?

Not really certificates, but there are always new products coming out to make our job easier, so I have to listen to the sales pitch of the sales rep and decide if it is a quality product.

When you were hired, did you receive professional training or was it basically "on-the-job training"?

I would say on-the-job training.

In a typical week, are your hours fixed or flexible? On what days do you tend to work overtime?

Depends how much work I have. Days always vary.

Is your work environment "hectic," "all work and no play," "serene," "laid back," or other? Briefly explain.

Hectic . . . getting materials to the job, talking to customers, making sure everything is done the way it should be.

What types of conflicts do you deal with?

Installers didn't understand the way I wanted the tile installed, or the customer changes their mind about something.

What issues have prevented your advancement?

Figuring out how to do more work, but keep the quality.

Is your position secure, or are you frequently looking for the next opportunity?

Yes, I most always have work.

How important is/was networking or connections in finding your current or other positions? Is it a factor in advancement once you're on the job?

It is always important to network with other people in the same industry, to learn better ways of doing things.

How much fulfillment do you get out of your career?

Seventy-five percent, but I could always use more money; I have two young children.

Do you feel that you are fairly compensated?

Yes; some jobs are better than others.

Are the benefits and vacation schedule fair?

No; I have to pay for my own benefits, and vacations are almost impossible.

If you could choose again, how much would money be a factor?

I think it is more important to base a career on what you like than how much you make.

Would you choose the same career path?

Yes, I think I would.

Any comments or words of advice for someone entering your field?

Talk to lots of people in the industry . . . better to learn from someone else's mistakes.

TRUCK DRIVER

Name

Robert C.

Location

El Paso, Texas

Education

High school

Total years in profession

15

Brief occupation description/goal of occupation

To pick up freight at point A and deliver to point B.

Why did you choose this career path?

To make better money than I was previously making.

What do you like about your occupation?

You're always in a different place every day; you get to see the country and make a good living doing it.

What do you dislike about your occupation?

City traffic; people using cell phones when they're driving; sometimes not getting enough sleep; not enough parking for trucks in the rest areas after 9:00 p.m. or 10:00 p.m.

What are the misconceptions about your profession?

That you're a paid tourist just sitting there and holding the steering wheel—there's a lot more to driving a truck than that.

On a scale of 1 to 10 (10 being great), how would you rate your occupation and why?

I think it's a 7. There are a lot of pros and cons, but the money's pretty good.

What factors or former positions led to this occupation?

I live in a city where the wages are low, so it was one of the few options I had without a college degree.

What career choices were most helpful?

Going to a good truck-driving school.

What career choices were least helpful/detrimental?

Almost going to a bad truck-driving school. There are a lot of trucking schools out there—you have to do some homework. The best way to find out about schools and trucking companies is to talk to the students or drivers that are there. Most people will tell you the truth that way.

**Did you have a mentor? If so, how did
you find them? Did they help?**

Yes, I had a few good mentors at the school and when I trained for
the first company I worked for.

What type of education was needed for your position?

At the time, it was two-and-a-half months, but now it's two to four
weeks. You now learn the basics and how to get your license, then
get paid to learn on the road.

Was your formal education necessary for this position?

Yes. You need a high school diploma or GED.

**Do you have to update your career with
ongoing training and certificates?**

Yes. It varies from state to state, but just like a regular license, you
have to renew it every two to eight years. Now, if you have a Hazmat
endorsement, you have to take a test every one to two years, and
after 9/11, you go through a state and federal background check.

**When you were hired, did you receive professional
training or was it basically "on-the-job training"?**

Yes. I went through a four-day orientation, and then I went on the
road with a trainer for six weeks.

**In a typical week, are your hours fixed or flexible?
On what days do you tend to work overtime?**

It all depends on the shippers and receivers; if one of them takes
too long to load or unload you, it can mean not getting much sleep
(sometimes no sleep) to get to the next place. This is not a nine-to-
five job Monday through Friday—at least not over the road. If you
get a local or semi-local job, then yes, but most local driving jobs
don't pay much unless it's union.

Is your work environment "hectic," "all work and no play," "serene," "laid back," or other? Briefly explain.

I think I've explained most of that already, but it is a job, and it can get very hectic with the way people drive—including other truck drivers. You have to be very patient, because road rage can happen very easily in this business. There are a lot of good things too—like the money and the scenery. The open road with very little traffic can be very serene and laid back.

What types of conflicts do you deal with?

Traffic and making appointments on time.

Do you interface with coworkers, groups, or vendors, or do you work alone?

Mostly alone, unless you're a team driver—then you have one other driver. But you can always talk to the other drivers on the CB or when you stop to get fuel at the truck stop.

What are your coworkers like?

Most of them are great people, but there are always a few bad apples.

What is management like?

Mine has been great. Most of the time they're trying to keep me happy.

Is input accepted, or do you fare better as a "yes man"?

Most input is accepted, but you want to have a little "yes man" going on at the same time.

What issues have prevented your advancement?

After driving for so long, you top out and only get a raise when the industry raises its rates; and with fuel prices right now, that's not going to happen.

Is your position secure, or are you frequently looking for the next opportunity?

There are lots of companies out there, and the demand for trucking is way up there, so the need is definitely there. I've been driving for longer than I really wanted to, and it was good to me—but yes, I'm always looking for new opportunities.

What would be your next career move?

Self-employment, but not in the trucking industry.

How much fulfillment do you get out of your career?

It is a rewarding career, but I wouldn't call myself fulfilled.

Would you choose the same career path?

Yes.

Any comments or words of advice for someone entering your field?

Just remember, it's a job, and it's definitely not for everyone; but it's a good living, and it has been a good career for me. Make sure to go to the schools and talk to the students; they'll give you the real story about the school. The school recruiter's job, just like that of the trucking company recruiter, is to bring you in and make money. So go to the people (one of which you are about to become) and ask them.

TRANSPORTATION CIVIL ENGINEER

Name

Megan S.

Location

Seattle, Washington

Education

Bachelor of Science

Total years in profession

5

Brief occupation description/goal of occupation

Analyze traffic, evaluate transportation networks, and write traffic impact studies.

Why did you choose this career path?

I narrowed it down from engineering (because I like problem solving) to civil (because I like the building/hands-on aspect) to transportation (because it seemed interesting, but probably was a wrong move ultimately).

What do you like about your occupation?

Generous pay, good benefits, intelligent people.

What do you dislike about your occupation?

I'm no longer interested in the field, and I feel like my work is meaningless or at least provides intangible benefits. Also, my future career path involves less analysis and more management and business skills, which I'm not at all interested in.

What are the misconceptions about your profession?

I don't think many people are aware of my specific job (transportation analysis), but in engineering in general, most students are not made aware of how many nontechnical skills are required (writing, business, communication, etc.). In this sense, I feel disappointed and misled.

Did you have a mentor? If so, how did you find them? Did they help?

I had several peers, but no one in a higher position that could have better prepared/informed me.

If you didn't have a mentor, would you have liked one?

Absolutely.

What type of education was needed for your position?

Bachelor of science in civil engineering.

Do you have to update your career with ongoing training and certificates?

Licensing is strongly preferred, but at the very least, training to stay up to date is necessary.

In a typical week, are your hours fixed or flexible? On what days do you tend to work overtime?

I typically work forty to forty-five hours per week, which can be somewhat flexible.

Is your work environment "hectic," "all work and no play," "serene," "laid back," or other? Briefly explain.

Workload is up and down, from very stressful deadlines to "nothing to do." In private practice (versus government), there is often a lot of pressure to stay "billable" rather than work on training or other opportunities.

What types of conflicts do you deal with?

Prioritizing projects and managing deadlines, and working with different people with different working styles.

What are your coworkers like?

Some are the typical "introvert" analytical engineer, while others are more business/sales motivated and more outgoing.

Is input accepted, or do you fare better as a "yes man"?

Input and innovation are almost always encouraged.

What issues have prevented your advancement?

My own lessening interest in current work, as well as apprehension about transitioning to different work, such as business and management.

Is your position secure, or are you frequently looking for the next opportunity?

Pretty secure, as my job is in high demand.

How important is/was networking or connections in finding your current or other positions? Is it a factor in advancement once you're on the job?

I'd say it's somewhat important, but not necessary.

What would be your next career move?

That's an excellent question. I haven't figured that out yet; hoping your book might help.

Do you relocate often? Are there travel requirements?

No, it's minimal to no travel.

Do you prefer going to work or leaving? Why?

Leaving. I'm not a people person, and all day I just want to get away from everyone and go do something else more productive or interesting. I despise dressing up for work (even "business casual"), building relationships with coworkers, and doing work that seems to have no tangible outcome.

How much fulfillment do you get out of your career?

Little.

If you could choose again, how much would money be a factor?

I knew this job would provide good starting pay, and stability was important to me. But now that I have saved up money and feel so unfulfilled, money will not be a primary consideration for my next career choice.

Would you choose the same career path?

Probably not.

Any comments or words of advice for someone entering your field?

You may be drawn into engineering because of your love of problem solving or data crunching, but the "hidden secret" is that the successful engineers spend most of their time talking to people, writing, marketing, and managing others. So, if this doesn't appeal to you, you might want to reconsider or modify your career choice.

MAMMOGRAPHER

Name

Janet H.

Location

Central North Carolina

Education

Bachelor of Science

Total years in profession

25

Brief occupation description/goal of occupation

Provide quality mammography as mandated by MQSA Mammography Quality Standards Act (federal standards).

Why did you choose this career path?

A dear friend was diagnosed with breast cancer found upon a screening mammogram.

What do you like about your occupation?

Each patient is a unique experience. Many are repeats from the years past, and we have developed a relationship.

What do you dislike about your occupation?

It's not considered a specialty field, even though an MD who can do anything in a hospital or with patients is not allowed to perform a mammogram. It's very emotionally draining, and not a glamor job. Each patient requires a sincere effort to make them comfortable, relaxed; their fear of the unknown makes them tense and less responsive to compression, which is necessary to obtain quality films.

On a scale of 1 to 10 (10 being great), how would you rate your occupation and why?

I would say 7. Low compensation; benefits are being reduced yearly, but federal jurisdiction mandates are ever increasing (quality control); it's considered low priority because it is a woman's disease, not a moneymaker, so salaries reflect this.

What factors or former positions led to this occupation?

I was tired of being a radiologic tech, which is quite a repetitive position. Mammograms require technical skills and sometimes imagination.

What career choices were least helpful/detrimental?

Obtaining a bachelor of science, which was not needed, but I thought it would help market my abilities within the system. I just went into deep debt.

What type of education was needed for your position?

A two-year degree, a radiologic tech certification, and then specialized on-the-job training and passing certification in mammography.

Do you have to update your career with ongoing training and certificates?

Yes, continuing education in mammography and radiologic technology.

When you were hired, did you receive professional training or was it basically "on-the-job training"?

I had to have radiologic tech certification in place; then I was allowed to learn mammography on the job.

In a typical week, are your hours fixed or flexible? On what days do you tend to work overtime?

Pretty much fixed at forty hours per week.

Is your work environment "hectic," "all work and no play," "serene," "laid back," or other? Briefly explain.

A lot depends on the patient. They can make or break your "laid back." It's becoming more and more demanding and harder to understand why when you are trying to help someone, they can turn on you.

What types of conflicts do you deal with?

Late arrivals, unscheduled patients, lack of supplies, each patient's different temperament. No matter how hard you try, you cannot please some.

What is management like?

Money. Do more with less.

Is input accepted, or do you fare better as a "yes man"?

Yes, ma'am!

What issues have prevented your advancement?

I do not have contacts at the main office. I have always been offsite; all who went back to school with me to obtain a BS have advanced (except me), and my radiologic director actually told me that I was too good at my job—no one else could handle it. I was sole operator for fourteen years—no on-site supervision.

Is your position secure, or are you frequently looking for the next opportunity?

Oh yes, it's secure, but I'm always looking for a change. I'm not going to jump from fire to frying pan and cannot afford to take a cut in pay.

What would be your next career move?

Out of direct patient contact.

Do you relocate often? Are there travel requirements?

My satellite office has been relocated six times within fifteen years, all within a ten-mile radius. It's very stressful for patients, because they never know where I will be from year to year.

Do you prefer going to work or leaving? Why?

That's a loaded question. I stated previously that your patients can make or break what started out to be a really good day. A lot of patients do not appreciate the effort we take to provide quality mammography. They do not realize we're trying to save their life.

How much fulfillment do you get out of your career?

My greatest satisfaction is knowing that I have a strong following of patients and knowing that I provide quality mammography for them.

Are the benefits and vacation schedule fair?

Reductions occur every year, to include losing paid-time-off accrual.

If you could choose again, how much would money be a factor?

A lot.

Would you choose the same career path?

I would have become a radiologic tech again. I would have chosen to stay in the hospital and become specialized in everything possible. I would have loved to have been involved in PACS (picture archival and communications system).

Any comments or words of advice for someone entering your field?

Specialize, socialize with other employees, go for every opportunity you can. Don't stay just a radiologic tech; there are too many graduates each year that can fill this need.

OFFICE MANAGER

Name

Kimberly H.

Location

Houston, Texas

Education

Some college

Total years in profession

13

Brief occupation description/goal of occupation

Managed daily operations for health care financial advisory and investment firms. Made decisions daily and worked with computer software for presentations, correspondence, and reports. I did presentations and arranged client meetings and office gatherings. I was relied upon for many jobs over the thirteen years I was employed.

Why did you choose this career path?

I was asked to join a former boss to open a Houston office of a New York–based firm, and it seemed like a good opportunity.

What do you like about your occupation?

I enjoyed my boss and liked what we did in terms of helping hospitals and other health-related organizations find the funds and help they needed to expand their business and/or introduce new products to the market.

What do you dislike about your occupation?

When joining the firm, we were a small company, and everyone's opinion mattered. We became a "bought-out" firm, first by a top investment firm, then by a group of private investors. My opinion became less and less valued and, by choice, I quit. I believe the company was more profitable in terms of the good it did in earlier years and had become a firm about a few in New York getting rich on the backs of the long-timers.

What are the misconceptions about your profession?

As an office manager, bosses sometimes thought I should remember everything immediately. While I always had information at the tips of my fingers, I was helping four or five local executives with their issues and helping regional executives, including the owners, with their needs. Problem was, I was working on many projects at the same time, and it was more difficult to keep them straight than my bosses wanted to recognize.

On a scale of 1 to 10 (10 being great), how would you rate your occupation and why?

My occupation: 10; my firm at the beginning: 10; my firm the last three years: 3.

What factors or former positions led to this occupation?

I started as a receptionist with a consulting firm at seventeen years of age. I was promoted within the firm to graphic design, then left for more money to join an investment firm. I didn't like the investment firm I was working for, and after four months, my new boss offered me a ground floor opportunity with another firm. I accepted the offer.

What career choices were most helpful?

I always chose to go the extra mile. Eighty percent of my success and the success of those I hired and trained was attitude and willingness. Also, stay sharp and keep your mind jogging at all times at all costs. Like a duck, I stayed calm on the surface and paddled like the devil under the water. Also, I was always honest, never took credit for someone else's work, and gave credit when due. Further, I accepted responsibility when I made mistakes. Overall, I chose to commit to doing my best work with the best attitude. Also, I listened more than I talked and thought carefully before I spoke. I would tell myself: think before you speak!

What career choices were least helpful/detrimental?

I wear my feelings on my sleeve and may have been taken advantage of at times. Also, I failed to delegate because I didn't want to let someone else do the work—not because I was selfish, but because I truly wanted to get it done right and not worry about it, for the good of my bosses. Also, while this is no longer a problem for me, failure to embrace change is a detriment.

Did you have a mentor? If so, how did you find them? Did they help?

Yes, I have had several. They helped a lot. Even now as a stay-at-home mom and PTO (parent teacher organization) president at my children's school, I am working off good advice received by a number of valuable people from over the years.

What type of education was needed for your position?

Generally, the person employed in my capacity had a college

degree. I did not. I had some college, but school simply wasn't for me.

Was your formal education necessary for this position?

No, but it required a good deal of common sense and the ability to think on your feet.

Do you have to update your career with ongoing training and certificates?

No, but I do stay versed in the computer and various software programs, in case I opt to return to the workforce.

When you were hired, did you receive professional training or was it basically "on-the-job training"?

No. I was self-taught on a number of software programs. I did have people to call on from other offices, but the resources were limited.

In a typical week, are your hours fixed or flexible? On what days do you tend to work overtime?

Flexible. About twenty-eight hours each week, but paid full time with benefits, including three weeks' vacation and insurance at no cost to me for myself, my husband, and two boys.

Is your work environment "hectic," "all work and no play," "serene," "laid back," or other? Briefly explain.

Hectic at times and relaxed at others. My bosses traveled, so when they were in town, it was busy. However, when they were away, I was able to catch up on things that had been neglected while they had been there keeping me busy.

What types of conflicts do you deal with?

At work, my local bosses wanted me to shield the corporate folks from local issues. I tended to agree to do this because corporate made big deals about small things.

Do you interface with coworkers, groups, or vendors, or do you work alone?

Yes—daily. While I was in the office alone a good deal of the time, we had people in regularly. Also, lots of phone interaction with executives, hospital administrators, accountants, attorneys, etc.

What are your coworkers like?

Two old-timers were wonderful. One younger Rice University grad was terrible. The other younger Rice grad was great. I hired an office assistant who was no good at all but looked really good. She got away with too much and stayed about four years when she should have been fired after a few months.

What is management like?

Management at corporate didn't listen. I think the owners who sold out lost their conscience. It saddened me. They sold out and made buckets of money leaving loyal employees out to dry.

Is input accepted, or do you fare better as a "yes man"?

At the end, I fared better as a "yes" person. In the earlier years, I gave my opinion, as did others. The company isn't the same, and I would argue that it was no longer a top-notch place to work. It had become just another corporate firm.

What issues have prevented your advancement?

I was at the top of my game. My bosses were Rice University grads (Houston). There was nowhere for me to go at the firm, but the pay was good, and I knew and liked what I did.

Is your position secure, or are you frequently looking for the next opportunity?

In the end, I considered other opportunities. For the first ten years, I never looked elsewhere.

How important is/was networking or connections in finding your current or other positions? Is it a factor in advancement once you're on the job?

Very important. I never burn bridges, and I walk in truth. It is the only way.

How much fulfillment do you get out of your career?

I was very fulfilled when working in the early years. It had a lot to do with management and how they treated their employees. Somehow that was lost in the end.

If you could choose again, how much would money be a factor?

A great deal. I enjoy work but, let's face it, I have a family to entertain, clothe, feed, save for, etc.

Would you choose the same career path?

Yes.

Any comments or words of advice for someone entering your field?

Be honest and go the extra mile. It does pay off in the long run. While at times you may feel taken for granted, when bonuses are passed around, those who do the little extras—and with a smile—are the ones who are rewarded. Plus, knowing you are doing your best allows you to sleep better at night.

FITNESS EDUCATOR

Name

Julie S.

Location

Western Florida

Education

Bachelor of Science

Total years in profession

26

Brief occupation description/goal of occupation

Educator for aquatic fitness professionals, providing hands-on training as well as distance education opportunities. My goal is to reach more people and expand the industry.

Why did you choose this career path?

It chose me. I have a degree in wildlife management and got involved in fitness to stay in shape, but fell in love with the benefits and wanted to share and lead.

What do you like about your occupation?

Meeting people from across the globe who share similar goals and interests. Making a positive difference in people's lives.

What do you dislike about your occupation?

We often do not receive the credibility or recognition that the industry deserves. It's frustrating that more people are not physically active or have the desire to be physically fit, but I guess you could say that is job security. I feel that my position is at the low end of the salary scale when compared to similar positions in other industries.

What are the misconceptions about your profession?

That fitness professionals are not well educated. Unfortunately, some of this was brought on by individuals in the profession who were not properly educated.

On a scale of 1 to 10 (10 being great), how would you rate your occupation and why?

A 10—I feel that I have the best job in the world. I can help people and make a positive difference in their lives when they want to achieve these goals. My job also encourages me to stay in shape; and as mentioned, I get to travel worldwide making friends and networking globally.

What factors or former positions led to this occupation?

Although I was always very active growing up, I hated participating in PE (physical education) classes! When I went to college, I realized that fitness was not about performance but about a lifestyle. I wanted to share this revelation with others, and having always preferred leading instead of following, moving into fitness instruction was a logical progression—but it took me five years to do this full time.

What career choices were most helpful?

Choosing to step out with a business partner into the next level.

Did you have a mentor? If so, how did you find them? Did they help?

Yes, I found my two mentors when attending a certification course in the field of aquatic fitness. They made all the difference in the world; I would never have pursued this career otherwise. Mentors are a huge part of being successful in any career.

What type of education was needed for your position?

There are no mandated education levels for the career, but many things are helpful. This career benefits more from continuing education and real-life experiences than having a designated degree!

Do you have to update your career with ongoing training and certificates?

Yes, and I am thankful for that. I love learning as much as I love educating, so having to keep current with trends and research findings is exciting and ensures that our industry does not fall behind.

When you were hired, did you receive professional training or was it basically "on-the-job training"?

I received some professional training, worked as an apprentice for a period of time, and then moved on to hands-on training—which is the most beneficial of all.

In a typical week, are your hours fixed or flexible? On what days do you tend to work overtime?

Flexible. I tend to work overtime most days of the week, actually.

I have my full-time position, a part-time position, and a volunteer position—all related to fitness.

Is your work environment "hectic," "all work and no play," "serene," "laid back," or other? Briefly explain.

Hectic, but very interesting; nothing is ever the same, which keeps me motivated (but also frustrated at times). We tend to have very tight deadlines and crazy schedules.

What types of conflicts do you deal with?

Deadlines and financial limitations.

Do you interface with coworkers, groups, or vendors, or do you work alone?

Fitness is definitely interactive, so all my projects involve working with others on some level—sometimes face to face, other times via the computer.

What are your coworkers like?

Dynamic and interesting, very diverse, sometimes opinionated and challenging—but we are working multiculturally, so there are many interpretations!

What is management like?

Excellent, but overworked and underpaid, which leads to stress.

Is input accepted, or do you fare better as a "yes man"?

Input is most always accepted, but there are times when it is best for all to accept decisions made and move on.

How important is/was networking or connections in finding your current or other positions? Is it a factor in advancement once you're on the job?

Networking is crucial in the fitness industry, as it is ever changing. Networking would definitely be a key consideration for advancing.

What would be your next career move?

Being able to add projects that could provide personal financial gains. Primarily now my focus has been on helping the industry, and it would be nice to look toward preparing for retirement.

Do you relocate often? Are there travel requirements?

Relocation is not necessary—work requirements are either accomplished via computer or travel (for hands-on teaching). Travel requirements are flexible.

How much fulfillment do you get out of your career?

My career is a significant part of my life. It has given me confidence and security and improved self-esteem.

Do you feel that you are fairly compensated?

Realistically, I have a decent salary and many benefits, and can support myself at the moment. However, I feel that compared to others with similar responsibilities in other fields, I am under-compensated for the time and dedication that I commit.

If you could choose again, how much would money be a factor?

Actually, not much . . . I would love to make more money, but not at the expense of having a job I do not enjoy!

Would you choose the same career path?

Yes.

Any comments or words of advice for someone entering your field?

Be flexible. The industry is ever changing, and if you are not willing to adapt, then you will not succeed. Help others, enjoy life, and appreciate your career opportunities . . . then you have become successful.

DIRECTOR OF CATERING

Name

Carole B.

Location

Baltimore, Maryland

Education

Some college

Total years in profession

14

Brief occupation description/goal of occupation

Responsible for all sales and planning of social and corporate affairs, currently for a privately owned restaurant in the Baltimore area.

Why did you choose this career path?

I love the planning of events and can trace it back to as far as high school, being on the prom committee and other school functions.

What do you like about your occupation?

The different people that I get to meet every day, and the sense of pride I feel once I make a person's event what they had envisioned it would be.

What do you dislike about your occupation?

The hours are grueling and there is very little time for a social life.

What are the misconceptions about your profession?

We get people every day who planned a birthday party for their Aunt Martha in 1979 and think that they can walk into the industry and plan events like a professional. There is a lot of work involved in planning truly expressive events. There are too many people who want something for nothing and take advantage of the extra little things we do to make their event one of a kind.

On a scale of 1 to 10 (10 being great), how would you rate your occupation and why?

10. There is no other job where you can do the same type of thing every day and have it change every day. I make a lot of new friends and have the time of my life. I wouldn't trade it for the world.

What factors or former positions led to this occupation?

I was the girl in high school who was always on the prom committee, the float committee, the homecoming dance committee. I guess I just got tired of planning things for free.

What career choices were most helpful?

Getting into the hospitality industry allowed me to learn a lot, starting from the bottom and working my way to the top.

What career choices were least helpful/detrimental?

Moving straight into the private planning field was not a good move. I did not have enough time in the industry to create events on the scale of my competition. Not having the capital that a large Fortune 500 company would have at their disposal made it hard to pay the bills.

Did you have a mentor? If so, how did you find them? Did they help?

My mother was always my mentor. She taught me to select something I was good at in life and to make the most of it, and that's exactly what I did. You have to be happy at what you do or you will never truly succeed.

If you didn't have a mentor, would you have liked one?

I would have liked to have had an industry professional take me under their wing and show me the ropes, but in my field, you learn from experience only.

What type of education was needed for your position?

I have some college, and a college degree is typically preferred, but I started a long time ago. I have years of experience working for me now.

Do you have to update your career with ongoing training and certificates?

I don't have to, but I try to as often as I can. This industry changes all the time, and to stay at the top of your game requires you to try new things. There is always room to learn and get better at what you do because there is always someone out there trying to outdo the last event with a bigger and better one.

When you were hired, did you receive professional training or was it basically "on-the-job training"?

Everything was on the job for me. No formal training, except for a light amount in certain software programs that we use.

In a typical week, are your hours fixed or flexible?
On what days do you tend to work overtime?

My hours are flexible, but we tend to see our busiest days on the weekends and around holidays.

Is your work environment "hectic," "all work and no play," "serene," "laid back," or other? Briefly explain.

Our environment is sometimes a combination of all these things. There are moments when you can joke around with fellow employees; there are hectic times when you and all your staff are in what we call "the weeds"; there are quiet times here and there; and then there are crunch times where we need to be "on point" and make things happen. That's what keeps us all on our toes and keeps things interesting. Oh, the stories I could tell you!

What types of conflicts do you deal with?

I deal with the public every day. There are always people who want things that you can't give them, or were expecting something different from what you actually gave them. We deal with people from all walks of life, with all different kinds of expectations. It's my job to make sure that they are getting what they feel like they paid for.

Do you interface with coworkers, groups,
or vendors, or do you work alone?

I mix and mingle with staff, vendors, personal clients, professional clients—pretty much everyone.

What are your coworkers like?

I have a great staff of people. They are all very professional, but in this industry you have a very diverse group of people that you can work with.

What is management like?

My management staff is currently a bit of a problem. The people I work for are not "restaurant people." They are people with money who thought that buying a restaurant would be fun. It is more hard work than they were prepared for.

Is input accepted, or do you fare better as a "yes man"?

Input is greatly accepted in the field as a whole. We want to hear your ideas, and we want your input on problems that you can foresee.

What issues have prevented your advancement?

I think my lack of a degree in the field, and that I refuse to travel because I like where I live. There are jobs in this field in every city in the nation; you just have to find the right spot for you, and I have found it.

Is your position secure, or are you frequently looking for the next opportunity?

This industry has a huge turnover as a whole, but we usually stay in the same field. I think that money drives most of us, so we would be foolish not to look for better opportunities. As I have more time in the field, I tend to look less for new places and want to stay more with where I am..

How important is/was networking or connections in finding your current or other positions? Is it a factor in advancement once you're on the job?

Networking is key in this field. Most restaurant and hospitality people know their competition and know employees from their competition. Burning bridges with people is not a good idea in this business as you never know when your paths might cross again . . . and they always do.

What would be your next career move?

Since my fiancé is a chef and I work the "front of the house," so to speak, we would like to own and manage our own small bed and breakfast with a small restaurant.

Do you relocate often? Are there travel requirements?

There are some travel times required, but this field does not allow a lot of time for that. I have relocated before, and due to the type of business, could again at any time, but I choose not to.

Do you prefer going to work or leaving? Why?

I like to go to work. Never know what new adventure the day may hold!

How much fulfillment do you get out of your career?

My career is my life, and if I hated doing it, then I would hate life. I'm glad I took my mom's advice and picked something that I was good at!

Do you feel that you are fairly compensated?

I feel as though people in this field should make more money. We work extremely hard and deserve every dime that we make. It's hard to make everyone happy . . . you should try it sometime!

Are the benefits and vacation schedule fair?

Vacation schedules are not, but benefits usually are. In our field it's very hard to schedule vacation as there are always events going on and really no down time. If you don't vacation, though, you burn out really quickly. It takes a certain type of dedicated person to do this work.

If you could choose again, how much would money be a factor?

Money would be a large part, but not my sole driving force.

Would you choose the same career path?

Yes, I would. I am a "foodie"—it's just what I do.

Any comments or words of advice for someone entering your field?

Work hard and never, ever say, "That's not my job." I am in management, but if I need to help the kitchen plate food or help the staff clear dishes, then I do it. If you want to be really and truly good at what you do, then you need to walk a mile in everyone's shoes. Never rule with an iron fist. A good manager appreciates, delegates, negotiates, and reciprocates. Do all those things with your staff, and they will go to bat for you whenever you need them to. A leader takes pride in what they do and teaches their staff to take pride in it as well. I don't care if you clean toilets for a living . . . take pride in it and you will be rewarded for it.

POST OFFICE MANAGER

Name

Janie K.

Location

Atlanta, Georgia

Education

Some college

Total years in profession

26

Brief occupation description/goal of occupation

Ended my career in mid-management postal service.

Why did you choose this career path?

Job stability, benefits, pay.

What do you like about your occupation?

A variety of jobs equals constant learning. Excellent benefits, pay, and stability.

What do you dislike about your occupation?

Only some personal problems with postal management.

What are the misconceptions about your profession?

That postal workers or government workers, in general, do not work.

On a scale of 1 to 10 (10 being great), how would you rate your occupation and why?

I really loved my jobs in the post office—from carrying the mail to sorting the mail to being timekeeper to being temporary supervisor. It was a variety of work.

What factors or former positions led to this occupation?

I took the civil service test in high school. My husband was in the navy, and government work was always available wherever I lived. I transferred to the postal service for more money and the option to work outdoors.

What career choices were most helpful?

The best choice I made was taking the initial civil service exam, and then keeping it current for several years until I started working for the Department of the Navy.

What type of education was needed for your position?

A high school education.

Do you have to update your career with ongoing training and certificates?

No, but many opportunities were available.

When you were hired, did you receive professional training or was it basically "on-the-job training"?

On the job.

In a typical week, are your hours fixed or flexible? On what days do you tend to work overtime?

A typical week at the post office was around fifty hours, with twelve-hour days not unusual. Mondays and days after holidays were standard overtime.

Is your work environment "hectic," "all work and no play," "serene," "laid back," or other? Briefly explain.

A varied environment, but generally it was laid back.

What types of conflicts do you deal with?

Meeting deadlines; scheduling of employees; timely submission of pay records to payroll; dissatisfied patrons.

What are your coworkers like?

Generally, like family.

What is management like?

Kind of "big brother-ish."

Is input accepted, or do you fare better as a "yes man"?

Input is accepted.

What would be your next career move?

Stay with government work.

How much fulfillment do you get out of your career?

It's very fulfilling.

If you could choose again, how much would money be a factor?

I would need enough to pay bills.

Would you choose the same career path?

Yes.

Any comments or words of advice for someone entering your field?

Look for a job with stability and the best benefits possible, and stick with it. You can't like everybody and everybody can't like you.

CHAPTER THREE

The Einsteins

PSYCHOLOGIST

Name

Marie H.

Location

Western Massachusetts

Education

Doctor of Education

Total years in profession

28

Brief occupation description/goal of occupation

Currently I work as the staff psychologist for the State Department of Mental Retardation. I am a consultant to the case managers and management team of the area office. We serve nine-hundred-plus people with mental retardation.

Why did you choose this career path?

I chose the field of psychology because I've always been fascinated by the internal and external forces in people's lives that make them do what they do. I've also wanted to be of service to others and make a difference in people's lives.

What do you like about your occupation?

I'm never, ever bored. Every person is unique. Every problem is a little different. There is always something new to learn and think about.

What do you dislike about your occupation?

Not much. Sometimes I wish that the decision-making process didn't take as long as it does. Meetings can seem interminable at times.

What are the misconceptions about your profession?

That all psychologists do the same thing. There are many, many sub-professions in the field.

On a scale of 1 to 10 (10 being great), how would you rate your occupation and why?

A 10 for me. I like to be active. I like challenges. I like working with people. I like thinking hard about difficult situations. I like helping people negotiate their differences.

What factors or former positions led to this occupation?

I started out as a secondary teacher. It didn't take long for me to realize that I liked working with the kids themselves more than I liked presenting subject matter. However, I am grateful that I have teaching experience. I also founded and managed a small human service agency for ten years. During that period, I developed management skills and marketing skills. Both areas continue to be very useful.

What career choices were most helpful?

Years of practice as a therapist. The more people you see, the more you come to appreciate the endless variety of approaches to life. It's also true that the more people you see, the more possibility there is that you've seen something somewhat like a person's problem before. This at least gives you a place to start.

What career choices were least helpful/detrimental?

A brief foray into marketing. For me it was too far away from direct work with people.

Did you have a mentor? If so, how did you find them? Did they help?

I have been fortunate to have had a number of mentors; all teachers at one time or another. Each was a role model for using theory and practice in patient and compassionate ways.

Do you have to update your career with ongoing training and certificates?

Yes. Continuing education credits are needed to keep my license. I absolutely support this. It's important to stay current with the field and to always be learning.

When you were hired, did you receive professional training or was it basically "on-the-job training"?

My current job largely assumed that the years of experience I already had adequately prepared me. I just had to learn a new administrative structure. The process required for licensure does a pretty good job of preparing one to be a psychologist. It requires supervised experience as well as study.

In a typical week, are your hours fixed or flexible? On what days do you tend to work overtime?

Monday to Friday, forty hours a week. Hours are fixed. However, at this level it is expected that I will stay until the job is done, within reason.

What types of conflicts do you deal with?

Conflict is central to this job. We deal with conflict between families and staff, professionals and laypeople, individuals and their caretakers. It's also true that growth and change often come with working through conflict. If you can't manage disagreements between reasonable (and sometimes unreasonable) people, you shouldn't consider this job.

Do you interface with coworkers, groups, or vendors, or do you work alone?

I'm constantly interfacing with others: vendors, case managers, other psychologists, families, etc.

What are your coworkers like?

Good people. All have at least a college degree. All work hard.

What is management like?

In my office, management is supportive, engaged, and receptive to input.

Is input accepted, or do you fare better as a "yes man"?

Input is invited and appreciated.

What issues have prevented your advancement?

None except the structure of a state system and the limited number and types of jobs for psychologists within it. Throughout my career, I have changed where I work when I wanted to change what I was doing.

How important is/was networking or connections in finding your current or other positions? Is it a factor in advancement once you're on the job?

Networking has been very important throughout my career. It's how I've found each new, and better, position. Having developed respectful relationships is often the difference when trying to get things done.

What would be your next career move?

If I were younger, I'd consider working toward a larger position at the next level up (regional instead of area). But at this point in my life, I'm content to consolidate.

Do you relocate often? Are there travel requirements?

No. One of my personal goals was to never have to relocate. The only travel I do is to meetings within state, but that isn't often.

How much fulfillment do you get out of your career?

A great deal. It is an important part of how I define myself.

Do you feel that you are fairly compensated?

Now—absolutely. That hasn't always been true. To be in human services has usually meant choosing not to make a lot of money. I strongly urge newcomers to the field to identify ways to specialize if they want to make a good salary.

Are the benefits and vacation schedule fair?

Yes, although going to work for the state three years ago meant going back to only two weeks of vacation a year. That's been tough because I was up to four weeks in my prior job as the administrator of a mental health clinic. However, the benefits of taking this job far outweigh that issue. Health insurance is great. Holidays, sick time, and personal time are competitive.

If you could choose again, how much would money be a factor?

I think I was naive about money when I was young. If I could do it all over, I would be more careful with money and do more planning for eventual retirement. I only wised up to the need for that in my fifties, and it is late to manage making a comfortable retirement for myself.

Any comments or words of advice for someone entering your field?

1) Build a satisfying personal life. This work is emotionally hard. To be a psychologist means that you are often dealing with people

when they are the most troubled, the most angry, confused, and upset, and the most challenging. It's very, very important to confront your own issues, develop a solid personal life, and keep very good boundaries. Otherwise, you will quickly burn out. 2) Get lots of training, both before and after graduation. This is an ever-developing field. You will stay excited by it if you are always learning new things. 3) Always, always find a way to have supervision. It is so easy to become inducted into a client's way of thinking. In our efforts to be on the client's side, we can lose sight of the bigger picture. Good supervision, whether by a senior psychologist or a peer supervision group, helps us avoid those pitfalls and keeps us intellectually honest.

SOFTWARE ENGINEER

Name

Byron D.

Location

Salem, Oregon

Education

Master of Science

Total years in profession

35

Brief occupation description/goal of occupation

Develop software for complex programs in different industries, such as industrial automation, embedded computer products, accounting, and financial systems.

Why did you choose this career path?

Because I am good with computers and enjoy developing software.

What do you like about your occupation?

The challenge of taking complex problems and producing easy-to-use software for the people who depend on it.

What do you dislike about your occupation?

Incompetent management.

On a scale of 1 to 10 (10 being great), how would you rate your occupation and why?

I would say 10. It's something that I would do as a hobby if I didn't do it for a living.

What factors or former positions led to this occupation?

High school computer math class, a bachelor of science, and a master of science in computer science, as well as writing my own computer games, operating systems, and compiles for fun while I was still in school.

What career choices were most helpful?

I make career choices based on enjoyment of the work rather than the money I can make.

What career choices were least helpful/detrimental?

Taking on projects because I needed the money. Big mistakes.

If you didn't have a mentor, would you have liked one?

Perhaps. I tend to be very independent and I'm not sure I would have been better off with a mentor. I have been more of a trailblazer in what I've done than a follower.

What type of education was needed for your position?

Computer science fundamentals.

Was your formal education necessary for this position?

No, but it has allowed me to perform at a level beyond my peers. This has allowed me to do the work I'm paid to do, on time, while leaving me time to provide much more value to my employers.

Do you have to update your career with ongoing training and certificates?

Independent study, yes. Certificates, no.

When you were hired, did you receive professional training or was it basically "on-the-job training"?

My employers expect me to know what I'm doing when they hire me.

In a typical week, are your hours fixed or flexible? On what days do you tend to work overtime?

Whenever I have started a new job, I've typically worked 8:00 a.m. to 5:00 p.m. After working with a company for a while, my hours become flexible and I rarely need to work overtime to complete my projects.

Is your work environment "hectic," "all work and no play," "serene," "laid back," or other? Briefly explain.

I've worked in all kinds of work environments. Over time they have all become laid back.

What types of conflicts do you deal with?

All kinds, both technical and personal.

Do you interface with coworkers, groups, or vendors, or do you work alone?

I've worked alone and as a team member, project lead, project manager, department manager, and mentor.

What are your coworkers like?

In general, my coworkers are usually technical professionals.

What is management like?

I've worked with some excellent management and I've worked with managers that have risen above their level of incompetence, and everything in between. I prefer managers who are people oriented, who know how to get the best out of their employees.

Is input accepted, or do you fare better as a "yes man"?

Definitely not a yes man.

What issues have prevented your advancement?

I've always achieved my goals that I've aimed for.

How important is/was networking or connections in finding your current or other positions? Is it a factor in advancement once you're on the job?

Networking has rarely been a contributing factor in helping my advancement.

What would be your next career move?

I will be working for an organization that encourages object-oriented technology; otherwise, I'll retire.

Do you relocate often? Are there travel requirements?

I've lived in the same house for the last fifteen years. I do not travel except for vacation.

How much fulfillment do you get out of your career?

Great fulfillment.

If you could choose again, how much would money be a factor?

Not much.

Would you choose the same career path?

Yes.

Any comments or words of advice for someone entering your field?

As I have told my kids, it doesn't matter what you do, just make sure you enjoy doing it.

CONSULTANT FOR NONPROFITS

Name

Jayne C.

Location

Austin, Texas

Education

Master of Science

Total years in profession

11

Brief occupation description/goal of occupation

Advising nonprofit organizations regarding community involvement, including volunteer management, as well as media and public relations, donor relations, grant writing, and governance basics.

Why did you choose this career path?

It was my second career; it chose me.

What do you like about your occupation?

Working with nonprofit organizations.

What do you dislike about your occupation?

Low pay.

What are the misconceptions about your profession?

That volunteers are "free"; that to involve them effectively, a nonprofit organization need only post some advertising asking for such and, perhaps, ask some volunteers to take on the responsibility of managing the others.

What factors or former positions led to this occupation?

Originally, I was a journalist, then a communications manager for nonprofits for ten years.

What career choices were most helpful?

Journalism was an excellent subject to major in as an undergrad at university, as was practical experience producing publications. The skills learned from this more than twenty years ago continue to be helpful in my current profession.

What career choices were least helpful/detrimental?

Taking a pay cut in order to get a job in the field I desired.

Did you have a mentor? If so, how did you find them? Did they help?

I have had mentors on the job, in the form of supervisors or the heads of the company.

What type of education was needed for your position?

Undergrad university degree is an absolute. Studying Spanish would have been very helpful.

In a typical week, are your hours fixed or flexible? On what days do you tend to work overtime?

My hours are flexible but often require overtime.

What types of conflicts do you deal with?

Competing priorities of other staff members, conflicting support requirements of paid staff and volunteers I supervise, and unrealistic requests from funders.

What are your coworkers like?

The volunteers are wonderful; fellow volunteer managers can be very "old school" and unwilling to face new realities in volunteer involvement.

What issues have prevented your advancement?

Lack of funds.

Is your position secure, or are you frequently looking for the next opportunity?

Volunteer managers are frequently targeted for staff cuts, per the misconception of what kind of support volunteers and those who involve them need.

How important is/was networking or connections in finding your current or other positions? Is it a factor in advancement once you're on the job?

Networking is absolutely fundamental to finding any position I have ever had.

What would be your next career move?

Expanding internationally.

Do you relocate often? Are there travel requirements?

I relocate often, and there are travel requirements.

How much fulfillment do you get out of your career?

A great deal.

If you could choose again, how much would money be a factor?

None.

Any comments or words of advice for someone entering your field?

Learn another language in addition to English and be able to work in both.

MS ACCESS DATABASE DEVELOPER/ ADMINISTRATOR

Name

Lisa H.

Location

Detroit, Michigan

Education

Some college

Total years in profession

9

Brief occupation description/goal of occupation

Design, develop, and administrate databases. Maintain knowledge of programming language to hard code custom functionality to create a wide range of data collection and reporting options.

Why did you choose this career path?

I was temping and learning many new software packages. I realized that I had a flair for them and enjoyed creating something that people could use to make their jobs easier.

What do you like about your occupation?

I can come in and sit with someone watching them do their job inefficiently, and then I can take a few weeks to develop a database system that can do their four-hour job in about thirty to sixty minutes. This gives the person the opportunity to expand their current duties and learn new things that can allow them to move higher in a company. I have seen more than one person get a promotion after utilizing a database I have written, because they are more productive, they are happier with their job (because the database does all the boring repetitive work), and they are eager to learn new things.

What do you dislike about your occupation?

Some users don't understand what I do, so they act like it's no big deal. Even though they know they can't do it themselves, they still treat me like I'm a glorified secretary and not a computer programmer.

What are the misconceptions about your profession?

The most common misconception about what I do is that because I know a lot about computers and software, I must be a complete geek with no social skills and an overinflated ego. That may be true about some computer people, but I remember what it was like when I was just learning how to use computers and programming languages. I know how scary it can seem at first, and I take pride in the fact that I am patient and understanding when dealing with users who may be intimidated by the computer.

On a scale of 1 to 10 (10 being great), how would you rate your occupation and why?

I would rate it an 8, because every day is a new challenge. I create things for people to use and solve new problems every day because people always want the software to do more, and I have to figure out how to get it to do that. Also, there is a great amount of respect for people who do the type of thing that I do, and it's nice to have some freedoms because my boss knows how hard it would be to replace me.

What factors or former positions led to this occupation?

I started out doing temp work as an admin and had the opportunity to play around and learn the program. Then, I was lucky enough to be in a position where my company made yearly training a requirement, and they paid for me to have a forty-hour course in programming, which only increased my flexibility in the tools and what I could get them to do.

What career choices were most helpful?

Being eager to learn and using my extra time at work to learn different features of all the software that was available to me.

What career choices were least helpful/detrimental?

Getting caught up in office politics almost led to me losing the best opportunity of my life.

What type of education was needed for your position?

Computers are one of the only fields that you can go to school and get a degree in, or you can just tinker around and learn enough to get a very good-paying position.

Do you have to update your career with ongoing training and certificates?

You don't have to keep up with the latest technologies, because there are always companies who do not have the desire or the financial resources to continually upgrade to the latest and greatest technologies available, but they also aren't going to be paying as competitively. If you want to make the big money, you have to keep up with the latest trends.

When you were hired, did you receive professional training or was it basically "on-the-job training"?

All my training has been on the job.

In a typical week, are your hours fixed or flexible? On what days do you tend to work overtime?

My hours are fixed, but I decide what hours I want to work, and I have the flexibility to change them as I need to, as well as the flexibility to leave when my family needs me. I never work overtime.

Is your work environment "hectic," "all work and no play," "serene," "laid back," or other? Briefly explain.

My work is challenging but not hectic. I have a lot to do, but not too much or too little. I love what I do for a living.

What types of conflicts do you deal with?

Dealing with people who don't understand the limitations of the system or its capabilities is the most frustrating.

Do you interface with coworkers, groups, or vendors, or do you work alone?

I have limited interaction with my coworkers. Mainly, I observe and ask some questions and then work independently until it's time to test and implement the software.

What is management like?

Supportive, knowledgeable, and progressive; they are open to new ideas and processes that will save them time and money.

Is input accepted, or do you fare better as a "yes man"?

Input is required. The "yes man" is frowned upon because management understands that to succeed in today's economy, you have to be constantly looking for more efficient ways to conduct your business.

What issues have prevented your advancement?

The fact that I do not have a degree.

Is your position secure, or are you frequently looking for the next opportunity?

I've moved around looking for new opportunities when they were in my best interest, but my positions have usually been secure.

How important is/was networking or connections in finding your current or other positions? Is it a factor in advancement once you're on the job?

Impressing the right people has helped me advance and opened up new opportunities to me on more than one occasion.

What would be your next career move?

At this point, the next step would be to go out on my own and begin doing freelance consulting work.

How much fulfillment do you get out of your career?

When I complete a database and see people using it, it makes me feel like I've really done something significant to help my coworkers. And then when my database is adopted into other departments or other satellite offices, it makes me feel very proud of what I do.

If you could choose again, how much would money be a factor?

I needed a good job that required little formal education but paid well, which is why I'm in this profession.

Would you choose the same career path?

Knowing what I know now, yes, I would.

Any comments or words of advice for someone entering your field?

Technology is the way of the future. Even if you don't plan on being in a technical field, knowing how to use and troubleshoot your computer will save you time and headaches and make you invaluable to your boss and coworkers, who are at the mercy of IT support.

COMMUNICATIONS LIAISON

Name

Michael S.

Location

Western Massachusetts

Education

Bachelor of Arts

Total years in profession

18

Brief occupation description/goal of occupation

Communications link between our engineering and marketing departments; improving communications between groups.

Why did you choose this career path?

I was a communications major.

What do you like about your occupation?

It's busy and challenging. I like a challenge.

What do you dislike about your occupation?

It's very political. The company is like a bureaucracy. Job security is always a concern.

What are the misconceptions about your profession?

None that I know of, although you can say in general that we rarely have an opportunity to get to the top working for a corporation.

On a scale of 1 to 10 (10 being great), how would you rate your occupation and why?

I would say 6. It's a job and I work independently, which is good, but there isn't much chance to move forward career-wise.

What factors or former positions led to this occupation?

Experience and longevity. I have a good reputation and work hard.

What career choices were most helpful?

Perseverance and helping others.

What career choices were least helpful/detrimental?

Helping others (sound ironic?).

What type of education was needed for your position?

A bachelor's degree or a few years of tech experience.

In a typical week, are your hours fixed or flexible? On what days do you tend to work overtime?

Flexible. I normally don't have to work overtime.

Is your work environment "hectic," "all work and no play," "serene," "laid back," or other? Briefly explain.

Hectic; I work for an $8 billion/year company that continues to increase sales by buying other companies. It's hectic, busy, exciting at times, but it's just another job. It would have been nice if college taught me all my options way back when instead of just the concept/idea that we get an education and work for someone else. Entrepreneurialism makes a lot of sense nowadays.

What types of conflicts do you deal with?

Management conflicts on how to do things better. Ideas on making life easier for the customer; high-end managers have no idea what customers desire or like and tailor business decisions to their liking and cost-cutting measures at the expense of customer satisfaction.

Do you interface with coworkers, groups, or vendors, or do you work alone?

I interface with other workers, departments, etc. but also work independently.

What are your coworkers like?

You want my honest answer? See the *Dilbert* cartoons . . . most are like *Dilbert* characters . . . how sad. But they're raised that way in the corporate environment—cubicle robots settling for less.

What is management like?

Some are good, but most are corporate boys. I don't mean to be stereotypical, but it's reality and very sad.

Is input accepted, or do you fare better as a "yes man"?

My ideas are accepted for the most part because I've been around a while and I'm respected, but they don't always listen.

What issues have prevented your advancement?

It's called the "Corporate Pyramid," and it limits who gets ahead often. If I had an advanced degree that would probably help, but no guarantees still.

Is your position secure, or are you frequently looking for the next opportunity?

As I stay there longer, I think it's less secure. I look sporadically for other opportunities.

How important is/was networking or connections in finding your current or other positions? Is it a factor in advancement once you're on the job?

It wasn't a factor, but I believe it often can be a factor in advancement.

What would be your next career move?

Being my own boss and no longer working for someone else.

Do you prefer going to work or leaving? Why?

Leaving. Work doesn't excite me and if I want to retire comfortably financially, then I need something more or better. Job security is in question as I get older, and the money I need and seek is not sufficient through the current channels.

How much fulfillment do you get out of your career?

I get fulfillment occasionally but not often.

If you could choose again, how much would money be a factor?

It's a big factor (60 percent), but time freedom/stress-free/happiness factors are important too (40 percent).

Would you choose the same career path?

No.

Any comments or words of advice for someone entering your field?

Yes. Consider not working for someone else. Consider all your options and look at being your own boss instead. The most successful people in America are entrepreneurs, and many didn't have stellar backgrounds when they started out. They just worked hard and somehow realized the opportunities that colleges and corporate America failed to acknowledge.

ASSOCIATE ENVIRONMENTAL PLANNER-ARCHAEOLOGIST

Name

Timothy K.

Location

Northern California

Education

Bachelor of Arts

Total years in profession

17

Brief occupation description/goal of occupation

I work for a transportation agency and ensure that archaeological/cultural sites are addressed in the planning of new roadways/altered roadways. If impacts to these resources are unavoidable, I lead/guide archaeological excavations to mitigate those portions of a site that will be damaged.

Why did you choose this career path?

I wanted a profession that required me to constantly think, and this profession requires that. Plus, I love to get away from office environments and work outside, which is a great bonus in this profession.

What do you like about your occupation?

I am constantly having to problem-solve and seriously think about the meaning and importance of what is around me. My job demands I have some knowledge of anatomy, botany, ethnology, genetics, linguistics, geology, geomorphology, chemistry, and many other fields so that you can piece together the past. Due to this, I am constantly learning new things and new ideas to help me in my job. Stagnation is not possible in my job. I also like the fact that my profession has meaning. Preservation of important archaeological sites and the interpretation of these provide us with context to our surroundings.

What do you dislike about your occupation?

The deadlines and expectations of management can sometimes be unrealistic. Since I work for a state agency, politics sometimes get in the way of reality.

What are the misconceptions about your profession?

Archaeology is always exciting and interesting. Sometimes (as with most professions) the mundane tasks can be mind numbing. Another aspect that can get to you is the paperwork. Good archaeology demands good recordkeeping. You must be able to reconstruct and interpret what you have found and justify what you have done. Lots of forms to fill out, lots of labels to produce, lots of databases to create.

On a scale of 1 to 10 (10 being great), how would you rate your occupation and why?

An 8. I can't think of anything I would rather do. I know very few jobs this diverse and demanding of thought. We work with the remnants of people's pasts, and we have to attempt to reconstruct their ways of life as well as their environments.

What factors or former positions led to this occupation?

I worked some labor/service-type jobs before and in college and found that I just didn't have to use my brain much. I wanted something obviously more involved.

What career choices were most helpful?

Attending an archaeological field school at the end of my college career. I was very interested in archaeology at this point but didn't know if I really wanted to pursue this as a profession. I headed out to Arizona and was immersed in Southwestern archaeology (excavations, laboratory work) for six weeks at a little ranch in the middle of nowhere, and I was hooked. After this, I just diversified my talents by working in a multitude of locations for a variety of organizations.

What career choices were least helpful/detrimental?

Not getting a master's degree in my field. I was having such a good time working as an archaeologist that I just kept putting this off. It delayed my development as an archaeologist. I probably should have done this a few years after leaving college once I figured this was what I wanted to do.

Did you have a mentor? If so, how did you find them? Did they help?

I met a person at my archaeological field school, a grad student, who asked me if I would volunteer and work on a project in Mexico once I graduated from college. This person really awakened me to the broadness of the field and its possibilities.

What type of education was needed for your position?

At least a BA, and as I said earlier, an MA is really a must as well. Due to recent changes in my field, you really now need an MA if you want to be certified in my field.

Was your formal education necessary for this position?

Absolutely—I was an anthropology major, and the varied background I received at college in this major has allowed me to succeed in my field.

Do you have to update your career with ongoing training and certificates?

I would say yes to this. My field is governed by state and federal law, and you have to clearly understand these to work well in my field. Also, there is always the need to learn new technologies as well as refined methods for accomplishing work.

Is your work environment "hectic," "all work and no play," "serene," "laid back," or other? Briefly explain.

How about interesting and stimulating on some days and some days straightforward?

What types of conflicts do you deal with?

I have to work with people who don't understand what I do, and there is sometimes the assumption that since I work in what is classified as the "environmental" field, I must have an agenda. I also sometimes have to tell work groups things they don't want to hear, and this obviously leads to conflict sometimes.

Do you interface with coworkers, groups, or vendors, or do you work alone?

I work on project development teams (coworkers) and with consultants, Native American tribes, and the public.

What are your coworkers like?

Varied. All are well meaning and believe in their professions. This includes biologists, geologists, engineers, and hazardous waste specialists. Some are easy to get along with, and some aren't.

What is management like?

Overall, I would say pretty good, although at the worker level you sometimes feel out of the loop. I think my organization makes efforts to keep people informed of what is going on organization-wise. As I stated earlier, sometimes we do have political pressure put on us to produce products (reports, clearances) with little consideration of the reality of a situation.

Is input accepted, or do you fare better as a "yes man"?

This has varied by where I have worked. Yes men can get ahead quicker, get promotions and such, but you also see a lack of respect for people of this sort. I think I am lucky to be in an office right now where well-thought-out and non-reactionary approaches to management are received well and accepted.

Is your position secure, or are you frequently looking for the next opportunity?

Secure. I have thought of taking a supervisory position in my field leading biologists, archaeologists, and planners.

How important is/was networking or connections in finding your current or other positions? Is it a factor in advancement once you're on the job?

Knowing people hasn't hurt me, especially since they can speak up for you when you are seeking a job. It certainly has been beneficial in my job by providing me sources for information that I may need to answer questions I have in my job.

What would be your next career move?

Supervisor of biologists, archaeologists, and planners.

Do you relocate often? Are there travel requirements?

I've relocated about every five to six years, but I am now where I want to be (location was the reason for relocating the last fifteen years). I am on the road about one night every two weeks.

How much fulfillment do you get out of your career?

Quite a bit. I love the people I meet in my profession, and I'm constantly learning new things.

If you could choose again, how much would money be a factor?

Not much. I knew getting into this field that I wasn't going to be making much off the bat (I worked in Mexico for room and board for six months). I've worked up the ladder to where I am today, and working for the state over the federal government (I worked for the US Forest Service and National Park Service before here) was certainly a factor in my choice to work here.

Any comments or words of advice for someone entering your field?

Go to archaeological field school, get a master's, don't tie yourself down to one job or location early on. Also, don't hesitate to ask another archaeologist questions. If you aren't constantly learning something new, something is wrong.

CREDIT RISK MANAGER– STATISTICAL MODELER

Name

Jim N.

Location

Chicago, Illinois

Education

Master of Statistics and Master of Business Administration

Total years in profession

7

Brief occupation description/goal of occupation

Manage the risk of credit card portfolios based on behaviors that customers display in using their card and on their credit bureau information.

Why did you choose this career path?

I chose what I enjoyed studying. A master's degree in statistics and an MBA in finance and international business were the perfect preparation for my career. I originally applied for a job with my company because the job description fit with what I had studied. Basically, the career path chose me . . .

What do you like about your occupation?

The focus on analytics to drive actions.

What do you dislike about your occupation?

Bureaucracy involved in working for a large corporation—especially a large bank where federal regulators add a whole new dimension to the craziness.

On a scale of 1 to 10 (10 being great), how would you rate your occupation and why?

It's a 9. It is not for everyone, but I really enjoy it. Merit is rewarded. Politics always will play a role, but when decisions are data driven, those who can best digest the data find themselves in the driver's seat (or at least riding shotgun!). I have been very blessed in both of those areas. I've been skilled enough to do some very good work, and lucky enough to have impressed some very good people who have helped me tremendously in my career. My only real complaint is the bureaucratic nightmare that my job entails.

What career choices were most helpful?

Leaving a job in Charlotte that I didn't like to take a job in Dallas with my current company that sounded like something I'd really enjoy. Also—deciding to have weight-loss surgery was a huge help—seriously! Severely overweight individuals face tremendous bias and discrimination in the corporate world. Not "looking" the part is a real problem.

What career choices were least helpful/detrimental?

The biggest harm to my career happened on two different occasions when I saw very poor decisions being made around me and I didn't voice any real issues with them. They were just bad decisions being made by people who didn't really know what they were doing. But they were my superiors, and they had ignored my advice, so I didn't raise the issue any further. It probably set me back a year or two in my career progress.

Did you have a mentor? If so, how did you find them? Did they help?

Yes, but not an official one. He hired me for my first job with the company two years out of grad school. I have consulted with him on virtually every major project I have worked on with the company. I speak with him at least weekly. In the last seven years, he has rehired me four different times in three different cities.

What type of education was needed for your position?

A master of business administration and/or graduate degree in statistics, economics, or finance. It is a real requirement.

When you were hired, did you receive professional training or was it basically "on-the-job training"?

On-the-job training, but to be considered for the job, I needed significant schoolwork in research methods, statistics, and economics and econometrics.

In a typical week, are your hours fixed or flexible? On what days do you tend to work overtime?

Hours are "flexible." I typically work ten- or eleven-hour days Monday to Thursday and try to get out on Fridays as close to noon as possible. Typically, I work about forty-eight to fifty hours a week.

Is your work environment "hectic," "all work and no play," "serene," "laid back," or other? Briefly explain.

Generally, fairly laid back—analysis takes time. But ad hoc projects suddenly appear on a fairly regular basis. Those make life very hectic.

What types of conflicts do you deal with?

The worst conflicts are between different functional areas within my division at the bank. It is conflict that is set up by design. We all have goals and objectives that are in conflict with those of other parts of the business.

What are your coworkers like?

Very, very smart. Very, very well educated. Very, very diverse. In the group of four employees that I manage, none of us are originally from the same country as anyone else in the group, and only one of us was born in the US (that would be me). I have a person from Russia, a person from Pakistan, a person from India, and a person from China.

What is management like?

Very well educated. Very diverse. Most are willing to admit that they do not have all the answers and actively seek input from others. Some, unfortunately, do not. Everyone hates working for those guys . . .

Is input accepted, or do you fare better as a "yes man"?

Input is accepted from most of the people senior to me. As my career has progressed, I have become more emboldened in giving my input . . .

How important is/was networking or connections in finding your current or other positions? Is it a factor in advancement once you're on the job?

Absolutely essential. I noted above that I've worked for one individual in four different positions in three different cities. He trusts me, knows my abilities, is quick to let me know of opportunities elsewhere in the company, and has been very helpful in "talking me up" for positions where I don't know the hiring managers directly.

What would be your next career move?

International—country risk manager or as a country manager of "decision management" (a set of heavy-duty analytic techniques for maximizing value in a credit portfolio).

Do you relocate often? Are there travel requirements?

Relocation—yes. I've moved three times for my company in seven years. Travel is different by assignment but is usually not very heavy.

Do you prefer going to work or leaving? Why?

On most days, leaving is the clear favorite. The days when I enjoy going in are when I am highly involved in a complicated analytical program. Those eat at your brain literally twenty-four hours a day until they're complete. Going to work means you can stop thinking about possibilities and start getting some answers. It's all there in the data.

How much fulfillment do you get out of your career?

A lot. But I have a very active family life as well, and I spend a lot of time volunteering as well with my church and with the Boy Scouts, etc.

Do you feel that you are fairly compensated?

Yes and no. I am pretty well compensated, but I know that if I were to leave my company right now, I would be worth 25–30 percent more "on the market," and I would have no trouble finding a job. No trouble at all. So, while I can't really complain too much—I'm making over six figures and get a bonus in the 30 percent–plus range—it's aggravating to know that the company posted my job externally with an advertised salary almost 50 percent more than I'm making right now.

If you could choose again, how much would money be a factor?

About the same as now. It is a factor, and there are some lines that have to be drawn. But fighting bitterly over the last 3 or 4 percent a year simply isn't worth it to me right now.

Would you choose the same career path?

Probably. It all depends on whether or not I would've had good enough grades to get into pharmacy school. Talk about a great job! But assuming I studied the same stuff in school, I would definitely take the same path I took already.

Any comments or words of advice for someone entering your field?

Learn how to manage people effectively—especially people living remotely. India and China will become major players in providing the analytic and modeling services that people in my field are currently providing. India and China are already big players in our industry, and they will continue to get bigger.

SOFTWARE TESTER

Name

Russ D.

Location

Dallas, Texas

Education

Junior college

Total years in profession

9

Brief occupation description/goal of occupation

Testing software and reporting associated problems.

Why did you choose this career path?

I was involved in the airline industry, and I had a friend who invited me to test the same software I was using already.

What do you like about your occupation?

Freedom of flexible working hours, including working from home. The ability to use my intellect and solve problems. Working with a variety of people and accomplishing a united goal.

What do you dislike about your occupation?

Time we have to test is always crunched, and software rarely gets tested to my expectations. Superiors tend to not listen to your ideas or implement your solutions, due to the fact that you are seen as inferior to the people who write the software; and their interests are often counter to yours. The job is monotonous.

What are the misconceptions about your profession?

The pay is better than one would think. People underrate the importance of the position.

On a scale of 1 to 10 (10 being great), how would you rate your occupation and why?

I would say 8, because of the dislikes previously mentioned.

What career choices were most helpful?

Getting connected with people through user groups you find on the internet, figuring out what the expected pay is, and interviewing for jobs. Learning new skills through work or on my own (e.g., database, office, network administration, general computer).

What career choices were least helpful/detrimental?

Staying in a low-paying position and not realizing that there are a lot of opportunities for testers.

Did you have a mentor? If so, how did you find them? Did they help?

I have lots of associates I work with, or some I don't work with, whom I ask what they would do in a situation I am having trouble with or if they know of any job openings in the field.

What type of education was needed for your position?

A four-year degree is very helpful, but a two-year degree works okay. If you get experience, that is the main thing!

Was your formal education necessary for this position?

It helped a whole lot, and I'm not really sure if they would have hired me without it.

Do you have to update your career with ongoing training and certificates?

Some people do, and I have in the past, but it is not very necessary.

When you were hired, did you receive professional training or was it basically "on-the-job training"?

On the job. All testing assignments are different, and you just usually go in and figure it out.

In a typical week, are your hours fixed or flexible? On what days do you tend to work overtime?

Overtime comes when a release is late and needs to be thoroughly tested. I have flexible hours, as previously mentioned.

Is your work environment "hectic," "all work and no play," "serene," "laid back," or other? Briefly explain.

It is from one extreme to the other, based on how close we are to releasing the next version of the software.

What types of conflicts do you deal with?

Communication of information about defects in the product is paramount here, plus some of the other issues I commented on.

Do you interface with coworkers, groups, or vendors, or do you work alone?

I interface with almost everyone, with questions, answers, and suggestions.

What are your coworkers like?

The ones who write the software usually keep to themselves; some have attitudes against testers since we find their mistakes.

What is management like?

Domineering and enjoys micromanagement with lots of communication. Sometimes she yells at people.

Is input accepted, or do you fare better as a "yes man"?

It is a combination. You are asked for your opinion, but it is usually rejected—and you need to learn to accept the rejection.

Is your position secure, or are you frequently looking for the next opportunity?

A little of both. It feels pretty secure, but there is always talk of being bought out or something.

What would be your next career move?

Something more along the automated testing lines. This is where you write software to test the software.

Do you relocate often? Are there travel requirements?

No relocation and no travel requirements.

How much fulfillment do you get out of your career?

About 75 percent.

Do you feel that you are fairly compensated?

Yes, for the most part.

If you could choose again, how much would money be a factor?

That will always play a big factor to me. I want to have enough to retire ASAP!

Would you choose the same career path?

I would stay in school longer and study harder to make good grades. I would become connected to smart instructors who could get me placed in more of an environment that I had chosen, instead of one I just got lucky to find.

Any comments or words of advice for someone entering your field?

It is better than most jobs and somewhat rewarding. It is a bit challenging at times, and there are a variety of personalities to deal with, but you only have to deal with them for a limited time, which is good.

INDUSTRIAL HYGIENIST

Name

William P.

Location

Newark, New Jersey

Education

Bachelor of Arts

Total years in profession

18

Brief occupation description/goal of occupation

Occupational health and safety: industrial hygienists
protect workers in many industries from hazardous
chemicals, noise, radiation, and other hazards that cause
illnesses or injuries on the job.

Why did you choose this career path?

I began in this occupation when I joined the USAF (air force). It was chosen for me because there was a need for industrial hygienists.

What do you like about your occupation?

Besides the technical aspects of identifying hazards, I enjoy learning about many different occupations and the people who belong to them. You meet a diverse set of people from all walks of life.

What do you dislike about your occupation?

The general public doesn't understand what industrial hygienists are and do when they first hear about us.

What are the misconceptions about your profession?

I wish people knew enough about industrial hygiene to have misconceptions.

On a scale of 1 to 10 (10 being great), how would you rate your occupation and why?

I would rate industrial hygiene with an 8 because it allows me to interact with people yet allows me to exercise my technical expertise.

What factors or former positions led to this occupation?

Seeking a career in a technical field led me to join the military. This is what introduced me to industrial hygiene.

What career choices were most helpful?

My bachelor's degree in a "hard" science immediately opened many doors for me when I left the military. The practical experience I gained in the USAF was also vital.

What career choices were least helpful/detrimental?

Not taking some introductory business courses in college or afterward.

Did you have a mentor? If so, how did you find them? Did they help?

I have mentors at the institution I currently attend for my master's degree. They are faculty members with many years of experience in industrial hygiene and related fields.

If you didn't have a mentor, would you have liked one?

A mentor in my early career would have been very helpful.

What type of education was needed for your position?

The USAF sent me to a special school for industrial hygiene before I was assigned to a duty station. Since then, I have taken many training courses to refresh my knowledge.

Was your formal education necessary for this position?

My bachelor's degree is essential for most positions in industrial hygiene. The master's degree will only open up more opportunities.

Do you have to update your career with ongoing training and certificates?

Periodically, I must take many refresher courses.

When you were hired, did you receive professional training or was it basically "on-the-job training"?

I was given class training at the beginning and then on-the-job training thereafter.

In a typical week, are your hours fixed or flexible? On what days do you tend to work overtime?

In a typical week my hours are fixed, although I can work overtime. As a salaried employee, I don't receive overtime.

Is your work environment "hectic," "all work and no play," "serene," "laid back," or other? Briefly explain.

My work environment is laid back.

What types of conflicts do you deal with?

Sometimes I deal with conflicts between workers and management. Sometimes a union is involved.

Do you interface with coworkers, groups, or vendors, or do you work alone?

I interface with all my coworkers. I also have to deal with vendors, contractors, and consultants, as well as our agency's "clients."

What are your coworkers like?

They are very amiable, easy to get along with, and very helpful.

What is management like?

Management is somewhat laid back, but they have prescribed ways of doing things.

Is input accepted, or do you fare better as a "yes man"?

My agency's middle management only occasionally takes input from employees.

What issues have prevented your advancement?

My chain of command has many relatively young individuals occupying the positions above me.

Is your position secure, or are you frequently looking for the next opportunity?

My position is secure, although I am constantly testing the job market.

How important is/was networking or connections in finding your current or other positions? Is it a factor in advancement once you're on the job?

Networking was indispensable in obtaining my current position.

What would be your next career move?

After I obtain my master's degree, I will attempt to become certified as a CIH (certified industrial hygienist).

Do you relocate often? Are there travel requirements?

I don't travel very far from the area where my agency is located. Other industrial hygienists with private companies often travel much more than I do.

How much fulfillment do you get out of your career?

I derive a great deal of fulfillment from my career.

Do you feel that you are fairly compensated?

Yes, I do.

If you could choose again, how much would money be a factor?

Money would not be a very big factor if I had the same opportunities that I have had.

Would you choose the same career path?

Yes, I would.

Any comments or words of advice for someone entering your field?

If possible, try to obtain a graduate degree before you obtain a job in the real world. There seems to be a high increase in salary if you have an advanced degree before you are offered a job. On the other hand, real-world experience is vitally important, so if possible, try to get an internship in your field of interest. Also, you should try to get a job while in school even if it isn't in your field of interest.

PROCESS ENGINEER

Name

Jason D.

Location

Southern Illinois

Education

Bachelor of Science

Total years in profession

4

Brief occupation description/goal of occupation

Process engineer for the world's largest fiber pellet–producing plant for animal feed. My goal is to complete capital projects for better efficiency of equipment and cost savings.

What do you like about your occupation?

Not very many times are any of my days the same. Usually, every day is different and I love it.

What do you dislike about your occupation?

Not getting paid for the overtime.

What are the misconceptions about your profession?

That all engineers have no personalities, but that is not the case with me. That was one of my goals when I graduated from college . . . to change the way that people (at least ten) think about engineers.

On a scale of 1 to 10 (10 being great), how would you rate your occupation and why?

An 8 because just about every day is different. Some days will be desk days and other days will be out in the plant solving process problems.

What factors or former positions led to this occupation?

I always loved trying to figure out how things work. I would take things apart just to find out how they worked.

What career choices were most helpful?

Knowing what I wanted to do before I went to college and taking my time when deciding on which job to take when I graduated. Don't rush into it!

Did you have a mentor? If so, how did you find them? Did they help?

Yeah, my father. He put a good head on my shoulders, and I owe it all to him!

What type of education was needed for your position?

A bachelor of science from college . . . in engineering!

Do you have to update your career with ongoing training and certificates?

I can, but it is not necessary!

When you were hired, did you receive professional training or was it basically "on-the-job training"?

Mostly on-the-job training. Swing shift . . . you have to love it!

In a typical week, are your hours fixed or flexible? On what days do you tend to work overtime?

Mostly fixed if you consider working nine- to ten-hour days fixed. As for overtime, I don't know. It all depends on how the plant is running. It runs twenty-four hours a day, seven days a week, 365 days a year!

Is your work environment "hectic," "all work and no play," "serene," "laid back," or other? Briefly explain.

I would say a little bit of both. When things are not going right, it can be hectic, but when things are running good, it's pretty laid back and a great time!

What types of conflicts do you deal with?

Equipment failures, flow problems, heat issues, chemical problems, metal strength problems, welding, finished product quality in terms of temperature, etc.

What are your coworkers like?

Depends on the day. Now that I'm in the feed house, the operators are great. My boss is great and so are the other engineers in my department.

What is management like?

Great. They are usually looking over your shoulder at least once a month, which is good. Pretty laid back.

Is input accepted, or do you fare better as a "yes man"?

Very accepted. The more you give, the better/faster problems get solved.

Is your position secure, or are you frequently looking for the next opportunity?

Very secure!

How important is/was networking or connections in finding your current or other positions? Is it a factor in advancement once you're on the job?

Not important. I can advance in the company by showing them my hard work and dedication to the job.

What would be your next career move?

Department superintendent.

Do you prefer going to work or leaving? Why?

Both—it all depends on the day. Mostly I enjoy going, but when it's nice outside, I love getting out of there to get on my motorcycle and go for a ride.

How much fulfillment do you get out of your career?

I would say 110 percent.

If you could choose again, how much would money be a factor?

Depends on the amount of debt I would be in, but I would say about 60 percent.

Would you choose the same career path?

Yes!

Any comments or words of advice for someone entering your field?

Be patient! Don't try to rush in and think you are going to solve the world's problems right off the bat, because you won't. Take your time when completing a project, and have it planned out to a "T" so you know what to expect when you see the finished product!

ELECTRICAL ENGINEER

Name

Scott H.

Location

St. Louis, Missouri

Education

Bachelor of Science

Total years in profession

14

Brief occupation description/goal of occupation

Programming automated machines. Design and program user interface to machine software. Set up and train customers on the details of the machine.

Why did you choose this career path?

I'm interested in electricity and like working with automation and machinery. Early as a college student I had a mind for math.

What do you like about your occupation?

I feel automation is like a large toy, like a train set as a kid. I enjoy programming a robot and then watching it do as I programmed. I like working with the many different manufacturers of equipment—it keeps me current in my field.

What do you dislike about your occupation?

Pressure to get things done with groups of people around waiting to see the results. The machines are always late and very important to some company's future. I hate working with so many equipment manufacturers. It can be too much, and I have to wonder why my company can't do the same thing as before. Many times I do not inspect the equipment we will be using.

What are the misconceptions about your profession?

That programming is easy. That is because all they see is typing and then a moment to think and then some more typing. Some people watching wonder why I need that moment to think.

On a scale of 1 to 10 (10 being great), how would you rate your occupation and why?

I feel I've got to do something to pay some bills. I would rate it a 7.

What factors or former positions led to this occupation?

College showed me I could achieve an education. Then I took what I considered at the time of graduation a lesser job with a machine manufacturing company that hired me to do sales. The machines had to be programmed.

What career choices were most helpful?

Choosing to get a BSEE (bachelor of science in electrical engineering), staying with college, leaving jobs that were taken just to get an income.

What career choices were least helpful/detrimental?

Taking jobs to just make an income. I hate being unemployed, and I have taken a job only to quit after a week.

Did you have a mentor? If so, how did you find them? Did they help?

In my job I have had people willing to help me get started.

What type of education was needed for your position?

An associate electrical degree of some type. My education (BSEE) is somewhat extreme for my occupation.

Was your formal education necessary for this position?

Yes. My education taught me how to think and solve problems. I did learn a great deal in programming and electrical fields.

Do you have to update your career with ongoing training and certificates?

I have had some courses on the different equipment I need to program the machine.

When you were hired, did you receive professional training or was it basically "on-the-job training"?

I have received some professional training, but for the most part it was on-the-job training. I have gone to robot manufacture courses or seminars. I also have spent many hours in a trial-and-error process.

In a typical week, are your hours fixed or flexible? On what days do you tend to work overtime?

I work a forty-five-hour week. If something is very hot or behind schedule, I put in as many as sixty hours. I mostly work a strict schedule of 8:00 a.m. to 5:30 p.m.

Is your work environment "hectic," "all work and no play," "serene," "laid back," or other? Briefly explain.

Very stressful at times. I get pulled in all different directions with it all being a priority.

What types of conflicts do you deal with?

I have to deal with management giving directions to set up technicians to do functions with the machines that are not programmed yet. Many times, people get in the way of the programming just trying to run the machine and having a difficult time because it is not programmed yet.

Do you interface with coworkers, groups, or vendors, or do you work alone?

All the above. I have a small group of engineers I might bounce ideas off, and I look for their feedback. I work with machine setup people. They turn the wrenches and assemble the components. I make it move. I look to vendors to tell me what products they have and what solutions they can provide.

What are your coworkers like?

I work with a great group of technicians. Most of them really know the job. They seem open to my ideas and seem willing to explain their positions.

What is management like?

Management can be a real source of stress. Positive input from management is never there. I answer to a lot of different departments within my company, and each one thinks their job is the most important. Management seems to work from their point of view by name-calling and intimidation tactics. I do not think too highly of management.

Is input accepted, or do you fare better as a "yes man"?

I sometimes can be a yes man, but for the most part I do stand up for what I want the machines to perform like.

What issues have prevented your advancement?

I seem to have a conflict going on with production demands. Therefore, I do not get work done in the time they demand. When all this happens, I can make some enemies with my attitude.

Is your position secure, or are you frequently looking for the next opportunity?

My position is secure. I feel I have proven my dedication to my employer many times. I do keep an open mind as to the possibilities of my company not selling machines and my not having anything to program.

What would be your next career move?

It would be into management.

Do you relocate often? Are there travel requirements?

I have never moved for my employment, but if I were to lose my job, I feel that in order to stay in my field I would have to relocate. I travel quite a bit for my company, on average 30 percent a year.

How much fulfillment do you get out of your career?

I enjoy many parts of my job. Working with customers is the most fulfilling. Solving problems and being needed to resolve issues are also.

Do you feel that you are fairly compensated?

More money would be nice. I take on a great deal of responsibility and do not get appreciated. It would not have to be a lot, just a small percentage of a raise every year.

If you could choose again, how much would money be a factor?

I was able to get to my position by being willing to take less money and prove my value. I do not think I could make a difference by demanding a better salary.

Any comments or words of advice for someone entering your field?

Work hard, gain experience, move on to a position that will reward you for your experience. Your greatest bargaining power comes from before you start your next job.

COMPUTER ANALYST

Name

Daveran M.

Location

Pittsburgh, Pennsylvania

Education

Some college

Total years in profession

19

Brief occupation description/goal of occupation

Analysis of PC problems and resolutions.

Why did you choose this career path?

Information technology is the way of the world—not to mention other more physically demanding careers yield a gold watch at retirement, possibly a pension, and a body racked full of pain.

What do you like about your occupation?

It's an easy-going, relaxed atmosphere, not physically taxing, and pays well enough to live comfortably.

What do you dislike about your occupation?

Nothing. I have complete liberty to do this kind of work anywhere; there's always a need for IT.

What are the misconceptions about your profession?

Like any, I guess, depending on what you're looking for—false promises from corporations to move up in the company type of stuff. That's the thing about IT, though—you're not bound by working for someone else.

On a scale of 1 to 10 (10 being great), how would you rate your occupation and why?

I would say 8, only because I haven't achieved what my ultimate goal is, as of yet.

What factors or former positions led to this occupation?

Where I'm from there was only one form of career that was highly successful at the time; when it was phased out to other entities for various reasons, the IT field was up and coming and a good fit for me.

What career choices were most helpful?

Post–high school education and working dead-end jobs for little to no money was enough for my eyes to be opened. It was necessary to get into something that was expanding in profitability and opportunity, or be poor and angry.

What career choices were least helpful/detrimental?

Opportunities that seemed too good to be true. I have been duped by a few, only to find they were only successful through deceit.

Did you have a mentor? If so, how did you find them? Did they help?

I have always been fortunate enough to have someone with wisdom who would help me with good advice. I didn't always follow their direction and soon found they were right and I was stupid!

If you didn't have a mentor, would you have liked one?

Definitely! That's like asking what you'd choose if you had a choice of cars between a four-cylinder and a V8.

What type of education was needed for your position?

Fortunately for me, I was able to secure an opportunity in this field without completion of my college education. My training in customer service helped, along with my upbringing in always being courteous and listening. Plus, I have a passion for helping people whenever possible.

Do you have to update your career with ongoing training and certificates?

No, that's not necessary, although it's good to have under your belt for skill level.

When you were hired, did you receive professional training or was it basically "on-the-job training"?

Mostly on-the-job training, along with prior experience.

**In a typical week, are your hours fixed or flexible?
On what days do you tend to work overtime?**

My hours are always the same, and I wouldn't change that for anything. I work to live; I do not live to work, if you understand.

Is your work environment "hectic," "all work and no play," "serene," "laid back," or other? Briefly explain.

Very laid back. Sometimes a little hectic in the a.m.

What types of conflicts do you deal with?

Service partner mishaps with their PCs, system outages, inquiries to resolutions, stuff like that.

Do you interface with coworkers, groups, or vendors, or do you work alone?

Yes, I communicate with coworkers, groups, and vendors.

What are your coworkers like?

Crazy! They're a great bunch of people to work with. Fun all the time.

What is management like?

My immediate manager is a man among boys, if you know what I mean, and the staff is very personal and not standoffish.

Is input accepted, or do you fare better as a "yes man"?

Input is a must for more proficient workflow. There is no "you do as I say, not as I do" here. We lead by example.

What issues have prevented your advancement?

My own interests. I like the freedom of not being tied into a nine-to-five setup.

Is your position secure, or are you frequently looking for the next opportunity?

Very secure, but I like to freelance also.

How important is/was networking or connections in finding your current or other positions? Is it a factor in advancement once you're on the job?

No. This is a wide-open field. If I had it any other way, I wouldn't be here.

How much fulfillment do you get out of your career?

I feel balanced and able to see clearly what I want in life. I couldn't see anything but drudgery in those other jobs.

Do you feel that you are fairly compensated?

For what I do for this company, yes. I can achieve the rest on my own.

If you could choose again, how much would money be a factor?

Only for necessity. I love this line of work, so money is not the only object.

Would you choose the same career path?

Most definitely!

Any comments or words of advice for someone entering your field?

Always keep an open mind to learn all you can and be a go-getter. No one can be successful looking for "handouts" in life. Love what you do, and do what you know you will love.

SENIOR SCIENTIST

Name

Nola

Location

New York City, New York

Education

Master of Applied Epidemiology

Total years in profession

9

Brief occupation description/goal of occupation

Senior scientist in the Australian Government Department of Health, Food Safety. The Government Department of Health is committed to developing and implementing health strategies to protect and promote health.

Why did you choose this career path?

Actually, it was a series of default options. I studied in the capital city of my country. I graduated as a medical technologist/microbiologist, and at the time there was a temporary vacancy in the government labs, which I found out about through a friend of a friend. Then, I did the master's in applied epidemiology as I felt it would give me more hands-on and deeper experience in my role in public health.

What do you like about your occupation?

The money and security were very good. The conditions, largely, were better than in any similar employment.

What do you dislike about your occupation?

Big wheels turn slowly . . . it seems that things take forever to complete. If you have very risk-averse bosses (and public service is full of them), it can be very frustrating trying to apply innovative solutions to repeating problems.

What are the misconceptions about your profession?

The same as for all public servants—boring, "faceless bureaucrats." That we do nothing, that we are all "politicians," that we don't have opinions.

On a scale of 1 to 10 (10 being great), how would you rate your occupation and why?

I give it a 6. On the plus side: great conditions, good salary, opportunity for promotion and development; on the minus side: stifling culture, slow progress, limited by the views of the government of the day, and you have many, many managers (state, local governments, public, industries).

What factors or former positions led to this occupation?

I lived in the capital city and seat of government, which was also the biggest employer at the time for new graduates. I think I chose science and government as safe options, as we had grown up poor children of immigrants. A job with the government was a dream come true for my parents.

What career choices were most helpful?

In the beginning I was very open to trying short-term vacancies and taking on new roles. The employment culture at the time was quite accepting of new graduates having lots of different experiences at the beginning of their career in public service (as opposed to being seen as fixed and narrow in outlook). I think this gave me exposure to a lot of people and job roles that I would otherwise have missed.

What career choices were least helpful/detrimental?

Fear-based choices. Staying in the government with a "safe and secure" job rather than taking a risk when I was younger and going with private enterprise or a non-government organization or being an artist.

Did you have a mentor? If so, how did you find them? Did they help?

Not until I was thirty. I met my mentor through organizing training courses, where the US EPA (Environmental Protection Agency) would travel abroad to deliver teaching in risk communication. He helped me realize that what I loved about my work was the people (public) and teaching.

What type of education was needed for your position?

A university degree in human sciences.

Do you have to update your career with ongoing training and certificates?

Not necessarily, but it helps with the salary and future opportunities. There are different sectors of public service that have different requirements.

When you were hired, did you receive professional training or was it basically "on-the-job training"?

On-the-job. Any professional training I undertook was that which I sought out, and my employers were supportive of this approach.

In a typical week, are your hours fixed or flexible? On what days do you tend to work overtime?

We work a standard week of 37.5 hours. We can work anytime between 7:00 a.m. and 7:00 p.m., but must be present between 10:00 a.m. and noon and 2:00 p.m. to 4:00 p.m. (core hours). You are not allowed to do more than nine hours per day. All extra time can be accrued to take as "flex time." Overtime is very rare, weekends even rarer. With higher positions and responsibilities, there appears to be a need to do extra hours on your own time, but this is flexible.

Is your work environment "hectic," "all work and no play," "serene," "laid back," or other? Briefly explain.

When I left, it was a dysfunctional mix of hectic and out of touch. Parts of my agency within the greater department were incredibly busy, while other parts were really slow. The work was not being managed well at the top, and the agency was really suffering as a result.

What types of conflicts do you deal with?

Internal politics! As a government agency dealing with food safety, we have to deal with the conflicts between industry and consumer views, overseas importers, governments, and different portfolios (such as agriculture, foreign affairs). These groups all have very different needs and viewpoints, and often the final policy or program must bridge these. Then we have to make it work in law!

Do you interface with coworkers, groups, or vendors, or do you work alone?

My job was very much team based, but there was also a lot of independent and autonomous work. The work was usually in project form, and as a project manager you would organize your team and your consultation strategy with the public.

What are your coworkers like?

Like anywhere, a mixture of nice, ordinary people. I suppose public service attracts and retains more conservative types who are happy to cruise toward retirement without too much surprise. But that could be my own stereotyped viewpoint!

What is management like?

Hopeless, risk averse, unimaginative. More interested in pleasing and appeasing their bosses than attending to the urgent issues. A lot of lip service. (This is why I am on a leave of absence.)

Is input accepted, or do you fare better as a "yes man"?

Yes men go straight to the top. A few years ago, it became the fashion to advertise standard selection criteria for job vacancies with the "desirable" criterion of "ability to challenge the status quo." I think this is funny to this day, because if you fulfilled this criterion, you would not fare so well generally (unless you got lucky and worked in a progressive unit).

What issues have prevented your advancement?

I am too happy to offer my opinion when something is really not working. Perhaps more importantly, I became disenchanted with the place I was working at and what I saw as a declining impact in public health.

Is your position secure, or are you frequently looking for the next opportunity?

My position is secure, and I am frequently looking for the next opportunity.

How important is/was networking or connections in finding your current or other positions? Is it a factor in advancement once you're on the job?

It was important in my case, as my first break was purely word of mouth. It's absolutely a factor once on the job; with so many people looking for jobs, it's a definite aid to be known and have a good reputation when going for promotions. However, you need to have the goods to back it up.

What would be your next career move?

If I stayed in my current job, I would be seeking a promotion to a management level or specialist scientific position, or possibly with a related but different department. I would also consider acting as an independent consultant in organizational training and subject-matter advice on a project-by-project basis.

Do you relocate often? Are there travel requirements?

I have not had to relocate for my job, and we tend to view travel as an opportunity. Depending on the project of the day or your position, there can be a lot of travel to meetings of expert scientific panels, conferences, public forums, and intergovernmental meetings.

How much fulfillment do you get out of your career?

I used to get a lot of fulfillment, but not so much recently.

Are the benefits and vacation schedule fair?

The best in the country.

Would you choose the same career path?

Absolutely not.

Any comments or words of advice for someone entering your field?

If you don't love it, give it some time until you know what the factors that influence your job are. Get a mentor, don't be afraid to make professional friendships, and approach people you admire to ask them about their experience and insights, but do build your own wisdom. That is, try on their viewpoints, but develop your own. Try everything you are interested in and don't be afraid to take a leap of faith, especially when you are young and straight out of university. Finally, if you feel you are not making a difference, remember that change is incremental and dependent on many people working together to do their little part.

APPLICATION DEVELOPER

Name

Rex C.

Location

Houston, Texas

Education

Some college

Total years in profession

19

Brief occupation description/goal of occupation

As an application developer, there is a sense of satisfaction when you're assigned a task to resolve and you design an application that not only solves the problem but increases employee productivity. I personally always strove to exceed the expectations of users and managers when developing applications. In most cases, I developed tools that were not a part of the original scope but turned out to be a great addition to the application design.

Why did you choose this career path?

I am a person who is able to analyze problems and see solutions, and as such I provide a tool that proves to be a great benefit in this industry. In addition, you can work with the latest in computer technology.

What do you like about your occupation?

The satisfaction of a job well done and the ability to work with others to arrive at a concentric solution. Then, the ability to work alone and demonstrate a product that is a direct match to the agreed solution. The income is not bad either. It just depends on how much time anyone is willing to invest.

What do you dislike about your occupation?

Sometimes people change their minds and ideas get shelved for other priorities, but this comes with the territory.

What are the misconceptions about your profession?

Certifications and degrees are required to even enter the field. This is not so. But education is a must. An individual with selective training, the ability to prove his skill, and some experience can quickly rise in the ranks, but education is ongoing. You can never stop learning or growing in this field. Like I said before, if you don't follow the flow of changes, it will hurt you in the long run.

On a scale of 1 to 10 (10 being great), how would you rate your occupation and why?

Being an applications developer is about an 8. There are areas where you could improve, but due to the political structure of most corporations, it is better to leave things alone than to intrude into areas in which other individuals are responsible. But the benefits and rewards for a job well done make what you do on a daily basis well worth it!

What factors or former positions led to this occupation?

I started in the computer industry as a salesperson. There, I quickly learned much more about the industry. I then worked for a major computer manufacturer as a technical support engineer. Within less than a year, I became a network support engineer, and then within another year I became a senior support engineer assisting other technicians. During this time, I learned programming languages. Then I entered the field as an applications developer for a web-based asset management company. It was there that they gave me the chance to show them my coding skills and I was able to grow even more.

What career choices were most helpful?

My best career change was to go from hardware-based technical support to software design and development. This one move opened more doors for me in the IT industry, since most hardware positions were now low pay or outsourced.

Always take the time to understand what your daily duties would be before taking a position. If you don't ask, you might wind up working in a job that you did not originally sign up for. Always ask the employer to summarize or describe a typical workday. For me, the more they could tell me, the better the job was for me. I loved to be challenged!

If you didn't have a mentor, would you have liked one?

Having someone who could explain how to make a specific function work in a programming language certainly would have reduced my learning time significantly! My only mentor was, and sometimes still is, the internet.

What type of education was needed for your position?

I did get an associate degree in computer science; however, with the exception of the programming classes, most of the education I received did not apply to the real-world scenarios that I run into on a daily basis.

Do you have to update your career with ongoing training and certificates?

Having certifications helps increase your value to any corporation. However, unless you have the experience to back up your training and certificates, then most employers see the certification as just an ability to pass a test and not real knowledge of the day-to-day duties that they need.

When you were hired, did you receive professional training or was it basically "on-the-job training"?

Every job I have worked has been a learn-as-you-go job. Each employer I worked for recognized my ability to think outside the box and learn new tasks quickly and took the risk of hiring me.

In a typical week, are your hours fixed or flexible? On what days do you tend to work overtime?

As an application developer, your workweek can be very unpredictable. There are times I have had to work till three o'clock in the morning doing a rollout of an application change due to problems. But, then again, there were just as many times that I was able to work from home or leave early for a job well done. Again, one must roll with the changes.

Is your work environment "hectic," "all work and no play," "serene," "laid back," or other? Briefly explain.

During the times you are actually working on code, it is sometimes hectic because you are under pressure to complete your project within a set time. Once that is accomplished and your slate is on hold or clean, you are given free time to pretty much do what you want to do.

What types of conflicts do you deal with?

Many times you have individuals who cannot come up with a concentric idea on how to accomplish a job. Many people are set in their ways and are resistant to change. Sometimes it becomes your job to sell the benefits of change.

What are your coworkers like?

The person who coined the phrase "You can please some of the people all the time, and all the people some of the time, but never all the people all the time," definitely understands my coworkers. My choice to minor in psychology proved to help me change my approach to each individual.

What is management like?

Most of the managers I worked for recognized my ability to meet or exceed the needs of others, so they pretty much only interacted with me to see what my schedule was like or to thank me for a job well done.

Is input accepted, or do you fare better as a "yes man"?

Yes men do not always get the job done in this field. Yes men only keep the status quo. One must be able to show ideas in a way that smooths the rough grain of management and coworkers.

What issues have prevented your advancement?

I should have finished my degree plan. I feel I could have been in a management role with more education.

How important is/was networking or connections in finding your current or other positions? Is it a factor in advancement once you're on the job?

Networking always helps get your foot in the door of some companies that otherwise would have looked over you or passed you by due to the flood of résumés. Keep your friends close, and your clients closer; you can always use them as a reference.

What would be your next career move?

To continue working toward a management role within the corporation.

How much fulfillment do you get out of your career?

It depends on the individual. If you like solving problems, thinking outside the box, and looking at things a different way, then this type of job can be very rewarding in itself.

If you could choose again, how much would money be a factor?

Not always. Sometimes, you must work for your money; other times, you can call your price. It depends on your job duties. For me, it would be location and how challenging the job is for me.

Would you choose the same career path?

I would have not changed a thing. Each job I have had prepared me for the next.

Any comments or words of advice for someone entering your field?

Learn as much as you can, and never quit learning. Be flexible and roll with the changes.

DEPENDENCY ATTORNEY

Name

Kerin C.

Location

Bakersfield, California

Education

Juris Doctor and Master of Arts

Total years in profession

5

Brief occupation description/goal of occupation

I represent abused and neglected children in dependency proceedings to determine what, if any, intervention by the court is needed based on family circumstances. We start with the initial petition for adoption or termination of the case as the family has resolved the problems that brought them before the juvenile court.

Why did you choose this career path?

I was a CPS (Child Protective Services) social worker for thirteen-and-a-half years, and I'm basically doing the same thing, only my new position has me actively representing children in court.

What do you like about your occupation?

You can help children with big problems.

What do you dislike about your occupation?

You see the worst of people. For instance, I've had to deal with parents who adopted a child and later molested or dumped them because the child had too many problems and they were not prepared to deal with the child's problems. Further, drugs are being used instead of parenting skills, and we don't have a choice, as too few are ready and willing to deal with major behavior problem children. In addition, we have to deal with some horrible child abuse situations.

What are the misconceptions about your profession?

There are never any success stories, and everything is just so bad the average person can't deal with it.

On a scale of 1 to 10 (10 being great), how would you rate your occupation and why?

I would say 8. I help children. We have major social work staffing shortages, so people are exhausted and mistakes are made, or work isn't completed in a timely manner.

What career choices were most helpful?

I started out to do special education teaching, and since I have a child development BA, the transition was fairly easy. Instead of getting a teaching credential, I got a master's in family and child counseling.

Did you have a mentor? If so, how did you find them? Did they help?

No, that is a major problem, as I frequently feel left out in the cold. Over the years, I've been able to develop relationships with colleagues who have been helpful. This has been very limited, however.

What type of education was needed for your position?

Juris doctor.

Do you have to update your career with ongoing training and certificates?

Yes, I am required to complete at least thirty-six hours every three years.

In a typical week, are your hours fixed or flexible? On what days do you tend to work overtime?

I rarely work overtime. It's generally in response to a trial or motion that must be filed. I rarely have to write motions.

What types of conflicts do you deal with?

Disagreements on how to handle a case. We're most likely to really fight over termination of services, denial of services to a parent, or whether or not sufficient evidence exists to keep a child out of the home. We also argue over relative placement.

Do you interface with coworkers, groups, or vendors, or do you work alone?

Daily, I deal with parent attorneys, county counsel, other child attorneys, social workers, foster parents, court-appointed special advocates, and relatives of children as well as the children.

What are your coworkers like?

Variable. Some are very isolated, others are helpful, and some are miserable and want all persons around them to be miserable as well.

What is management like?

Upper management doesn't understand our job or its importance, as the main goal of the office is criminal defense.

Is input accepted, or do you fare better as a "yes man"?

It depends. I have a long history in CPS, so I can say things because I know the history of the profession, even though I worked at two other counties before taking this position.

Is your position secure, or are you frequently looking for the next opportunity?

It's secure, but I'm always willing to talk about new opportunities. I have a home, so unless I am very certain the new job will be a good fit, I have no plans to move on.

How important is/was networking or connections in finding your current or other positions? Is it a factor in advancement once you're on the job?

Not at all—I applied because of a job listing on the internet, and they had a dependency opening. The office was under orders from a judge to hire another dependency attorney when I applied.

What would be your next career move?

Either another dependency position or possibly a district attorney office.

Do you relocate often? Are there travel requirements?

No. I relocated when I changed positions and there is no reason for me to have to relocate, as dependency cases are only heard in one courthouse in this county. I travel for training purposes only, and generally I choose which opportunities I want to attend.

Do you prefer going to work or leaving? Why?

Leaving; there is life after work, and I used to be a workaholic. This job can consume someone because of the vast problems you see daily, so it's important to keep your life balanced.

How much fulfillment do you get out of your career?

I can't complain, yet I don't jump up and down about what I'm doing. Some days are great and other days the abuse case put on my desk will be overwhelming. If the case is bad (e.g., serious sexual abuse or a significant burn), I have trouble reading through the case and learning the details as necessary for trial purposes.

If you could choose again, how much would money be a factor?

Not much. I started to teach, and this pays as well or better than teaching.

Would you choose the same career path?

Probably, as I'm always looking around at possible opportunities. I like having an exit plan in case this gets to be too much.

Any comments or words of advice for someone entering your field?

Be careful to take care of yourself. We, the profession, didn't create the problem. We are the mop-up crew, and it's important to keep your own needs in perspective.

SENIOR TECHNICAL ACCOUNTANT

Name

Clara P.

Location

Boston, Massachusetts

Education

Bachelor's in Business Administration

Total years in profession

8

Brief occupation description/goal of occupation

The technical accounting group offers centralized resources related to guidance, review, or other accounting assistance needed by the subdivisions mostly related to regulation and tax codes (GAAP, SEC, Tax, etc.), but generally all encompassing.

Why did you choose this career path?

Everyone needs an accountant, and it was the best way to secure a job.

What do you like about your occupation?

The challenge, although ever-changing guidelines can be frustrating. I am luckily surrounded by very smart individuals who make it easy to bounce ideas off and better understand issues at hand.

What do you dislike about your occupation?

The long hours, fire drills . . . your personal life is usually put on hold when deadlines have to be met.

What are the misconceptions about your profession?

That accountants don't have personalities—or are plain dorks.

On a scale of 1 to 10 (10 being great), how would you rate your occupation and why?

I would rate it an 8.5; it's not as good as being part of the operations team, but it sure is a great way to get close to the results!

What factors or former positions led to this occupation?

Definitely having experience in the "public" arena as an auditor. It is the best exposure you'll ever get, even if you decide to work for the private sector.

What career choices were most helpful?

Making the decision to be part of a six-month internship was difficult since it disappointed me not to graduate with the rest of my class; yet, those were the three best lost months of my life, since they put me slightly over the top of the rest of the candidates. Being a December graduate, there were more jobs and fewer applicants.

What career choices were least helpful/detrimental?

Settling for a job because I wanted a more "comfortable" schedule. In a short period of time, I realized I missed the challenge, and it was the only way to get ahead in my profession.

Did you have a mentor? If so, how did you find them? Did they help?

Of course I have a mentor! Everybody needs a mentor! I actually have several of them, each very knowledgeable in different areas. I know most of them through work, and they have helped in looking at issues in different lights—usually that I wouldn't have thought of on my own.

What type of education was needed for your position?

A bachelor's degree, at the least.

When you were hired, did you receive professional training or was it basically "on-the-job training"?

Professional training for the first few; afterward, it has mostly been on-the-job training.

In a typical week, are your hours fixed or flexible? On what days do you tend to work overtime?

Hours are flexible in terms of being responsible for getting your work done. An average day is 8:30 a.m. to 6:30 p.m., but when deadlines have to be met, no one looks at the clock.

What types of conflicts do you deal with?

A major conflict we deal with is when the operations group doesn't understand a specific guideline that needs to be adhered to, but doesn't believe they are wrong.

What are your coworkers like?

Extremely smart, professional, personable.

Is input accepted, or do you fare better as a "yes man"?

Input is accepted.

Is your position secure, or are you frequently looking for the next opportunity?

My position is secure—until my boss deems it isn't.

How important is/was networking or connections in finding your current or other positions? Is it a factor in advancement once you're on the job?

Networking is important, but having a good reputation and communication with your past employers is even more important.

What would be your next career move?

Within the same company, next level up.

Do you relocate often? Are there travel requirements?

I have not relocated to date . . . no travel requirements.

How much fulfillment do you get out of your career?

A lot.

Do you feel that you are fairly compensated?

Yes, given the expectations.

If you could choose again, how much would money be a factor?

A lot.

Any comments or words of advice for someone entering your field?

If you need constant positive reinforcement, accounting is not the right choice. It is challenging and can be rewarding depending on how hard you want to work, but for the most part, there will usually be an open position. If you decide on accounting, don't let others scare you out of doing public. It is one of the best ways to have exposure to issues/companies/individuals that you otherwise will not have shortly after graduation. It definitely offers as much or as little as you would need it to.

INSURANCE ADJUSTER INVESTIGATOR

Name

Walter P.

Location

Boston, Massachusetts

Education

Bachelor of Science

Total years in profession

18

Brief occupation description/goal of occupation

I generally deal in a face-to-face manner with insureds, their attorneys, and others for the purpose of investigating potential fraud in insurance claims and adjusting said claims as necessary.

Why did you choose this career path?

I started as an adjuster solely; my employer identified my ability to detect fraud and steered me in that direction.

What do you like about your occupation?

There's nothing like the feeling of having a long-term investigation all come together at the end and not only being able to deny payment on the claim, but to have the district attorney prosecute the same for fraud.

What do you dislike about your occupation?

Having to hold my tongue. People will really talk down to you, threaten you and your family/coworkers, etc. You essentially have to swallow your pride and continue to do your job.

What are the misconceptions about your profession?

That it is only an insurance company and it is okay to cheat them. People don't understand insurance and the coverages they are provided with when they buy a policy—it covers more than just them and their automobile.

On a scale of 1 to 10 (10 being great), how would you rate your occupation and why?

I would say 6. While the work can be satisfying, it is never-ending. Something goes on 24/7/365 and you can never finish it all. People are constantly angry and yelling and screaming at you if they don't get their way/what they are looking for.

What career choices were most helpful?

Adjusting claims prior to becoming an investigator provided me with the background necessary to know and understand insurance.

If you didn't have a mentor, would you have liked one?

It would have been beneficial for one of my coworkers to have taken me under their wing, but it did not happen. I took it upon myself to be a mentor for several coworkers after this, and they have all told me they benefited greatly from this.

Do you have to update your career with ongoing training and certificates?

I have taken numerous courses related to the industry and my specific job.

In a typical week, are your hours fixed or flexible? On what days do you tend to work overtime?

When you work in an office environment (as I have most of my career), the hours are fixed only in that you have to work 8:00 a.m. to 4:00 p.m. at a minimum. You cannot get the job done in 37.5 hours, and there are few who work less than fifty hours per week that are successful in their job.

Is your work environment "hectic," "all work and no play," "serene," "laid back," or other? Briefly explain.

When I worked in the office, it was hectic. The biggest problems were meddling supervisors and managers who brought work to a standstill by calling meetings that ninety-nine times out of a hundred were not necessary and could have been handled via an email. From home, the interruptions are essentially nonexistent and you set your own pace.

What types of conflicts do you deal with?

Face to face, over the phone, via written letter, etc. In the office, tensions run high and coworkers get on each other's nerves as well.

Do you interface with coworkers, groups, or vendors, or do you work alone?

When in the office, interfacing is a daily part of the job. From home, there is some email and phone interaction, but you are essentially on your own.

What is management like?

Current management is hands off; do your job, post your results, and they will not bother you. For my prior employer, management was just the opposite—they had little to nothing to do and were far too involved in the entire process.

Is input accepted, or do you fare better as a "yes man"?

Input is accepted when sought from management. If they are not looking for it, don't volunteer it, because it only falls on deaf ears.

What issues have prevented your advancement?

If you don't know someone in management who takes an interest in your career, your name does not get out there and you're going on an uneven ground. Also, the insurance industry has a high proportion of female workers and the "old girl network" is alive and well. For my prior employer, management was often selected based upon the makeup of the community. Each branch office had a similar makeup based upon the community makeup and the personal preferences of the office manager.

Is your position secure, or are you frequently looking for the next opportunity?

My position is secure. I'm very happy where I currently am and another opportunity would have to be overwhelming for me to consider it.

How important is/was networking or connections in finding your current or other positions? Is it a factor in advancement once you're on the job?

Networking is essential. Who you know is vastly more important than what you know.

What would be your next career move?

Management level in the insurance industry.

Do you relocate often? Are there travel requirements?

No relocation necessary. Travel is daily but is covered via car and seldom goes more than three hundred miles round trip in one day.

How much fulfillment do you get out of your career?

It is somewhat satisfying but can get redundant at times.

If you could choose again, how much would money be a factor?

Get as much money as you can as quickly as you can.

Would you choose the same career path?

I've done this to death at this point, so trying something else intrigues me. However, you can become trapped easily when your job is secure, you have decent benefits, and you have a family to provide for.

Any comments or words of advice for someone entering your field?

If you don't have thick skin or hate dealing with the public, this is not the occupation for you.

TAX ACCOUNTANT

Name

Robert F.

Location

Phoenix, Arizona

Education

Master of Business Administration; Bachelor of Science in Electrical Engineering

Total years in profession

12

Brief occupation description/goal of occupation

I do business accounting for small- to medium-size businesses, prepare taxes for businesses and individuals, and review tax problems of businesses and individuals and resolve them with the Internal Revenue Service and state tax departments.

Why did you choose this career path?

I enjoy working with people and I enjoy the challenge of resolving problems that others are reluctant to take on. Working as a tax accountant provides me with day-to-day contact with clients for accounting and normal tax preparation work for steady income, while the tax problems brought to me require thought and understanding of challenging tax regulations. Resolving these challenges requires a working relationship with the IRS and trust of the client that is being represented to bring issues to a resolution acceptable to both parties.

What do you like about your occupation?

The peace of mind knowing that I am helping businesses and individuals to avoid or resolve tax issues with the IRS and state tax departments, and keeping businesses informed financially of what they are doing correctly or incorrectly with their revenue.

What do you dislike about your occupation?

The second half of the year after tax season often is slow. It is when new business can be sought but existing clients don't want you to provide new services that could increase your revenue. It also is when the accounting records for businesses who don't keep or do accounting records must be done as their tax filings were postponed and extensions were filed. It means poring through checking account statements and credit card statements and recording all entries into spreadsheets to determine what was earned, spent, and taxable versus non-taxable.

What are the misconceptions about your profession?

That it's boring. It is a detailed profession and does require the ability to concentrate and have a good understanding of math (arithmetic, accounting, and tax rules). Without those, this field is not for you.

On a scale of 1 to 10 (10 being great), how would you rate your occupation and why?

I give it an 8. It's challenging mentally, and having to be persuasive can be tiring. New tax rules and laws are always in flux.

What career choices were most helpful?

After years of running my own business and learning accounting as a necessity, and after selling that business, I wanted something more to keep busy, so I began an accounting service. After a year or so, I realized that not only was tax preparation needed, but also tax representation was needed when the IRS challenged or demanded more tax be paid. Tax courses are available through the IRS.

What career choices were least helpful/detrimental?

Accounting as a profession is not one that is highly regarded by most students while in college, yet it is a necessary one to the business community. It doesn't have the glamor or provide the income that computer science or a field in engineering does. However, in time it can provide for great financial rewards and esteem.

What type of education was needed for this position?

Since I had the BSEE degree, it was easiest to simply take the accounting courses needed and to use the IRS courses to gain tax knowledge. Normally, a BS in business with a major in accounting and tax is needed and a master's in science is even better.

Do you have to update your career with ongoing training and certificates?

If you are going for either the certified public accountant (CPA) or the enrolled agent (EA) status, then there are continuing professional education (CPE) requirements for both each year.

When you were hired, did you receive professional training or was it basically "on-the-job training"?

Since I started my own business in accounting, I did not. I did have a full-charge bookkeeper I worked with in my previous business who helped guide me to fully understand all of the accounting functions of my business. I also had a CPA who helped me to understand the basics of my taxes for over ten years.

Normally, one would be assigned to work with another more senior accountant to receive guidance or the training needed. Additionally, an overview presentation could be done in a larger firm to orient a new accountant.

In a typical week, are your hours fixed or flexible?
On what days do you tend to work overtime?

During the tax season, the hours are anything but normal. They can run between eighty and 120 hours a week in order to complete the work in a private practice. After the tax season, a normal week's work runs from thirty to forty hours. Accounting and tax firms, large and small, experience the same craziness as well.

Is your work environment "hectic," "all work and no play," "serene," "laid back," or other? Briefly explain.

As the owner, I set my own pace, but I have to stay focused and committed to working so that my clients' work is completed punctually.

What types of conflicts do you deal with?

There are two types. One is with clients, though rare, where they don't like the results of my work. These sometimes can be heated and need to be defused.

The second is with the IRS, though these are strictly disagreements where each case is determined on its merits as evidence is presented to the IRS to prove a client's position.

How much fulfillment do you get out of your career?

Some. The work is often challenging, and keeping the clients pleased with the outcome is gratifying.

Would you choose the same career path?

Not necessarily. My health played a good bit into why I chose this field at this time.

Any comments or words of advice for someone entering your field?

If you enjoy working with numbers and with people, this is a great career.

CHAPTER FOUR

The Rockstars

ARCHITECTURE DESIGNER

Name

Jennifer C.

Location

Los Angeles, California

Education

Master of Architecture

Total years in profession

5

Brief occupation description/goal of occupation

Working as a designer, I am responsible for AutoCAD drafting, client interactions, design development, and construction administration for projects that range in size from sixteen-square-foot renovations to seven-thousand-square-foot new construction.

Why did you choose this career path?

I love architecture. There was never a thought in my mind that I should be doing something else.

What do you like about your occupation?

I love designing and developing solutions for various problems.

What do you dislike about your occupation?

I dislike clients who don't value my opinion.

What are the misconceptions about your profession?

That architects make a great salary. For the amount of education that most architects have, the profession tends to be one of the most underpaid professions out there.

On a scale of 1 to 10 (10 being great), how would you rate your occupation and why?

I would say a 10. I absolutely love what I do.

What career choices were most helpful?

Spending years as an intern was helpful to gain knowledge of the industry.

What career choices were least helpful/detrimental?

Because I didn't take business classes while at college, I lack the business sense needed to be more profitable.

Did you have a mentor? If so, how did you find them? Did they help?

Yes, my professor while at USC (University of Southern California). I continued to work for him during my internships. He gave me experience in the benefits of graduating from USC and professional experience, and he continues to advise me on certain projects.

What type of education was needed for your position?

Minimum is a bachelor of architecture, a five-year degree from an accredited school, or a three-year master's of architecture if you have a bachelor's degree in a different subject.

Do you have to update your career with ongoing training and certificates?

Yes. I need to stay current on trends and new technologies.

In a typical week, are your hours fixed or flexible? On what days do you tend to work overtime?

Hours are based on the projects that are due. Overtime is expected at all architecture firms.

Is your work environment "hectic," "all work and no play," "serene," "laid back," or other? Briefly explain.

Laid back on a daily basis. When something is due, the environment changes to all work, no play.

What types of conflicts do you deal with?

Meeting a client's budget and time schedule.

Do you interface with coworkers, groups, or vendors, or do you work alone?

I interface with clients, coworkers, contractors, vendors, etc.

How important is/was networking or connections in finding your current or other positions? Is it a factor in advancement once you're on the job?

Networking is extremely important. My office survives on referrals.

What would be your next career move?

Designing something, maybe landscape, clothing, textiles.

How much fulfillment do you get out of your career?

I love my career.

If you could choose again, how much would money be a factor?

Money plays a small role. My time is a much more important factor.

Would you choose the same career path?

Yes.

Any comments or words of advice for someone entering your field?

A lot of time is devoted to architecture for little pay. Only do it if you truly love it.

EDITOR, EDUCATIONAL PUBLISHING

Name

Sandra M.

Location

Chicago, Illinois

Education

Bachelor of Arts

Total years in profession

40+

Brief occupation description/goal of occupation

I conceive and direct the development of instructional programs (print and nonprint) for a diverse population, from preschool to college, including special-needs and bilingual students.

Why did you choose this career path?

I had a professor in college who encouraged me to use my writing talents in a career other than teaching.

What do you like about your occupation?

Educational publishing is a highly creative, stimulating profession that serves a useful purpose—educating today's students to succeed in tomorrow's world. It's a career in which one never stops learning.

What do you dislike about your occupation?

The work can be stressful—tight, unforgiving deadlines for bringing a product to market with a great deal of money at stake.

What are the misconceptions about your profession?

Most people outside the profession do not realize that editors in the educational side of publishing do more than copyediting. We start with a blank piece of paper—or in today's world, a blank screen—and conceive and develop complex, large-scale projects in concert with experts in the educational community.

On a scale of 1 to 10 (10 being great), how would you rate your occupation and why?

I would say 10. The work is creative, the people in the profession are intelligent and diverse, and the end product serves a useful purpose to society.

What factors or former positions led to this occupation?

It's a very difficult profession to break into. I was lucky; I broke in at the bottom and worked my way up the career ladder.

What career choices were most helpful?

Two career choices were helpful: starting at the bottom and constantly broadening my experience.

What career choices were least helpful/detrimental?

A detrimental career choice is making a job change for a higher position or more money with a company that does not reflect a compatible work philosophy or work environment.

If you didn't have a mentor, would you have liked one?

Certainly!

What type of education was needed for your position?

A college education in any subject; a master's is helpful but not necessary; broad knowledge in general is especially useful.

Do you have to update your career with ongoing training and certificates?

No formal training or certification is required; however, everyone in the field must be well informed on the latest research, best practices, market conditions, etc. to survive. In addition, individuals must independently stay abreast of the changes in the work process brought about by technology.

In a typical week, are your hours fixed or flexible? On what days do you tend to work overtime?

Hours are definitely not fixed—whatever it takes to create a quality product within the constraints of tight deadlines.

What types of conflicts do you deal with?

Getting highly creative people to work together as a team. Mediating the desires of the sales and marketing people (who reflect today's views) and the content and curriculum development people (who must create a product that stands up today and yet will meet the needs of the market, often well before those needs are documented).

Do you interface with coworkers, groups, or vendors, or do you work alone?

I interface with coworkers, teacher practitioners, university researchers, vendors, independent contractors, etc. around the nation. For most of my career, I worked in house; now I work from home, so the interface is either occasional face-to-face meetings or through internet communications.

What are your coworkers like?

Highly intelligent, highly creative, diverse backgrounds.

What issues have prevented your advancement?

I started in this profession when few women were in nontraditional professions. Advancement came from hard work and being especially good at what I do. Not until the mid-1970s were women in educational publishing capable of moving into management positions.

Is your position secure, or are you frequently looking for the next opportunity?

No positions are secure today. In my situation, age is now part of the issue.

What would be your next career move?

Working independently in the same career field.

Do you relocate often? Are there travel requirements?

I've relocated three times, to three different parts of the country—once by my own choice, once for a promotion, and the last for a company change. I've traveled to forty-two states in my work over the years.

How much fulfillment do you get out of your career?

An immense amount of fulfillment.

If you could choose again, how much would money be a factor?

Money is a factor only if the compensation is unfair.

Would you choose the same career path? Any comments or words of advice for someone entering your field?

It's a tough field to break into. Learn as much as possible about the field and be willing to start at the bottom.

COPY EDITOR AND PROOFREADER

Name

Patricia W.

Location

Western Massachusetts

Education

Bachelor of Arts

Total years in profession

28

Brief occupation description/goal of occupation

Entails reading manuscripts, articles, and printed materials to make sure they adhere to the style of the publisher and that they are grammatically correct, there are no misspellings, and the text is consistent. The goal is to make them ready for publication.

Why did you choose this career path?

I answered an ad in the newspaper for a production assistant in a small publishing company. The position utilized the skills I honed as a secretary. I love to read and am detail oriented, so it was a perfect match for me.

What do you like about your occupation?

I can work in house or as a freelancer. Since my first child was born, I have been a freelancer, which allowed me to stay at home while I raised my children. It allows me to work on a part-time or a full-time basis. I enjoy learning new things through the manuscripts I read.

What do you dislike about your occupation?

Pressures of deadlines and never knowing when a job is going to be coming in. Publishers usually allow the authors and others flexibility in the schedule, but by the time it gets to me they want it yesterday. Usually, I get little or no lead time. A call comes in one day and the assignment arrives the next.

What are the misconceptions about your profession?

That spell-check can do the same thing that I can.

On a scale of 1 to 10 (10 being great), how would you rate your occupation and why?

I would say 10. It is gratifying to catch an inconsistency or mistake that would make the author look like a complete idiot. I enjoy reading something and making sure that it is correct and makes sense. I like the idea of being a gatekeeper of the language.

What type of education was needed for your position?

A college degree.

Do you have to update your career with ongoing training and certificates?

I have to have updated reference materials.

**In a typical week, are your hours fixed or flexible?
On what days do you tend to work overtime?**

Flexible. I work overtime on Saturdays and Sundays.

What types of conflicts do you deal with?

Once in a while an author will not like the changes I have made. Sometimes I get conflicting instructions for completing an assignment.

Is your position secure, or are you frequently looking for the next opportunity?

There seems to be plenty of work out there for me.

How important is/was networking or connections in finding your current or other positions? Is it a factor in advancement once you're on the job?

Very important. People I've worked for will recommend me to someone else or use me again for another job.

What would be your next career move?

I might go work full time in a publishing house.

How much fulfillment do you get out of your career?

I get a lot of fulfillment out of my career.

If you could choose again, how much would money be a factor?

It would be one factor but not the major one.

Any comments or words of advice for someone entering your field?

Read a lot. Get training if available. Some colleges have a publishing procedures course. Be willing to take any kind of job in publishing to get your foot in the door.

JOURNALIST

Name

Dennis L.

Location

Los Angeles, California

Education

Bachelor of Arts

Total years in profession

4

Brief occupation description/goal of occupation

When stuff happens, I write it down. That's my sarcastic summary of my job. I'm an observer and recordkeeper of major and also, more than I care to admit, some minor news events breaking in my newspaper's coverage area.

Why did you choose this career path?

I tried my hand at it in college with the student newspaper and loved it.

What do you like about your occupation?

I love the freedom it affords me. My job is essentially to seek out curious, interesting things and people. For people who love to explore, love to talk, and are generally inquisitive, my job is perfect.

What do you dislike about your occupation?

It's not a job a lot of people retire from. It's a young person's job that doesn't give bonuses, humongous raises, or any of those lucrative things I have still yet to experience.

What are the misconceptions about your profession?

That every story is exciting and fresh. For every great story I write, there are five mediocre ones I have to write. This is especially true if you stay at the same paper over a long period of time—you'll inevitably have to cover the same events, folks, and themes again and again.

On a scale of 1 to 10 (10 being great), how would you rate your occupation and why?

It's a 6.5. It started as an 8, but even hobbies get old.

What career choices were most helpful?

Before I worked for a newspaper, I interned with a public relations group and accidentally networked with a group of former reporters. I was able to use their contacts to land my current job. When my college peers had no foot in the door, I had an entire leg in most interviews even before I handed over my résumé.

What career choices were least helpful/detrimental?

I once joined another professional group to network. It did nothing for me. Proof that not all networking is equal.

Did you have a mentor? If so, how did you find them? Did they help?

I don't have one mentor, but I'm pretty social at work, so I learn how things work/what's going on by talking to a couple different folks at the office.

What type of education was needed for your position?

A bachelor's degree at a minimum.

Do you have to update your career with ongoing training and certificates?

No, but I do highly recommend writing workshops. They are very helpful.

In a typical week, are your hours fixed or flexible? On what days do you tend to work overtime?

My schedule is very flexible, but at the same time my personal life has to be very flexible too. It's common for city meetings or some other story/event I'm covering to go well into the night.

Is your work environment "hectic," "all work and no play," "serene," "laid back," or other? Briefly explain.

Hectic during deadline time. Other times, it's a standard office. Get your work done and no one will complain.

What types of conflicts do you deal with?

An occasional reader or source. It's expected when you deal with the public so much.

Do you interface with coworkers, groups, or vendors, or do you work alone?

Both coworkers and the general public. It takes a team to put out the newspaper, not one person talking to a lot of other people to write a story.

What are your coworkers like?
My fellow reporters are an interesting lot, usually smart, good people skills, a few anal people, but that's expected in any work environment.

What is management like?
Usually the same as reporters.

Is input accepted, or do you fare better as a "yes man"?
Input is accepted, but be prepared to defend your position. Debates in the newsroom are very common.

What issues have prevented your advancement?
My age, my inexperience relative to my peers, a small number of higher positions. It's hard to move up in newspapers unless someone dies or quits.

Is your position secure, or are you frequently looking for the next opportunity?
Newspapers are notoriously under threat of falling under. It's an industry losing ground to television and the internet. Not sure where the future will take it.

What would be your next career move?
A career change.

Do you relocate often? Are there travel requirements?
If I wanted to move to another newspaper, I would probably have to relocate, but I don't plan to. Lots of local travel. Nothing exotic or too far.

How much fulfillment do you get out of your career?
Quite a bit, especially when I write a great story or realize I've made

a difference in some way. Interacting with the public, you hear whether you had an impact or not.

Do you feel that you are fairly compensated?

I would have said yes two years ago, but now my friends are starting to eclipse my earnings, which worries me.

If you could choose again, how much would money be a factor?

A very substantial one.

Would you choose the same career path?

No.

Any comments or words of advice for someone entering your field?

Choose a career with your interests in mind, but don't make a career decision with fear as a motivating factor.

PROFESSIONAL MUSICIAN

Name

Ron J.

Location

Fort Worth, Texas

Education

High school

Total years in profession

26

Brief occupation description/goal of occupation

Side musician for a major artist on tour worldwide; also, producing custom recording sessions, as well as playing on these projects, mostly for unsigned writers and/or artists.

Why did you choose this career path?

I love it. I can play on a recording session for twelve hours straight, then come home and still have the desire to play even more.

What do you like about your occupation?

Obviously, the travel worldwide . . . I have been to nearly every country over the years, all on someone else's "nickel." And the promoters treat all of us like royalty, to some degree. It is indescribable, to say the least.

What do you dislike about your occupation?

There are scammers out there preying on a lot of people who have the funds to record a project but end up losers because these thieves stole their dreams. Makes the rest of us look bad—and also makes it harder to convince them that we won't treat them the same.

What are the misconceptions about your profession?

That it is the "life of Riley." In reality, it is feast or famine. If I don't self-promote, I starve—plain and simple. And the travel isn't always the greatest either—flight delays, security issues, weather, etc.

On a scale of 1 to 10 (10 being great), how would you rate your occupation and why?

It's a 10! Of course! Like I said earlier, regardless of any downfall with travel, etc., I can always "escape" if needed with my instrument. I don't know too many other professionals who will work a full day, go home, and continue with it for hours on end.

What factors or former positions led to this occupation?

Simply out of boredom, we went downtown one day and I bought a cheap guitar. I took a few lessons from a local guy. Then, I was inspired by a stepcousin who was an excellent guitarist and I was hooked! Then a friend of mine recommended me to sit in for him on a recording session. I knew right after that day that I had found my future.

What career choices were most helpful?

Self-promoting sounds cheesy, I know, but the only other way I can describe it might be networking. Also, I moved to Nashville to expand my network of contacts. That, in turn, brought me back to the Dallas area.

Did you have a mentor? If so, how did you find them? Did they help?

Yes, and too many to mention. Some were distant mentors and others local.

What type of education was needed for your position?

None required, but it sure would have helped to have at least the basics in the beginning. Word of mouth and reputation seem to be the biggest requirements, along with the right contacts.

When you were hired, did you receive professional training or was it basically "on-the-job training"?

With this career, if you aren't prepared, you can be canned before the end of the first rehearsal!

Is your work environment "hectic," "all work and no play," "serene," "laid back," or other? Briefly explain.

Every session is different, but almost always a laid-back and enjoyable day. As far as traveling with the artist, most of the time it is laid back, unless there is a flight delay or some other "act of God."

What types of conflicts do you deal with?

Budget seems to be the biggest. Some clients want more than they have contracted for. Makes it hard to tell them they ran out of money versus time.

Do you interface with coworkers, groups, or vendors, or do you work alone?

Mostly with the client directly, and then the hired musicians. With the artist, I usually deal with the sound companies primarily, and the promoters secondarily. As far as performances, I work with five other musicians for the single artist.

What are your coworkers like?

They are the best in the business, and I am honored to be onstage with them. They take their "jobs" as seriously as I do, but they also have superb attitudes.

What is management like?

Our manager is our "Jesus." He has to deal directly with the artist on a daily basis, 24/7. I would not want his job . . . ever. He is another great man to be associated with.

Is input accepted, or do you fare better as a "yes man"?

Absolutely! Anything we can do to "streamline" the organization, they are all for it. I have suggested and we have made some drastic changes since I came on board.

Is your position secure, or are you frequently looking for the next opportunity?

No job is 100 percent secure. But I will also say that this particular artist seems to have a more personal attachment with all his "employees." But I have also tried to make sure that if this job ended today, I would have networked enough that I would only miss this income for a few months, maximum.

How important is/was networking or connections in finding your current or other positions? Is it a factor in advancement once you're on the job?

It's 100 percent important. I landed this position because of my reputation and network. I've tried as best I can to never burn any bridges, maintain a network of friends, and always strive to be more than reliable and well prepared for any performance date or session.

What would be your next career move?

I would enjoy knowing more about marketing and the inside track as far as how the major producers and record labels function. I see more growth with the internet as a huge marketing tool also.

Do you relocate often? Are there travel requirements?

I seem to have moved about every ten years. Travel is almost always required in one way or another. Not a problem for me . . . I love to travel, and I keep a bag packed and ready to go all the time.

How much fulfillment do you get out of your career?

If I were rich-rich, I would still do this. If I were rich-rich-rich, I would probably do it for free!

Would you choose the same career path?

Absolutely without a doubt, hands down.

Any comments or words of advice for someone entering your field?

Education, education, education, education, education; practice, practice, practice, practice, practice.

COSMETOLOGIST

Name

April H.

Location

Eastern Kentucky

Education

Some college

Total years in profession

6

Brief occupation description/goal of occupation

Cosmetologist—hair design, nail artist, massage, spa, makeup.

Why did you choose this career path?

I love to make people feel good about themselves.

What are the misconceptions about your profession?

That hairstylists are basically uneducated and paid to serve. We are very educated and are to be paid for our services, not treated as servants.

On a scale of 1 to 10 (10 being great), how would you rate your occupation and why?

I would say 10. It is fun, always changing, and exciting.

What factors or former positions led to this occupation?

I love art (I was a high school art student) and this is my artistic outlet.

Did you have a mentor? If so, how did you find them? Did they help?

My cosmetology instructor was my biggest inspiration. She was so encouraging.

What type of education was needed for your position?

In the state of Kentucky, 1,800 hours need to be completed in the areas of anatomy, trichology, skin care, nail care/art, principles of hair design, and massage, as well as basic knowledge of ethnicity and different traits of ethnicity. Also, we study different facial shapes and features in order to enhance and minimize different areas with makeup. We are required to complete an examination in practical and theory after our 1,800 hours by the Kentucky State Board of Hairdressers and Cosmetologists.

Do you have to update your career with ongoing training and certificates?

Yes, as well as complete six hours of CEU (continuing educational unit) classes per year.

When you were hired, did you receive professional training or was it basically "on-the-job training"?

I was well trained before I was hired.

In a typical week, are your hours fixed or flexible? On what days do you tend to work overtime?

Most days end in overtime because someone always needs work done.

Is your work environment "hectic," "all work and no play," "serene," "laid back," or other? Briefly explain.

The environment in my salon tends to be busy, but we try to keep the atmosphere relaxing and serene.

What types of conflicts do you deal with?

Most are clients who are not pleased with their service for some reason or another, or scheduling conflicts.

What are your coworkers like?

Energetic and trendy.

What is management like?

Very sophisticated and professional.

Is input accepted, or do you fare better as a "yes man"?

Input is accepted and encouraged.

What issues have prevented your advancement?

None. I advance on my own talent.

Is your position secure, or are you frequently looking for the next opportunity?

Secure, but in the beauty industry, you are always looking for more exposure.

How important is/was networking or connections in finding your current or other positions? Is it a factor in advancement once you're on the job?

Very important. Most of my clientele is built on "word of mouth," so the more people I connect with, and the more people they connect me with, the better my business.

What would be your next career move?

I have owned my own salon, but I will one day open an all-day salon/spa/fitness center with a small diner for all-day service.

How much fulfillment do you get out of your career?

I am very fulfilled.

Would you choose the same career path?

Yes.

Any comments or words of advice for someone entering your field?

Never give up, and always believe in your own talent and ability.

TELEVISION PRODUCER

Name

Diane

Location

Los Angeles, California

Education

Bachelor of Arts

Total years in profession

5

Brief occupation description/goal of occupation

Find locations to shoot, negotiate price and terms, and obtain city, county, and video permits. Interview contestants to be used in post-production to put the story together. Direct cameras to follow story and also to acquire footage needed for the show. Write scripts and work with editors to make the best television program in the time we are given.

Why did you choose this career path?

I wanted to write and produce for television or movies. I wanted to work in a creative environment. I am not a suit type of person.

What do you like about your occupation?

I love the exchange of creative ideas. I love putting the stories together out in the field as well as on my computer. Then seeing the scripts play out for others and their reactions, good or bad, is something that I wouldn't give up. There's nothing like the rush you get when you're with people and they laugh, cry, hate, or love what they're watching. It's the instant gratification of a job well done. If there are opinions on my work, that means I'm doing a good job.

What do you dislike about your occupation?

The hours, days, weeks, and months without a break. But then there are the weeks that you can afford to be unemployed between jobs that other professions don't have. I dislike that and the potheads. Some smokers can work and smoke, others only think they can.

What are the misconceptions about your profession?

That everyone does drugs. Not true. Everyone wants to be an actor. So untrue.

On a scale of 1 to 10 (10 being great), how would you rate your occupation and why?

I would give my occupation an 8. I get to meet and trade ideas with successful and respected people. I get to wear flip-flops to work on a daily basis. I get to lead a team and make choices in my work that millions of people get to see.

What factors or former positions led to this occupation?

Logger, tape dubber, story editor, associate producer, segment producer.

What career choices were most helpful?

Taking chances. I left successful shows to either move up or make more money. It hasn't ever hurt me. Knowing where I want to go as far as positions are concerned. I kept my eye on the prize.

What career choices were least helpful/detrimental?

Staying at a company out of loyalty; those days are over. Companies today demand your loyalty, but they're not loyal in return. I had to look out for myself.

Did you have a mentor? If so, how did you find them? Did they help?

I've had many. I found them by working hard, and they'd want to get me promoted. I learned early on hard work does pay in the long run. Today some of my mentors are now my equals and great friends.

Was your formal education necessary for this position?

Yes and no. It gave me an advantage as far as understanding story and how different techniques make plot lines stronger or more intriguing. The confidence of directing people previously made me trust my instinct in the field. Script writing and directing also helps.

When you were hired, did you receive professional training or was it basically "on-the-job training"?

On-the-job training. Pretend like you know it and learn it behind everyone's back.

Is your work environment "hectic," "all work and no play," "serene," "laid back," or other? Briefly explain.

All the above. It's minute by minute. You never know when a bomb will drop or when you might leave at a decent hour or even early. A good day is knowing you can go out to eat and not eat at your desk.

What types of conflicts do you deal with?

You name it. From personalities, to financial, to talent.

Do you interface with coworkers, groups, or vendors, or do you work alone?

The only time I work alone is when I'm writing a script. Otherwise, there are vendors, coworkers, groups . . .

What are your coworkers like?

Very different from one another; some are quirky, uptight, loud, quiet. A wide range of people.

What is management like?

Lately management has been great. The higher-ups look to you and count on you to make decisions. Once in a while you get an ego man on top, but now it's better for management to work with you rather than above you.

Is your position secure, or are you frequently looking for the next opportunity?

Looking for my next opportunity. I am hired on a weekly basis. If a TV network pulls the show, I am out of work. If a show gets canceled, I'm out of work. And at the end of any of my contracts, I'm out looking for my next one.

How important is/was networking or connections in finding your current or other positions? Is it a factor in advancement once you're on the job?

So important! I wouldn't be employed without them. A huge factor in advancement has to do with your relationships with people. There is no tenure here.

What would be your next career move?

Senior producer, supervising producer, co-executive producer.

Do you relocate often? Are there travel requirements?

No, I do not relocate because LA is the city of entertainment. Travel is required when shooting the show sometimes. It depends on what I have signed on for.

How much fulfillment do you get out of your career?

I'm not really sure. Sometimes I'm fulfilled and other times I'm not. It really depends on the project. Currently I'm fulfilled because the premise is great. I've only worked on a few shows where I got nothing out of it.

If you could choose again, how much would money be a factor?

I don't know. It is more about the job, but the money isn't bad. I couldn't complain and say it would have nothing to do with it.

Would you choose the same career path?

Yes.

Any comments or words of advice for someone entering your field?

Take chances. The more you gamble, the more your odds go up for gain.

K–12 ART TEACHER

Name

Bette B.

Location

Northeast Maine

Education

Master of Arts

Total years in profession

31

Brief occupation description/goal of occupation

Goal: to teach children about art history and use of materials—and to give them the opportunity and facility to explore and express their own creativity.

Why did you choose this career path?

It was what I liked best in college and what I excelled in. My minor was math. One summer at the end of my sophomore year, I decided to stay on campus and take additional classes in order to graduate early. I took three art classes and aced all three. The only math class I took (Theory of Equations) was a washout. That pretty much decided my course.

What do you like about your occupation?

I liked the idea of being the only art person in the school. I was on my own to plan and create lessons that I felt worked for the kids, within the framework of the state guidelines.

What do you dislike about your occupation?

I was asked to do anything and everything artistic in the school, from bulletin boards to backdrops for student performances. I was also an on-call advice person for all teachers who wanted to try something "arty" in their classrooms but did not know how to proceed, and generally asked me to advise them about twenty minutes before they wanted to teach the lesson.

What are the misconceptions about your profession?

That it is easy. It is probably one of the most difficult professions around. Although art teachers don't generally have scads of papers to grade every evening, they are always planning lessons and experimenting with materials (especially at the elementary level).

On a scale of 1 to 10 (10 being great), how would you rate your occupation and why?

I give it a 10. Teaching art was a relatively painless way to make a living and have fun doing it. It also helped when younger kids applauded after a demonstration before a lesson. I could tell instantly that we were on the same frequency. How rewarding!

What factors or former positions led to this occupation?

I did a lot of my own art. I did one or two exhibits. I think the idea of doing art as part of making a living was intriguing.

What career choices were most helpful?

After three years of middle school, I told my supervisor that I was out unless he had an elementary position for me. Within a month there were three openings at the elementary level in art. I felt like I died and went to heaven!

Did you have a mentor? If so, how did you find them? Did they help?

Each new teacher was given a mentor in the school, not necessarily in the same subject area. Mine was a science teacher whose room was directly across from mine. His advice was not to smile in class for at least six months. I tried, but I cracked up in laughter during the third week. Oh well! I also could call my supervisor at any time (about twenty miles away). Also, there was another art teacher at the school with whom I could talk.

What type of education was needed for your position?

At least a bachelor's degree. I was later encouraged to pursue a master's, because my supervisor said it would be good job security and more money. So I did.

Do you have to update your career with ongoing training and certificates?

Yes . . . every five years.

When you were hired, did you receive professional training or was it basically "on-the-job training"?

I already had student teaching . . . everything I've learned since then has been pretty much on the job. When the "computer age" hit the schools, there were many in-services that I took.

**In a typical week, are your hours fixed or flexible?
On what days do you tend to work overtime?**

Pretty much our hours were M–F, 7:30 a.m. until 2:45 p.m. I often got to school early to prepare by or before 7:00 a.m., and many days stayed late to work in the art room or attend meetings.

Is your work environment "hectic," "all work and no play," "serene," "laid back," or other? Briefly explain.

It was mostly hectic and constantly active. There is little time to "relax" with kids around all day.

What types of conflicts do you deal with?

I dealt mostly with student-to-student conflicts. There were sometimes attitude issues with other staff members, but I was often able to adjust to these by diplomacy.

Do you interface with coworkers, groups, or vendors, or do you work alone?

I interfaced with coworkers and parents intermittently. Mostly I was one on twenty or one on thirty with students.

What are your coworkers like?

Most were very professional and hardworking. They had their students' welfare and learning uppermost in their minds.

What is management like?

I had all kinds in thirty-one years. Most principals and supervisors were well prepared and worked hand in hand with teachers. There were a few occasions when they were obviously having personal issues that affected their job performance and, consequently, all the teachers' work environments as well.

Is input accepted, or do you fare better as a "yes man"?

Most times, input was welcomed and often implemented, if cost was not a factor.

What issues have prevented your advancement?

I did not want to advance to administration, in art, or within the school. The pay would have been better, but I'm not an office, parent-relations person. I liked being in the classroom.

How important is/was networking or connections in finding your current or other positions? Is it a factor in advancement once you're on the job?

Sometimes in education, if you want to get into something else, it is nice to know somebody higher up. But in my school system, if someone wanted to try something different, there were ways to go about that.

What would be your next career move?

I have been trying to get the energy to pursue my own art. We have beautiful vistas where I now live, and I enjoy landscape painting.

Do you relocate often? Are there travel requirements?

I do not travel very often now. When I taught, I had two or more schools to service for a number of years, so I was often at one school on certain days or weeks and another other days or weeks. I was always home at night.

Do you prefer going to work or leaving? Why?

Both. I found that if I was "down" in the morning, being around the kids would cheer me up. In the afternoons, I was sometimes so exhausted that I wondered if I had the stamina to drive in the traffic for twenty minutes to get home, and sometimes wished I could just sack out in the classroom.

How much fulfillment do you get out of your career?

I really enjoyed my job.

Are the benefits and vacation schedule fair?

Summers off . . . what more could you ask? Benefits were good while I taught.

If you could choose again, how much would money be a factor?

In what? Taking a teaching job? Probably not at all. With today's requirements on teachers and laws restricting discipline in the schools, I would not teach at all.

Would you choose the same career path?

No.

Any comments or words of advice for someone entering your field?

Don't . . . unless you are going into the private sector where parents seem to support "education" and student behavior better. I feel there is a possible outlet for passionate teachers with the home-schooling sector. I feel that energetic teachers could form mentoring agencies for parents to help them teach their kids. Something like Sylvan, but far more involved, as it would be the parents who would be taught.

ENGLISH PROFESSOR

Name

Wade T.

Location

Hartford, Connecticut

Education

Doctor of Philosophy

Total years in profession

10

Brief occupation description/goal of occupation

Teach writing (remedial, composition, technical/business)
and introductory literature courses (survey, American
literature, children's literature, folklore)

Why did you choose this career path?

I enjoyed reading and writing from high school on up. I also enjoyed teaching, which I discovered when my judo teacher asked me to take over a class one night when I was a teenager.

What do you like about your occupation?

The change in scenery between office and classroom rather than sitting at the same place for eight hours; the ability to use my brain a little bit planning course materials; the chance to interact with students in the classroom and to solve problems on my feet as I answer their questions or encourage their thinking; the pleasure at watching students using their minds and moving to the next steps in examining the world; the flexible schedule.

What do you dislike about your occupation?

The way work needs to be brought home constantly (we get great vacations but we can rarely ever leave the work back at the office; a forty-hour week is not enough to do the job properly); the piles of essays written by some students who do not really want an education but rather the piece of paper (a diploma); the rising ease and acceptance of routine plagiarism among students; the increasing tendency for administration to see students as "customers" rather than "students" (this is education, not business); the low regard much of the public seems to have for "true" liberal higher education (in other words, the value placed upon "training" rather than wide education; training is for jobs, education is for life; people do not seem to see the difference).

What are the misconceptions about your profession?

That we do not do much work; that we do not actually read the essays (I read them twice at least); that we are in the jobs for the summer vacations (a good teacher is so burned out by May that the summer is a recovery period, if indeed the teacher does not have to work during summer to make ends meet).

On a scale of 1 to 10 (10 being great), how would you rate your occupation and why?

For a community college professorship, I rate the job between 6 and 8 because the value will fluctuate depending on the level of course you get to teach. But teaching at this level (junior or community college) does not allow time for a lot of creative writing or research writing (as is done at the university level), nor can you offer advanced courses (they stop at the sophomore level). I have the feeling that I am educating students so that they can take the great courses at someone else's university. That can be tough on the spirit if you attained the PhD level (qualifying you for a university job) but had to teach at the junior-college level because of the state of the job market.

What factors or former positions led to this occupation?

My personal interests in culture, history, and hobbies (I write fiction as my hobby) led to this profession. I also worked as a corporate writer for many years as I was finishing the PhD. I also taught part time at colleges to gain experience during that period. So my interests, education, and work experience allowed me to have this job.

What career choices were most helpful?

Teaching part time to gain experience; working as a corporate writer to see how language skills are applied in the workplace.

What career choices were least helpful/detrimental?

Teaching too long at a community college can make you seem like "damaged goods" if your ultimate goal is to teach at a university. The most damaging decision was to stay in one locale (New England) for the job search (I was married and had a family, so my mobility was restricted), because one usually has to travel widely to find a university teaching job.

Did you have a mentor? If so, how did you find them? Did they help?

I had two English professors who became my friends, and one in particular who became my good friend over the many years during undergraduate, graduate, and post-graduate life.

What type of education was needed for your position?

A master's degree for a community college, although enough out-of-work PhDs exist even here that in some cases a PhD is useful to get a community college job (yet in other cases they will hold it against you because they will think you would not be happy at a community college; you can't win sometimes!).

Do you have to update your career with ongoing training and certificates?

Not formally, but we are expected to attend conferences and seminars in general, and if we do not show some effort at being active in our profession, then that might result in missing out on a promotion or tenure decision.

In a typical week, are your hours fixed or flexible? On what days do you tend to work overtime?

Two or three days per week may involve overtime depending on how much writing you have assigned, or how challenging your course material is (if you constantly update your courses, you can never just fall back on the previous semesters' course plans).

Is your work environment "hectic," "all work and no play," "serene," "laid back," or other? Briefly explain.

Moments of sheer terror and joy followed by a total collapse of psychic energy until the next class or the next day. Stay in good physical shape and have nonacademic hobbies (I recommend sailing and small-boat building).

What types of conflicts do you deal with?

Conflicts with students who think they deserve an A (but don't)—not often, though.

What are your coworkers like?

Fellow professors are usually witty and charming, but overworked just like me, so there's little time for interaction.

What is management like?

Utterly disconnected from reality unless they were recent professors.

Is your position secure, or are you frequently looking for the next opportunity?

Secure. Community college populations are growing as the nation declines in prosperity (or the social-class gap).

What would be your next career move?

None. Once a professor for several years, you are stuck. Rarely could you be hired elsewhere unless you have won major recognition somehow.

How much fulfillment do you get out of your career?

Hard to say. More than other jobs, surely. But still I think I would prefer to be on the first Mars expedition, or live like explorer historian Tim Severin: have great adventures, then publish books about them. But being a community college professor isn't a bad thing.

Do you feel that you are fairly compensated?

I didn't go into English to become rich, nor should you. Humanities professors are paid lower than science/tech professors, community college professors are paid lower in general, and we all earn less than people with similar educations in private businesses for the most part. But I don't complain. We do not work during the summer, so we are not paid for the summer; our salaries may seem low because of that but are relatively fair in an imperfect world.

Are the benefits and vacation schedule fair?

We have a lot of vacations, but the public doesn't understand that the shorter ones such as winter break and spring break are often filled up with exam/essay grading, course planning, or campus committee meetings. As said above, we have summer off, but then we are not paid for that time off as is fair, so if you have big bills, you need to work during the summer. The health benefits are very good.

If you could choose again, how much would money be a factor?
Not at all.

Would you choose the same career path?
I started with a BA in anthropology and switched to English for graduate work as I moved into folklore studies. I think now I would have stuck to anthropology, my first love (and I still could have studied folklore, which is part of both anthropology and literary studies). I would have read great books and written stories as a hobby, so, yes, I would have stuck to anthropology, but still, that would have led me to a teaching career. I would not want to give that up.

Any comments or words of advice for someone entering your field?
Some things you can't teach; you have to live them. The world is sometimes too big to advise about it. So—no advice, just an observation: If you have curiosity and a spine, and an honest mirror, that's good. That's the best you can hope for, and no small thing! Good luck!

PIANO TEACHER

Name

Beverly W.

Location

Northeast Wisconsin

Education

High school

Total years in profession

19

Brief occupation description/goal of occupation

I own, manage, and work at a music store, which I started in December 1999. I continue to try to expand with more instructors and students. I also teach piano in the business.

Why did you choose this career path?

I love music and also like being my own boss.

What do you like about your occupation?

I like the people I work with and the people I meet. I don't mind the book work, and it's great to watch the students learn the piano.

What do you dislike about your occupation?

I have not been able to grow the business to what I had hoped. It seems to be at a standstill, and I need more income to make it worthwhile.

On a scale of 1 to 10 (10 being great), how would you rate your occupation and why?

I would rate it at an 8. It feels great to be a business owner, and I enjoy what I am doing. If the income were higher, I would rate it a 9 or 10.

What factors or former positions led to this occupation?

I taught piano at a local music store for seven years prior to starting my own business. The condition of their studios and the nonexistent waiting area are what prompted me to find something better for everyone.

What career choices were most helpful?

Probably just the fact that I took piano lessons myself as an adult, besides having a music background. Just staying involved in music in one way or another is what led me to this profession.

Did you have a mentor? If so, how did you find them? Did they help?

My mentor would be my sister, who equally loves music. This was the first business venture that I have tried that she has totally supported me in. She helped me with decorating and getting everything set up and even loaned me some furniture to use initially.

If you didn't have a mentor, would you have liked one?

It would have been nice to have someone who had experience in running a studio to give me advice.

What type of education was needed for your position?

The fact that I took bookkeeping in high school and worked part time in an office my senior year helped. I learned how to do our personal finances and taxes, which has helped me in the management end of this business. And, of course, I needed to know how to play the piano in order to teach it.

When you were hired, did you receive professional training or was it basically "on-the-job training"?

Since it is my own business, I had nothing to base it on, as all other studios in the area were my competitors. I was literally "flying by the seat of my pants." I just went with my instincts.

In a typical week, are your hours fixed or flexible? On what days do you tend to work overtime?

My hours are very flexible. I typically spend more hours at the computer twice a month when I complete the book work and pay the other instructors. I typically teach only two days a week, but initially, I taught four days. These hours are all after school.

What types of conflicts do you deal with?

Returned checks (occasionally), irresponsible instructors, and occasional scheduling conflicts. Room conflicts between instructors. In general, just keeping everyone happy.

Do you interface with coworkers, groups, or vendors, or do you work alone?

I try to communicate with my instructors personally as often as possible. I do a lot of emailing also. I take all calls for scheduling lessons from new students. I only work alone when I'm at home at the computer.

What are your coworkers like?

I feel I have the most wonderful group of instructors. I don't feel that I am their "employer," because, technically, they are independent contractors and I am just providing them with a place to teach. However, it is my decision as to who will work at the studio. Most are middle aged with lots of teaching experience, and most do have music degrees. I believe in surrounding myself with people better than myself.

Is input accepted, or do you fare better as a "yes man"?

I always ask for input from the instructors. I want everything to run as smoothly as possible, and I certainly don't have all the answers as to how to do that.

Is your position secure, or are you frequently looking for the next opportunity?

My position is secure, as my business is becoming increasingly popular.

How important is/was networking or connections in finding your current or other positions? Is it a factor in advancement once you're on the job?

I needed to know other instructors in order to have enough business in the beginning. Since then, I have instructors calling me looking for a place to teach almost weekly.

What would be your next career move?

As I am getting older, I don't anticipate a major career move at this time. I recently took on a part-time job finding host families for foreign exchange students. I hope that will grow into the extra income that I would like to have.

Do you relocate often? Are there travel requirements?

I have been in the same city for thirteen years, and I doubt that I will move elsewhere, because my main business is here.

How much fulfillment do you get out of your career?

I get much fulfillment out of teaching students to play the piano and watching them grow in all aspects over the years that I have them, and I get many compliments and thanks from my instructors and students alike for giving them a nice environment in which to teach and learn.

Do you feel that you are fairly compensated?

As I said before, no. I feel I should be compensated quite a bit more for the time and energy that I put into the studio.

Are the benefits and vacation schedule fair?

I have no benefits of my own, and the only vacation that I take is when I decide to take one. But then I lose income, so I don't take off very often.

If you could choose again, how much would money be a factor?

I would probably still do the same thing. Even though I complain about not having enough money, I am basically pretty happy.

Any comments or words of advice for someone entering your field?

Thoroughly check out your competition and do your research. Even though on paper it looked like I could make good money, in reality it doesn't happen. There are too many variables like students that don't show up or don't pay; and the summers are tough because too many students take off or come sporadically.

PROFESSIONAL BODY PIERCER

Name

James D.

Location

Eastern South Carolina

Education

Some college

Total years in profession

1

Brief occupation description/goal of occupation

Professional body piercer. I pierce clients on places of their body they choose to beautify. My goal in my occupation is to own my own body piercing and tattoo studio.

Why did you choose this career path?

I chose this career because I love the body modification industry. I modify my body for pure vanity.

What do you like about your occupation?

I love the fact I can change someone's life by just a simple piece of jewelry.

What do you dislike about your occupation?

Well, the one and only thing I dislike about my job is when I have to do personal area piercings and the client has bad hygiene.

What are the misconceptions about your profession?

People think we are bad people because we may have piercings and tattoos, which society calls unprofessional.

On a scale of 1 to 10 (10 being great), how would you rate your occupation and why?

It's a 10, because I love waking up every morning and going to work.

What factors or former positions led to this occupation?

My big brother has been into this industry for many years. I also remember being in kindergarten, watching the National Geographic movies, and falling in love with the early body modifications.

What career choices were most helpful?

Becoming a professional piercer.

What career choices were least helpful/detrimental?

Working in retail.

If you didn't have a mentor, would you have liked one?

My only mentor was myself. I would have liked one, because I would have gotten into this industry, professionally, a lot earlier.

What type of education was needed for your position?
Apprentice and ARC (American Red Cross) certifications.

When you were hired, did you receive professional training or was it basically "on-the-job training"?
Professional and on-the-job training.

In a typical week, are your hours fixed or flexible? On what days do you tend to work overtime?
Fixed; mainly Fridays are pretty busy, so I might have to stay past posted hours.

Is your work environment "hectic," "all work and no play," "serene," "laid back," or other? Briefly explain.
I would say all the above, because there are a lot of risks in this industry.

What types of conflicts do you deal with?
Product failure.

What are your coworkers like?
My coworkers are awesome.

What is management like?
I am the piercing manager. I have to make sure we have everything in order to do the job.

Is your position secure, or are you frequently looking for the next opportunity?
Pretty much secure, but if a better opportunity arrives, I might consider accepting.

How important is/was networking or connections in finding your current or other positions? Is it a factor in advancement once you're on the job?

Networking is very important; the more people that come into the shop, the more money is made.

What would be your next career move?

My own piercing studio.

Do you prefer going to work or leaving? Why?

I prefer going to work, because I deal with a large variety of people.

How much fulfillment do you get out of your career?

A lot.

Do you feel that you are fairly compensated?

Yeah, but more would be nice.

Are the benefits and vacation schedule fair?

No benefits—but if I need vacation time, it's there.

If you could choose again, how much would money be a factor?

Money is not a factor as long as you are happy and the bills are being paid.

Would you choose the same career path?

Yes.

Any comments or words of advice for someone entering your field?

It's a long journey, but well worth it.

WRITER

Name

Suzanne C.

Location

Los Angeles, California

Education

Bachelor of Arts

Total years in profession

11

Brief occupation description/goal of occupation

I have written everything from newsletters to magazine articles to short stories to newspaper articles to website copy. I currently write training materials for a Fortune 500 company.

Why did you choose this career path?

I started writing because I'm a storyteller.

What do you like about your occupation?

I work at home and can balance my schedule so that I have time to work on personal writing, like the young adult novel I just finished.

What are the misconceptions about your profession?

That writers can't make money.

On a scale of 1 to 10 (10 being great), how would you rate your occupation and why?

I would say a 10. My job is challenging; the bar is always being raised. I write materials, people train against them, and sales results are achieved. It feels very good to see the actual impact of my work.

What factors or former positions led to this occupation?

I began pitching magazines to sell stories and ended up freelancing for teen magazines. That led to writing for an educational website. When the website folded, I was out of work and temping for a homebuilder when my boss learned that I was a writer. He asked me to develop training for him, and it all fell into place.

What career choices were most helpful?

Freelancing. Pitching is hard. It prepares you for anything.

What career choices were least helpful/detrimental?

I had a "gotta eat" job as an assistant to an assistant working at a company that bought airtime for infomercials. It wasn't detrimental, but it wasn't helpful!

Did you have a mentor? If so, how did you find them? Did they help?

My boss is my mentor. He's taught me a lot about developing training and processes and instructional design.

What type of education was needed for your position?

Bachelor of arts.

Was your formal education necessary for this position?

My formal education taught me how to write. I went to Emerson College in Boston, which was very hands-on. We learned a skill and were taught how to use it—it worked!

When you were hired, did you receive professional training or was it basically "on-the-job training"?

On-the-job training.

Is your work environment "hectic," "all work and no play," "serene," "laid back," or other? Briefly explain.

It's mostly laid back. Work gets hectic toward the end of the month when I'm on deadline, but most of the time I'm able to manage my time so that I don't feel incredibly rushed or under horrible pressure.

What types of conflicts do you deal with?

Very little conflict.

Do you interface with coworkers, groups, or vendors, or do you work alone?

I team up with a sales expert, but he is in Phoenix, so we telecommute.

What are your coworkers like?

Most of them are ambitious and able.

What is management like?

Strong development-wise, but there's a definite culture of accountability, so it's pretty hands-off.

Is input accepted, or do you fare better as a "yes man"?

Input is welcome and expected.

How important is/was networking or connections in finding your current or other positions? Is it a factor in advancement once you're on the job?

Networking was very important when freelancing. Establishing relationships with editors and publishers is huge.

What would be your next career move?

Sell my novel and become a full-time novelist.

How much fulfillment do you get out of your career?

A lot. I get fulfillment out of seeing results.

Do you feel that you are fairly compensated?

Yes.

If you could choose again, how much would money be a factor?

Money is important, but I believe I could make money at another career.

Would you choose the same career path?

Yes.

Any comments or words of advice for someone entering your field?

Don't believe what they say. You can be a working writer. Just write and pitch, write and pitch.

GRAPHIC DESIGNER

Name

Nicole B.

Location

Houston, Texas

Education

Bachelor of Fine Arts

Total years in profession

3

Brief occupation description/goal of occupation

I design anything for print or web.

Why did you choose this career path?

I have always wanted to be an artist; I just didn't want to starve—this is the closest thing I could find.

What do you like about your occupation?

I really enjoy the creativity and freedom I have.

What do you dislike about your occupation?

I really dislike clients who ask you for a new creative take, and then make you make so many changes it ends up looking like everything else you see.

What are the misconceptions about your profession?

Not very many people know what we do in our profession, and if they have any idea, they think we just do T-shirts.

On a scale of 1 to 10 (10 being great), how would you rate your occupation and why?

It's a 10; I love my career choice. I get paid to draw, illustrate, and design—which I have done in my spare time my entire life.

What factors or former positions led to this occupation?

When I was ten years old, I saw a billboard for a designer closeout shop. It said, "The closer you get, the cheaper we are." It had an image of a bulldog in what looked to be a mohair sweater, but then you got closer and it looked like a feather boa, and then you got closer and you noticed it was just spray paint splotches. I thought that someday I wanted to do that, to be creative, yet functional. I have always been creative and artistic, but I had to figure out how to make it into a career.

What career choices were most helpful?

I chose to pack my things and move away from my rural hometown to a very large city where I had more of a chance to work in my chosen career.

What career choices were least helpful/detrimental?

Waiting until my final semester of school to get an internship. If I could do it again, I would have at least tried to get a receptionist job at a design firm while I was in school, just to be around other creative people all day long.

Did you have a mentor? If so, how did you find them? Did they help?

I had a mentor who was a professor at my university. He did help, and he always pushed me to think as far outside the box as I could.

If you didn't have a mentor, would you have liked one?

I would have liked one outside my school.

What type of education was needed for your position?

You need at least an AA (associate in arts), but I have my BFA.

Was your formal education necessary for this position?

It was very necessary.

Do you have to update your career with ongoing training and certificates?

You have to be up on all the latest software.

When you were hired, did you receive professional training or was it basically "on-the-job training"?

I had to know everything before I was hired.

In a typical week, are your hours fixed or flexible? On what days do you tend to work overtime?

My schedule is flexible. I usually work from ten o'clock to six o'clock, M–F, but some days if I have a deadline or a print run, I will work later.

Is your work environment "hectic," "all work and no play," "serene," "laid back," or other? Briefly explain.

My work environment is pretty laid back, but you have deadlines you have to meet.

What types of conflicts do you deal with?

The only real conflict I deal with is clients who don't really know what they want.

Do you interface with coworkers, groups, or vendors, or do you work alone?

I interface with other designers, printers, paper vendors, web designers, my boss, and clients on a day-to-day basis. But when it comes to actually designing, I work alone.

What are your coworkers like?

My coworkers are pretty laid back, but some don't have a very good work ethic, so, being the art director, I sometimes have to be on their case to make them meet deadlines, which we always make.

What is management like?

Management is me, but my only boss is very laid back and lets me handle the other designers. But I'm laid back until there is a deadline that they are getting close to not making.

Is input accepted, or do you fare better as a "yes man"?

Input is always accepted. Someone might have a better or different idea to make your campaign/design better.

What issues have prevented your advancement?

I am at the highest place I can be—other than the owner's position. All I can hope or ask for is a raise. I'm still young, so I don't get paid as much as someone with more experience would get.

Is your position secure, or are you frequently looking for the next opportunity?

My position is secure, but I'm always looking for a better opportunity. In my field, there is always something better until you get your dream job.

How important is/was networking or connections in finding your current or other positions? Is it a factor in advancement once you're on the job?

Networking is always important. I wouldn't have found this position without knowing the people I know.

What would be your next career move?

I would like to find a larger advertising firm or design firm to move to but would like to keep my position and title of art director.

How much fulfillment do you get out of your career?

I get quite a bit of fulfillment when I drive around town or pick up a magazine and see something I have designed.

Do you feel that you are fairly compensated?

I feel fairly compensated for my experience, not the job I do. If I were compensated for the job I do, I would be paid at least $20,000 more than I am now. I know others that graduated with me who make a lot less than I do now.

If you could choose again, how much would money be a factor?

Money is always a big factor, but I can't see myself in any other career.

Would you choose the same career path?

I would choose my same career path, but I might have done more research on the school I chose to attend.

Any comments or words of advice for someone entering your field?

Talk to as many designers that are already in the field as you can before you start school. They can help you choose what school to go to and let you know what will be expected of you.

ART MODEL

Name

Jill F.

Location

New York, New York

Education

Doctor of Philosophy

Total years in profession

5

Brief occupation description/goal of occupation

I am a model, usually nude, for life drawing and painting art classes, workshops, small groups, individual artists, and photographers.

Why did you choose this career path?

I needed the money, and it appeals to my dance and yoga background.

What do you like about your occupation?

I like choosing challenging poses and poses that will best reflect the purpose of the class (group, artist, etc.). I am very flexible and strong, and I like the feeling I get holding poses on one foot or stretching in ways that are severe. I get a good workout and I get wonderful feedback, which helps a lot. I also like working freelance.

What do you dislike about your occupation?

I dislike that it wears me out. Also, I want to be a child psychologist and am not making enough money to go back to graduate school.

What are the misconceptions about your profession?

I am not sure. That art models are exotic or erotic? That we are all women? That we are not professional? That we are flaky and unintelligent?

On a scale of 1 to 10 (10 being great), how would you rate your occupation and why?

An 8. It is good fun for now. I am loving the art classes—I am gaining so much knowledge about art, it fascinates me. (I was a fine arts major in high school and have always loved to draw and paint, but I didn't pursue it.)

What factors or former positions led to this occupation?

Modern dance, yoga. I wanted to challenge myself to love and accept my body because I have had an eating disorder with body image issues.

What career choices were most helpful?

Well . . . I think this career choice was most helpful, as was my decision to open a cat-sitting business (at the same time). I couldn't work full time, or really at all, and these two jobs gave me the flexibility I needed and the cash to make up the balance that pays my rent. But I don't consider what I am doing now a "career." Art model, PhD?

What career choices were least helpful/detrimental?

My choice to become a professor. I had no support from my department, there were no jobs, and I found teaching bored students humiliating and degrading. I hated the university politics and the catty, petty environment. I spent most of my life in school to find out I hated what I prepared myself to do.

If you didn't have a mentor, would you have liked one?

Yes!

What type of education was needed for your position?

I'd say to be a good art model you need to know about art—the different art movements through history, the different poses that were frequent within the movements. You also need to know about space and planes and lines and how to draw. You need to know what the students and artists need from you; otherwise, what good will you do them? You have to be quick and creative and very smart.

When you were hired, did you receive professional training or was it basically "on-the-job training"?

On-the-job training. Actually, I was never trained. I was told what models do by another model and then I went to a class, took off my clothes, and did it.

In a typical week, are your hours fixed or flexible? On what days do you tend to work overtime?

My hours are flexible. I could work six days a week or I could work one day a week. The schedule tends to be heavy in the winter and the fall when schools are in session. In the summer there is not as much work. However, you can still work with artists' groups and individual artists on their exhibits.

Is your work environment "hectic," "all work and no play," "serene," "laid back," or other? Briefly explain.

I would say the work environment has been laid back; however, I get very nervous beforehand.

What types of conflicts do you deal with?

Occasionally, I will be late and the artist will be worried about me, or worried I forgot about the assignment. It has never been a problem, really. I haven't faced any conflicts.

Do you interface with coworkers, groups, or vendors, or do you work alone?

I work alone, although I make a point to talk with the professors and with the model coordinator and with the artists. I don't really see much of other models.

What issues have prevented your advancement?

I am five feet and three quarter-inches tall, so I can never become a fashion model, but I don't want to.

Is your position secure, or are you frequently looking for the next opportunity?

The job is never secure. There will always be work out there, but there are slow periods when there isn't as much.

How important is/was networking or connections in finding your current or other positions? Is it a factor in advancement once you're on the job?

Networking is very important. Most of my jobs have come from referrals through other models.

What would be your next career move?

I'd like to save so I can take a psychology course to begin my climb back into graduate school, where I want to study child psychology.

Do you relocate often? Are there travel requirements?

I never relocate. I travel by subway and bus to different parts of the city, and sometimes it takes up to an hour to reach an assignment.

How much fulfillment do you get out of your career?

I get more fulfillment out of this career than I have any other.

Do you feel that you are fairly compensated?

I think I should be paid more.

If you could choose again, how much would money be a factor?

If I could choose again, I would go way back to when I graduated from undergrad, work as an art model then, and save my money and go to school for psychology to become a psychologist.

Would you choose the same career path?

No way. Although I would work my way through school as an art model, I just wouldn't do the academic high theory route.

Any comments or words of advice for someone entering your field?

For art modeling, network. Make contacts. Go to art departments and find out who the model coordinator is and sign up to be a model. When you do go to work, bring a robe and a cloth to spread out for you to stand, sit, lie on. Always bring water and something to eat, because the work is more demanding than it sounds and you could faint. Tie your hair back. Just find out who is in charge of every art facility and every organization that holds art classes and tell them you are available as an art model. Volunteer to do photo shoots with photography students. They won't be able to pay you, but you will get some experience and also some photos that you can have for your portfolio and to send out via email. Be persistent! Talk to other models and ask where they work and how they got the job. Tell them you are just starting out and ask if they have any advice.

ACTOR

Name

Todd M.

Location

Los Angeles, California

Education

Bachelor of Arts

Total years in profession

15

Brief occupation description/goal of occupation

Theatrical/commercial actor. My goal was to make a decent living strictly performing. I wanted to rely on no other source of income other than one from acting, either on stage, TV, or film. My goal was to provide for my wife and two boys, in the hopes of providing regular/steady income.

Why did you choose this career path?

Performing was in my blood. There was no other profession that even piqued my interest. I felt alive and creative when I was in front of a live audience or camera. I knew I had the talent and drive, but I did not know how many obstacles I would face.

What do you like about your occupation?

I loved entertaining people, watching their reactions while I played a certain character. I loved the creativity of improvisation, working off another character and feeling so alive. The satisfaction from a good performance is like no other experience. The adrenaline rush was very similar to that of winning a big game.

What do you dislike about your occupation?

I never liked the uncertainty of when the next job would be. Not knowing when your next gig or paycheck would come provided an incredible amount of stress on myself and, of course, my family.

What are the misconceptions about your profession?

It is said that if you persist, keep focused, and study hard you will be successful. I would have to say that would hold true for most professions, but not the entertainment industry. It is really a "who you know" business and one that requires an incredible amount of networking.

On a scale of 1 to 10 (10 being great), how would you rate your occupation and why?

As a working actor, it was a solid 10, but as soon as it became irregular, the rating dropped off the charts. If I remained single, it probably would've stayed at the top of the charts.

What factors or former positions led to this occupation?

In college I was asked to perform in numerous student films and commercial productions. I caught the bug and continued my theatrical studies way beyond my college graduation.

What career choices were most helpful?

It was imperative to get the formal training under my belt. I studied with five incredibly talented instructors and gained completely different perspectives from each one. I utilized what worked best for me and kept to it.

What career choices were least helpful/detrimental?

I was continually being referred to one agency after another. I was never really successful with any one of them as they were all second rate. I even obtained a manager, which never amounted to much.

If you didn't have a mentor, would you have liked one?

I always wished I'd had a mentor. I was never quite able to make that kind of connection/relationship. I felt that I was close a couple of times, but it turned out that I was more of a threat to their careers.

What type of education was needed for your position?

It is not required that an actor have a specific educational background; however, in my heart it is mandatory. It is through education that an actor can relate to scripted material, life, and emotional experiences.

Do you have to update your career with ongoing training and certificates?

If you are a working actor, it is imperative that you keep your chops up, which requires ongoing training or performances. They say one can get rusty if this part of the brain is not used. I have to agree with that, as I kept busy for fifteen years.

When you were hired, did you receive professional training or was it basically "on-the-job training"?

I had many years of individual and class training; however, I always learned a great deal on the job working with various directors and performers.

In a typical week, are your hours fixed or flexible? On what days do you tend to work overtime?

In the world of acting, one can expect to work any hour of any day. There is no such thing as fixed hours in the entertainment industry. The only thing fixed is the desire to succeed.

Is your work environment "hectic," "all work and no play," "serene," "laid back," or other? Briefly explain.

All the above. In performing and working, one must endure the full gamut of emotions and work environments. It can surely be an emotional roller coaster.

What types of conflicts do you deal with?

The first conflict deals with getting the job audition. Soon to follow will be getting through the rest of the audition process to eventually getting the offer.

Do you interface with coworkers, groups, or vendors, or do you work alone?

It is very rare that one works alone, unless they are doing a monologue. An actor works with other actors, agents, and managers, and sometimes publicists and lawyers.

What are your coworkers like?

All actors are very different types of individuals, all with high levels of ego. Some work really well with you while others see you as a threat. Still, all in all, actors belong to a unique fraternity and usually cover each other's back.

What is management like?

Agents and managers are mostly on the lookout for themselves. It is a very cutthroat business, and they will usually send talent out for the sake of getting themselves a commission.

What issues have prevented your advancement?

Once I got married, I had to stop thinking about myself. I couldn't just leave the house and say I was attending a party in Hollywood. At least not a lot of the time.

Is your position secure, or are you frequently looking for the next opportunity?

In the world of entertainment, you are always looking for the next opportunity. Reading the trades and calling on friends, agents, and managers was all part of the process.

How important is/was networking or connections in finding your current or other positions? Is it a factor in advancement once you're on the job?

Networking/connections are key to being successful, maybe even more than having the talent itself. The industry is a tight niche, and it requires a ton of persistence in breaking into it.

What would be your next career move?

I am currently involved with a writing project, a series for cable television. From a writer's perspective, it is just a jump away from producing.

How much fulfillment do you get out of your career?

I was completely fulfilled while I was acting. It felt so right and so good that I look back now and say I wish I had another go at it.

Do you feel that you are fairly compensated?

When I performed I was fairly compensated. When I wasn't working there would be no compensation.

If you could choose again, how much would money be a factor?

Money actually plays a great factor. I invested quite a bit of money (probably more than I earned in the long run) in photos (8x10s), résumé reproductions, acting classes, wardrobe, and various other expenses. I always believed, though, that it takes money to make money, and I still do.

Would you choose the same career path?

If I had another chance at it, I would probably give it another try. If it's in the blood, there is no getting around it. You either have it or you don't. It is not something you can learn.

Any comments or words of advice for someone entering your field?

You must be persistent and know there is nothing you want more. You must train professionally and be ready at all times to perform at will. You must network and never take no for an answer. You must live to act and act to live.

TECHNICAL WRITER

Name

Melissa P.

Location

Boston, Massachusetts

Education

Bachelor of Arts

Total years in profession

Almost 4

Brief occupation description/goal of occupation

I am a technical writer (my official title is information developer) working for a pharmaceutical software company.

Why did you choose this career path?

I knew that I wanted to get my degree in English because I love to read and write, and I wasn't sure how to translate that passion into a marketable skill—the college technical writing program seemed like a good fit, and it certainly has turned out to be.

What do you like about your occupation?

My job allows me to work independently and to make decisions without consulting every person on the team. I manage my time and my projects by myself, and I'm constantly challenged by documentation and new software to learn. Plus, unlike some other careers, you have actual deliverables that you can look at and see what you can accomplish (and show in job interviews to prove your talents), and that is a great feeling.

What do you dislike about your occupation?

Technical writers don't get the same respect as engineers/ developers in software companies, so we and our processes are sometimes an afterthought to people.

What are the misconceptions about your profession?

A lot of people think that technical writing is boring—and I used to be one of those people! Even when I was going through the tech writing program in college, I said that I would work for any company but a software company.

On a scale of 1 to 10 (10 being great), how would you rate your occupation and why?

For me, my occupation is a 10—a perfect fit. I am fastidious about details and always want to know the "why" behind a question. You need these skills to succeed in the career, and if you have them, you will have immense satisfaction every day because every day, you accomplish something new.

What factors or former positions led to this occupation?

I love to write, and I wanted a great salary—the decision was easy for me.

What career choices were most helpful?

I started out at a small, non-public company where I worked in a team of two to create all the documentation for the company. On the plus side, I had tons of control and we got good bonuses. On the negative side, there were no processes and we received very little direction from our supervisors, so we were left on our own to figure things out.

What career choices were least helpful/detrimental?

At a smaller company, technical writers are not as respected as they wish they would be—and sometimes even their managers don't stick up for them. Try to judge the respect level that writers get in a prospective company, and make sure your supervisor and his/her supervisor recognize the value of documentation.

If you didn't have a mentor, would you have liked one?

I would like a mentor—and am looking for one in my company. Unfortunately, we don't have a mentoring program in place, so I am trying to figure out how to choose one and approach the topic with him/her.

What type of education was needed for your position?

I received a bachelor of arts in English, and I participated in the technical writing and technical communication program my senior year.

Was your formal education necessary for this position?

Absolutely—do not attempt technical writing without formal training in it.

Do you have to update your career with ongoing training and certificates?

Not yet, but I am considering getting an MBA or taking additional classes in the field.

When you were hired, did you receive professional training or was it basically "on-the-job training"?

At my first job (with a small company), training was definitely on the job—and sometimes I had to deliver it! My current company has full-time trainers who teach customers how to use the software, so I can sit in on those classes when I want to learn more.

In a typical week, are your hours fixed or flexible? On what days do you tend to work overtime?

In general, you work longer hours when you're closer to a release, and you have no control over when the release is.

Is your work environment "hectic," "all work and no play," "serene," "laid back," or other? Briefly explain.

At my first job, definitely hectic, all the time—but there was a strong community and I truly felt like I had a lot of friends there, and that made it bearable. My current job is laid back in general, unless it's close to a release time, and then things get hectic. But releases are generally scheduled well in advance, so you can plan for when you will be working longer hours.

What types of conflicts do you deal with?

I am working to develop a style guide for my team, and some people are pushing back—no one wants to be told how to write.

Do you interface with coworkers, groups, or vendors, or do you work alone?

I work in a team of two documenting a product, and I also work with engineers to understand application functionality. I don't work with outside vendors.

What are your coworkers like?

My coworkers are great. Most of the people on my team are fifteen years (or more) older than me. I am happy with the situation because they have a lot more experience than I do, and I can learn from them.

What is management like?

My managers are on my team, so they know exactly what I do.

Is input accepted, or do you fare better as a "yes man"?

With engineering, it depends—I request application changes all the time, and usually, people listen to me (but that is not always the case with other teams). Within my own team, everyone is expected to provide input and suggestions to improve processes, which is great.

What issues have prevented your advancement?

In general, you can't advance if someone already has the position that you want, and a lot of technical writers don't change jobs frequently. Sometimes you have to move companies to get ahead.

How important is/was networking or connections in finding your current or other positions? Is it a factor in advancement once you're on the job?

I got my first job through networking (a graduate of the same program contacted the professor), and I found my second job online. However, I've networked to bring other people in to my companies.

What would be your next career move?

I'd like to become a documentation manager.

How much fulfillment do you get out of your career?

A lot—it is a satisfying career, and I feel like I have a lot of options if I were to change jobs again.

Do you feel that you are fairly compensated?

I feel like I am overpaid—and that's a great feeling.

Are the benefits and vacation schedule fair?

Great benefits—health care is paid for 85 percent and I had three weeks' vacation to start. One glaring omission—no 401(k) match. I'm hoping it might happen in a few years.

If you could choose again, how much would money be a factor?

Money was one of my main motivations for entering this career, and I can't say that I've been disappointed.

Would you choose the same career path?

Definitely.

Any comments or words of advice for someone entering your field?

Choose your company wisely—figure out what your criteria are (size of company, age of coworkers, number of people on the team, respect level that writers get, whether your manager is a writer, whether documentation is part of engineering, if there is a defined career path, etc.) and try to find a company that matches them. And if you have the luxury of holding out until you find a good match, do it—better to wait than be stuck in a job that you don't like but don't want to leave because you think it will look bad on your résumé. And—try to get a mentor who can help you determine your criteria and can help you find a job and figure out the best way to succeed. A mentor would have helped a lot in the beginning of my career.

CHAPTER FIVE

The Good Kids

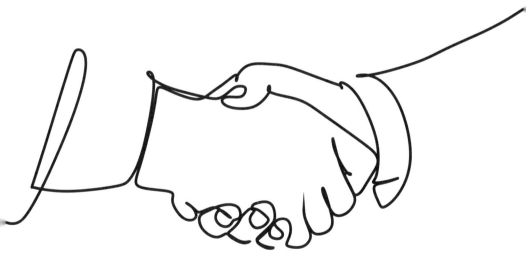

EDUCATIONAL CONSULTANT

Name

Lynn G.

Location

Chicago, Illinois

Education

Bachelor of Arts with some master's work

Total years in profession

5

Brief occupation description/goal of occupation

As an educator, I serve as a trainer and consultant for after-school programs while simultaneously developing curriculum and tutoring individuals one on one.

Why did you choose this career path?

I realized that in many ways, I enjoyed talking about writing more than I enjoyed writing itself. This led me into the world of individualized academic support, which led me to get my master's degree to teach full-time. It's amazing to watch and track a child's or adult's progress as they learn.

What do you like about your occupation?

It can be very flexible, especially if one is comfortable tutoring.

What do you dislike about your occupation?

While the field is extremely rewarding, it is also an area that is underfunded by the government. Many educators pay a lot out of pocket, even though pay is not spectacular.

What are the misconceptions about your profession?

One misconception is that teachers will always be poor.

On a scale of 1 to 10 (10 being great), how would you rate your occupation and why?

I'd give it a 9. I am constantly learning in order to be able to teach. There are plenty of professional development opportunities out there, no matter what your educational interests. I often have a great deal of flexibility (summers are great), and there is always more to learn. Education is a great field for those who bore easily.

What factors or former positions led to this occupation?

Having a strong writing background helped, since having knowledge in the area(s) you want to teach will always help make your educating that much stronger. I was always working with kids and adults. I started out as a writing consultant, which got me part-time gigs as a literacy tutor, which got me a full-time job as an adult educator, which helped me find high-paying part-time jobs once again.

What career choices were most helpful?

Always keeping an eye out for what jobs are out there. Just getting a small amount of tutoring experience and a bachelor's degree can help you bring in lots of potential career choices.

What career choices were least helpful/detrimental?

Sometimes I had my hand in too many part-time jobs. I couldn't pass up a good-paying job, even if it only offered a few hours a week. It made me burn out until I cut back on hours.

What type of education was needed for your position?

A bachelor's degree with three to five years of experience in education, training, and programming.

Was your formal education necessary for this position?

My English undergraduate degree helped. My partially completed master's in education helped cinch the deal.

Do you have to update your career with ongoing training and certificates?

Many full-time classroom teachers do need ongoing professional development credits each year. I take part in (or lead) over seventy-five hours of training in different subjects per year, though it is not required.

In a typical week, are your hours fixed or flexible? On what days do you tend to work overtime?

My hours are generally fixed from nine o'clock to five o'clock. I work overtime if I have an educational grant that I need to write, which usually takes a great deal of time.

What types of conflicts do you deal with?

Sometimes school principals are difficult to deal with and cause programmatic issues to evolve.

Do you interface with coworkers, groups, or vendors, or do you work alone?

I interface with others, including educators and other administrative staff.

What is management like?

Management is busy and not extremely well versed in education. They are well versed in other areas of direct service programming.

Is input accepted, or do you fare better as a "yes man"?

Input is accepted, as I am seen as knowing more about educational issues than others in the administrative office.

What issues have prevented your advancement?

There are no other jobs in this agency that are directly educational in focus, so upward movement is not possible.

How important is/was networking or connections in finding your current or other positions? Is it a factor in advancement once you're on the job?

Networking is a big deal in the field of education. I found my current job through a web search but had plenty of other leads due to educational colleagues.

What would be your next career move?

Becoming either a classroom teacher or a director of education for another nonprofit or for-profit company dealing with literacy or after-school issues.

Do you relocate often? Are there travel requirements?

I do not relocate. There are frequent local travel requirements in order to get to satellite centers. There are infrequent long-distance travel requirements for professional association conferences.

How much fulfillment do you get out of your career?

During times when my job is busy and varied, I get a lot of fulfillment.

When I'm working on special projects, I see a lot of intrinsic value to my job.

Do you feel that you are fairly compensated?

Yes and no. As the position grows to oversee more educational centers, I feel I deserve more money than I'm getting.

If you could choose again, how much would money be a factor?

I turned down a job for $6,000 more a year because I thought this job would be less stressful and more rewarding. I was right, but I sometimes wish I could've bargained more.

Any comments or words of advice for someone entering your field?

Start volunteering or working part time in child care, tutoring, or education as early as possible. You can gain great experience working just a few hours a week, and education is a field that requires a lot of practice and reflection. Getting some of that while in college or post–high school will serve you well. The sooner you are certified and experienced, the sooner you can leverage your experience for more money. And don't avoid education because you think you won't make enough money. There are plenty of ways to keep evolving as you get older, and you can always make extra cash working very part time since people always need tutors.

REGISTERED NURSE

Name

Betty I.

Location

Bridgeport, Connecticut

Education

Some college; diploma, Registered Nurse program completed

Total years in profession

23

Brief occupation description/goal of occupation

ICU (intensive care unit)/emergency department staff nurse

Why did you choose this career path?

I became interested while working as a medical secretary in a dermatologist's office.

What do you like about your occupation?

I can work three twelve-hour shifts. I can work 7:00 a.m. to 7:00 p.m. or 7:00 p.m. to 7:00 a.m.

What do you dislike about your occupation?

Lifting. Exposure to blood and needle sticks. Exposure to tuberculosis, AIDS, and Hepatitis B and C.

What are the misconceptions about your profession?

That it is high-paying and a very "clean" profession.

On a scale of 1 to 10 (10 being great), how would you rate your occupation and why?

I would say 4. Too many risks. Very heavy lifting (one hundred pounds or more).

What factors or former positions led to this occupation?

I was a medical secretary and certified nursing assistant.

What career choices were most helpful?

My time as a nursing assistant.

Did you have a mentor? If so, how did you find them? Did they help?

The employer/department manager assigns a preceptor (teacher/trainer) when new. The preceptor can last a few hours to six weeks.

What type of education was needed for your position?

Some college; a three-year diploma program in a large teaching hospital.

Was your formal education necessary for this position?

You need to know all the bones, muscles, tendons, and organs in the body, as well as how they work (in detail). You also need to have courses in psychiatry and sociology, and nutrition. Basic CPR for a health professional; advanced cardiac life support (ACLS); pediatric advanced life support (PALS).

Do you have to update your career with ongoing training and certificates?

Yes. CPR every year. ACLS and PALS every year. Certificate in Trauma Assessment every year. If you are certified in the state as a CCRN (critical care registered nurse), you need to take an exam every four years; if you are certified by the state as an ER (emergency room) nurse, you need to take an exam every four years, or every eight years if you provide a certificate that you obtained one hundred credits per year. All this is besides the general licensing exam that you take upon graduation from nursing school or a degree program.

When you were hired, did you receive professional training or was it basically "on-the-job training"?

Mostly on-the-job training. Mainly "baptism by fire," or "sink or swim" philosophy.

In a typical week, are your hours fixed or flexible? On what days do you tend to work overtime?

Fixed, but most times there is so much work and so few staff that you usually do overtime. I have done many sixteen-hour shifts. By CT law, we are not allowed to work over twenty hours in a two-day period without eight hours of downtime.

Is your work environment "hectic," "all work and no play," "serene," "laid back," or other? Briefly explain.

Very hectic and extremely high stress. In ICU and ER, you never know what's going to come in the door and how much one-on-one time a patient will need until he's stabilized, and then you are still responsible for him and anywhere between two and twelve others.

What types of conflicts do you deal with?

Drunk, drugged people who are combative cause conflict. There are also conflicts with other staff. In the ER, sometimes there are conflicts with police, EMS, and paramedics. Conflicts with family members of patients also occur.

Do you interface with coworkers, groups, or vendors, or do you work alone?

You cannot work completely alone; sometimes you need help, and so you have to help others. Responsibility for the patient in my care is mine.

What are your coworkers like?

You have to be cool headed, even tempered, and able to handle stress well. If a coworker does not do her/his share of the work, there is anger and resentment.

What is management like?

My ER manager was a former army nurse. She was extremely strict.

Is input accepted, or do you fare better as a "yes man"?

Input is accepted. More of the younger doctors ask and value nurses' opinions. The doctor is no longer considered God.

What issues have prevented your advancement?

None. Sometimes employers do not promote from within, which is the only problem.

Do you prefer going to work or leaving? Why?

Leaving. This type of nursing takes a severe toll on your body and health. You cannot deal with extremely intense situations without it affecting your health.

How much fulfillment do you get out of your career?

Only the satisfaction of saving a life. The money is not much.

Do you feel that you are fairly compensated?

No, not at all. If you are in an ER, in an ICU, or with any patient in a hospital, if something goes wrong (e.g., heart arrhythmia, choking, cardiac arrest), the nurse will be the one who saves your life, because your family doctor is going to be home in bed or out somewhere.

Are the benefits and vacation schedule fair?

You have to sign up for your vacation a year in advance; only two RNs can go on vacation at the same time from one department.

Would you choose the same career path?

No.

Any comments or words of advice for someone entering your field?

Do not expect to make much money.

HIGH SCHOOL ENGLISH TEACHER

Name

Stephen W.

Location

San Bernardino, California

Education

Master of Arts—Education

Total years in profession

15

Brief occupation description/goal of occupation

Teach high school English courses to ninth, tenth, eleventh, and/or twelfth graders.

Why did you choose this career path?

I was an English major in college and unsuccessful at real estate sales, and everyone in my family taught school.

What do you like about your occupation?

Teaching a class well, when students respond, is one of the most rewarding things a person can do.

What do you dislike about your occupation?

Teaching thirty-eight students for forty-eight minutes, five times a day, is very stressful. Constant discipline problems, due to the end of "the paddle" in education, impede positive progress. The stress built to the point, with me, that I suffered heart failure from prolonged high blood pressure. Most teachers don't last that long these days. The facts: three out of five teachers quit during the first five years, eight out of ten quit in the first ten years. I lasted fifteen years.

What are the misconceptions about your profession?

The biggest misconception is that teaching is a rewarding profession. Financially, it's mediocre. Aesthetically, it has moments, hours, but at best it has good days along with the bad days. Schools used to be well organized, safe, and calm.

On a scale of 1 to 10 (10 being great), how would you rate your occupation and why?

I would rate teaching as a 1 because it costs too much in time and money to become a teacher, only to discover, like eight out of ten, that it is not the profession for a lifetime they'd hoped to find.

What factors or former positions led to this occupation?

The fact that my mother and sister were excellent teachers and enjoyed pension and vacation benefits, along with my love of English, led to my decision.

What career choices were most helpful?

Once I decided to become a screenwriter and started working toward that goal, something I really wanted to do, I was a lot happier.

What career choices were least helpful/detrimental?

I chose to teach a class of "at-risk" students at the start of my career. This, although common, is a bad way for a novice teacher to begin.

Did you have a mentor? If so, how did you find them? Did they help?

I found another teacher who coached me through the first couple of years. He helped me a lot.

What type of education was needed for your position?

Education requires too many classes of theory and not enough on practice. It requires five years of college!

Do you have to update your career with ongoing training and certificates?

You have to continue your education indefinitely. Every time you renew your credentials, you have to submit 150 hours of "continuing education" approved by the state.

When you were hired, did you receive professional training or was it basically "on-the-job training"?

I was lucky to get "new teacher" training designed to help beginning teachers.

In a typical week, are your hours fixed or flexible? On what days do you tend to work overtime?

Teachers work various hours, depending on the tasks they take on.

Is your work environment "hectic," "all work and no play," "serene," "laid back," or other? Briefly explain.

The environment is very hectic—kids constantly bickering with each other and with you, and ignoring their work.

What types of conflicts do you deal with?

Gang members want to beat you up for disciplining their "cousin." Principals want to reprimand you for teaching something off the curriculum, because the class is noisy, because you fail too many students. Parents call you racist. Students tell lies "trying to get you fired" or fall in love with you.

What are your coworkers like?

Most teachers are too busy to socialize, but many are stressed.

What is management like?

Management likes to hide from the problems.

Is input accepted, or do you fare better as a "yes man"?

Be a "yes man" if you teach. Nobody listens, really. They might ask for input, but it's patronization.

Is your position secure, or are you frequently looking for the next opportunity?

Tenure makes one feel secure, but actually, given the high stress levels, one becomes their own threat to employment.

What would be your next career move?

I am now a screenwriter collecting a disability pension that finances my creative efforts.

Do you relocate often? Are there travel requirements?

Teachers should never move because they lose seniority and place on the salary schedule.

How much fulfillment do you get out of your career?

I feel proud to have taught, but disappointed in myself as a teacher.

If you could choose again, how much would money be a factor?

Money is a big factor.

Would you choose the same career path?

No. I would avoid teaching because it is no longer secure, benefits are vanishing, and working conditions are horrible.

Any comments or words of advice for someone entering your field?

Don't teach unless you can't imagine doing anything else.

HIGH SCHOOL GUIDANCE COUNSELOR

Name

Casey P.

Location

New York City, New York

Education

Master of Science

Total years in profession

2

Brief occupation description/goal of occupation

I work with high school students and their parents. Everything I do revolves around helping them to succeed academically, though that often involves leaving "academia" to delve into the personal areas of their life that are affecting their ability to succeed.

Why did you choose this career path?

I originally went into nonprofit after college because I knew I wanted to contribute to society, but I found I wasn't fulfilled. During that time, I volunteered to be a counselor to preteens who were going through their parents' divorce. It was because of this experience that I decided to go into counseling. The decision to do counseling in schools was because my boyfriend (who would become my husband) was a teacher and I thought we would have a wonderful quality of life if we were on the same vacation schedule—I have been right!

What do you like about your occupation?

At the high-school level, there is quite a lot of paperwork and not that much counseling. Some people dislike this ratio, but I love it. I enjoy organization and having tasks laid out for me.

What do you dislike about your occupation?

I dislike that I spend a lot of time and energy trying to help my kids and their parents deal with their struggles, but more often than not, they do not take my advice.

What are the misconceptions about your profession?

So many people, including teachers, think that guidance counselors do little to no work. They see that I have my own office and computer, can take my lunch when I want to (when all hell is not breaking loose in my office with a student and/or parent), can go to the bathroom when I need to, etc.

On a scale of 1 to 10 (10 being great), how would you rate your occupation and why?

For me, this job is a 10. It really fits my personality and my wants and needs as an individual. I receive decent pay and I have a great schedule.

What factors or former positions led to this occupation?

My volunteer work was the biggest influence, followed by the fact that my husband is a teacher.

What career choices were most helpful?

I was fortunate to have a boss at my last job who allowed me to rework my schedule to allow me to leave early once a week for my master's classes and eventually for my practicum (one hundred hours in an actual school).

If you didn't have a mentor, would you have liked one?

Yes, I would have liked to have had a mentor. It would have been nice to talk about my experiences and receive advice and sympathy.

What type of education was needed for your position?

A master's degree in education, school counseling.

Was your formal education necessary for this position?

Yes. I had my undergraduate degree in behavioral science. If I had not had that major, I would have had to take prerequisite classes, and that would have set me back timewise.

Do you have to update your career with ongoing training and certificates?

At a certain point, you need to get what's considered "thirty above," which means an additional thirty credits above your master's—all in guidance. Also, to even get the job, you need certificates in violence prevention and child abuse.

When you were hired, did you receive professional training or was it basically "on-the-job training"?

I already had four hundred hours in the field between my internship and practicum, but that barely prepared me. It was really on-the-job training. I learned more in two weeks on the job than in all my classes.

**In a typical week, are your hours fixed or flexible?
On what days do you tend to work overtime?**

My hours are fixed to a certain extent, but you never know when a crisis will occur and you are expected to stay. Also, there are certain times during the school year when you know you will be working overtime—during schedule changes, night school sign-ups, etc. But you do get paid overtime for these times.

Is your work environment "hectic," "all work and no play," "serene," "laid back," or other? Briefly explain.

Completely depends on the day. Some days are totally chill and I can catch up on a lot of paperwork and filing, and other times I do not even get a moment to breathe.

What types of conflicts do you deal with?

I deal with all conflicts: students and teachers, students and parents, students and security, students and social workers. The issues we discuss are truancy, behavior, personality, medical, emotional, mental—anything and everything.

What are your coworkers like?

My coworkers are dedicated individuals who are overworked and underpaid and underappreciated. And yet we all show up for work every day!

What is management like?

My administration is very student oriented and good to their staff.

Is input accepted, or do you fare better as a "yes man"?

Our school is very open to input.

Is your position secure, or are you frequently looking for the next opportunity?

It's secure in that you can be an invaluable asset to the school and they will not want to let you go, but you can be "excessed" in the early years. This means that if the budget does not allow for your position, you have to leave the school. You are still guaranteed a job from the Department of Education, but you will be out of your current school.

How important is/was networking or connections in finding your current or other positions? Is it a factor in advancement once you're on the job?

It is the number-one reason I am in my job today. There was a hiring freeze going on when I was looking for my job. No guidance counselors were being hired anywhere. It is because a principal at another school where I completed my practicum was impressed with me but was unable to hire me, so she called another principal who was interviewing me and gave me an outstanding referral. I am forever in her debt.

What would be your next career move?

In another year, I will have three years of experience. That is how many are needed to enroll in another master's program for administration. Once I complete that degree, I will have the opportunity to become an assistant principal.

How much fulfillment do you get out of your career?

It cannot be measured. Getting paid to help children is a dream come true.

Do you feel that you are fairly compensated?

I believe all educators should be paid more than what they are getting, but for now, early in my career, I am happy with my salary. And because I have financial goals, I take on every extra job I can at the school to pad that salary.

Are the benefits and vacation schedule fair?

Absolutely! Many people think educators get too much vacation, but believe me, we need every ounce of it! We give so much between the vacations that we need that time to recharge so we can come back and give even more!

If you could choose again, how much would money be a factor?

It definitely plays a huge factor. If this job only paid basic wages, I could not stay in it because I would not be able to make ends meet. That is not the life I want. Luckily, this job pays enough for me to have a decent quality of life.

Would you choose the same career path?

Yes! I am very happy with my choices and the outcomes.

Any comments or words of advice for someone entering your field?

Be ready to work very hard, to give in ways that your degree will not prepare you to give, to practice patience, and to keep your emotions in check. Also, be sure to have your own outside support system that you can turn to when the job overwhelms you.

PUBLIC EDUCATION TEACHER

Name

Patty

Location

Boston, Massachusetts

Education

Bachelor of Arts and Master's in Education

Total years in profession

20+

Why did you choose this career path?

I came to this via social work. I had been a social worker and was very frustrated with the system and how it handled children, in particular the follow-through of their daily routines once removed from their biological family setting. I thought I would have more of an impact on children if I were able to work with them in their everyday life.

What do you like about your occupation?

The pros of the job are the obvious ones. Working with children is very rewarding in simple ways—smiles, laughter, and watching students grow in their own thinking. Knowing that someday these students will grow to run our businesses and our country and knowing that you may have made an impact on someone's life is incredible. Really, where else can you go and be surrounded by future lawyers, businessmen, politicians, artists, etc.?

What do you dislike about your occupation?

The correcting and planning of daily work can be time consuming and tedious. The funding and grants that we depend on to make programs work can end at any time and, in fact, have. The outside influences, media, and politics that blame all problems on teachers and schools, and choose to end funding that helps students and families who do not and cannot help themselves; this, in fact, is very much a con of the job.

What are the misconceptions about your profession?

Bankers' hours are indeed a misconception. On the average, a teacher not only works the school day, but far beyond that day, correcting work and planning lessons, meeting with families, etc., as well as seeking funding and writing grants, organizing summer institutes and, in general, overseeing the needs of all the students in the present class and classes that came before.

On a scale of 1 to 10 (10 being great), how would you rate your occupation and why?

I love my job. I love the excitement in a child's eye when they learn something new . . . I love when a former student returns to share college acceptances. I love seeing the whole child and knowing that person will inevitably make a difference in my own life.

What factors or former positions led to this occupation?

I chose my career after viewing life from a different side. Being a social worker and a counselor unlocked many doors to lifestyles that I was unfamiliar with. I couldn't seem to make an impact or a significant difference for my clients. The children in all these cases tugged at my heart . . . now I work with kids and get to know them and their families before a crisis arrives, and maybe if I am lucky I can help prevent the crisis; plus a major bonus . . . I laugh all day . . . kids have the greatest sense of humor, and they are open and honest about everything.

How did you get where you are at now?

Work and studying and listening to others who know far more than I.

What career choices were most helpful?

Social work most definitely improved my teaching. Did it improve my chances of being a teacher? Of that I am not sure.

Did you have a mentor? If so, how did you find them? Did they help?

I did have a mentor. Cambridge provides new teachers with mentor teachers. Mentor teachers have a breadth of teaching experience and knowledge that they can impart to a new teacher. Mentor teachers are great sounding boards for just about all the things that come into play in teaching.

How much fulfillment do you get out of your career?

At times I get great fulfillment, and at times I have much frustration.

The best part of teaching is watching someone succeed . . . you can have a firsthand view of that.

What type of education was needed for your position?

In Massachusetts you need a master's degree in education and a minor in another field. You also need to pass a teaching test and get certification status.

Was your formal education necessary for this position?

Some of my education was not useful . . . not to say it was a waste. It was what I made of it; in retrospect, I think eighteen years old is very young to make educational decisions that may affect your whole life.

If you could choose again, how much would money be a factor?

I go back and forth on that . . . I would have to give up a lot in order to make the money my peers (outside of teaching) make. I do not think I would do things differently.

What type of hours do you typically put in in a usual week and what do they consist of?

In school by 8:00 a.m., hopefully out of the school building by 4:30–5:00 p.m. Hours spent preparing at home vary from two to sometimes four or five hours, depending on the curriculum and the students.

What are your coworkers like?

For the most part . . . hardworking, caring, and smart people. Our teachers come from a variety of ethnic backgrounds; they speak more than one language and have come to teaching through a variety of avenues . . . lawyers, economists, pilots, counselors, to name a few.

What would be your next career move?

I am contemplating this . . . most definitely a related field . . . some sort of community work.

What is management like?

We are fortunate enough in our school to basically manage ourselves. We design and implement our own curriculum; we are in charge of how we spend our monies and what programs we want . . . we are different from many schools in this respect.

What types of conflicts do you deal with?

City administration, budget cuts.

Is the pay satisfactory?

In comparison to other teachers, yes.

How important is/was networking or connections in finding your current or other positions? Is it a factor in advancement once you're on the job?

Absolutely—sharing strategies and finding funding is all done through networking.

Worst aspect of the job?

If I had to pick, the pay.

TEACHER OF ENGLISH AS A SECOND LANGUAGE

Name

Amy R.

Location

Massachusetts

Education

Master of Arts

Total years in profession

10

Brief occupation description/goal of occupation

I teach English to children whose families speak other languages. I teach in a small, urban public school system.

Why did you choose this career path?

I love working with people from around the world. I love learning about other cultures. I love language. I like helping people. I like working with kids.

What do you like about your occupation?

I find great satisfaction in helping others learn our American culture, history, and language. Working with kids is very rewarding, uplifting. I feel very "needed" in my work. I feel like I make a big difference in people's lives, people that most others would never take notice of or care about. I feel very privileged to be able to help people realize the American Dream.

What do you dislike about your occupation?

The adults, the bureaucrats, the people who have never taught a child or worked in a classroom (or even spent any significant time in a public school as an adult) who make the decisions that affect education. We work in substandard conditions with substandard materials and supplies. We have local, state, and federal governments who cry oceans "for the sake of the children" and don't have a clue. Testing, testing, testing, testing . . . when can I teach again?

What are the misconceptions about your profession?

"Those who can, do. Those who can't, teach." "All that time off, work from 9:00 a.m. to 3:00 p.m., all those weekends, holidays, and vacations, and the whole summer off." Teachers get paid to work only about eight months a year when you factor in vacations and holidays!

On a scale of 1 to 10 (10 being great), how would you rate your occupation and why?

Overall, I guess it's become a 7. If I could retire tomorrow, I would. I don't know how much I'd miss it. I would miss the kids and the teaching, but not all the other crap, which encompasses most of my day and mental energy. It used to be all about teaching kids.

What factors or former positions led to this occupation?

I grew up in a community with plenty of immigrants. I peer-tutored ESL (English as a second language) in high school and college, all while preparing to become a veterinarian. I spent a year studying abroad, and continued teaching and tutoring overseas while learning firsthand what it was like to be an "immigrant for a year."

Did you have a mentor? If so, how did you find them? Did they help?

My first year teaching, I was blessed to have a more experienced teacher latch on to me, out of the kindness of his heart. He was my savior. We became close friends.

What type of education was needed for your position?

A master's degree in teaching English as a second language and certification/licensure throughout the Commonwealth of Massachusetts.

When you were hired, did you receive professional training or was it basically "on-the-job training"?

Sink or swim.

Is your work environment "hectic," "all work and no play," "serene," "laid back," or other? Briefly explain.

We just finished two weeks of "hectic" state testing for third and fourth grade. Two weeks before that was a week of "hectic" state testing too. Never "serene," always busy. I like that my days are filled with energy. Often I don't have time for bathroom breaks.

What types of conflicts do you deal with?

What types of conflict don't I deal with? Conflicts with students, administrators, parents . . . people have written books about this.

Do you interface with coworkers, groups, or vendors, or do you work alone?

In my position, in an average day, I work with about seven classroom teachers, a guidance counselor, two administrators, a nurse, three custodians, six cafeteria workers, three secretaries, and about 100–120 children ages six to eleven years old.

What are your coworkers like?

As varied as humans can be! We're all working for the common goal of educating children, but we have different ideas of how to do that.

What is management like?

Administration can be a real anchor around my neck. I've requested a transfer to another building this year. Specifically, "any other building in the city."

What issues have prevented your advancement?

Lack of professional respect on the part of my administrators, "seniority," and long friendships (not between my administrator and me).

Is your position secure, or are you frequently looking for the next opportunity?

I can always get transferred to another position and building in the district as long as it's within my certification area. However, layoffs are from the bottom up in seniority. Also, I have a very rare, and much coveted, certification. A certified ESL teacher with a master's degree in ESL is a hot commodity, especially in an urban school district.

How important is/was networking or connections in finding your current or other positions? Is it a factor in advancement once you're on the job?

It was helpful in getting my résumé looked at by the "right person" in a district I wanted to work in.

How much fulfillment do you get out of your career?

Depends on the day/year. This year, not much, hence the transfer request.

If you could choose again, how much would money be a factor?

Not any more than it was.

Would you choose the same career path?

I ask myself that every day.

Any comments or words of advice for someone entering your field?

Work in a classroom for a full day, for a full year. Talk to a lot of teachers doing what you want to do. Don't believe the misconceptions. It's no cakewalk.

SOCIAL WORKER AND REHABILITATION COUNSELOR

Name

Arthur F.

Location

Boston, Massachusetts

Education

Master of Social Work

Total years in profession

24

Brief occupation description/goal of occupation

I have the opportunity to work with individuals who are seeking to make changes in their lives. I facilitate and support this process.

Why did you choose this career path?

While in college and during summer break, a long-term social worker recommended that I consider the field. I had not even considered it before then. My great respect for this man (and his impact on others) brought me awareness of the profession.

What do you like about your occupation?

I get to help people and get paid for it!

What do you dislike about your occupation?

Progress can sometimes be slow.

What are the misconceptions about your profession?

Many believe that social workers are all "bleeding heart liberals" and "Goody Two-shoes." This profession is one that allows you to help others in ways that fit with your own beliefs and values.

On a scale of 1 to 10 (10 being great), how would you rate your occupation and why?

I would say 8; I don't rate it a 10 only because social workers do not get the respect that is deserved. I am very proud of my profession!

What career choices were most helpful?

Investigating a wide variety of employment (including self-employment) opportunities within the profession—some of which were nontraditional for social workers and rehabilitation counselors.

What career choices were least helpful/detrimental?

I once took a job because it seemed the right thing to do at the moment and did not give it the objective and reasoned thought I should have. I also did not research the organization and the person I was to work for.

If you didn't have a mentor, would you have liked one?

Yes, I would have loved to have had a mentor.

What type of education was needed for your position?

A master of social work, as well as licensure.

Do you have to update your career with ongoing training and certificates?

Yes, frequently.

When you were hired, did you receive professional training or was it basically "on-the-job training"?

It was primarily on-the-job training.

In a typical week, are your hours fixed or flexible? On what days do you tend to work overtime?

Currently fixed—I have control over this (for the most part).

What types of conflicts do you deal with?

As in many careers, you have to deal with some people that you may consider to be unpleasant and even amoral, but this is the exception rather than the rule.

Do you interface with coworkers, groups, or vendors, or do you work alone?

I work alone yet interact with many others both in person and by telephone.

What is management like?

There is minimal interaction with management.

Is input accepted, or do you fare better as a "yes man"?

Neither. I am able to function independently within my role.

What issues have prevented your advancement?

None—I choose to be in the role that I am in!

Is your position secure, or are you frequently looking for the next opportunity?

My position is very secure.

How important is/was networking or connections in finding your current or other positions? Is it a factor in advancement once you're on the job?

My current position was found by responding to an advertisement. Past positions were facilitated by connections. Some private consulting work also came about as a result of connections and networking.

What would be your next career move?

Increased private (self-employment) opportunities (part time).

Do you relocate often? Are there travel requirements?

I have in the past and actually spent a few years doing a lot of travel throughout the US and internationally. These trips were part of some very nontraditional (for social workers and rehabilitation counselors) jobs that I became involved in.

How much fulfillment do you get out of your career?

Lots!

Do you feel that you are fairly compensated?

My compensation is fairly fair. I am not paid what I am worth, but I am getting there!

If you could choose again, how much would money be a factor?

I might have done a better job when negotiating for a job to start out at a higher rate of pay. Once in the job, it is very difficult to renegotiate your pay.

Any comments or words of advice for someone entering your field?

Take the time to learn about all the opportunities in the field. Do not rely solely on "common wisdom" because you may miss a lot!

RECREATION COORDINATOR

Name

Sandra D.

Location

Austin, Texas

Education

Bachelor of Arts

Total years in profession

12

Brief occupation description/goal of occupation

Responsible for the programming and implementing of activities for the entire nursing home population, the volunteer program, and all required federal/local paperwork for the department.

Why did you choose this career path?

I loved working with older people and doing something meaningful. Also, it wasn't the same every day.

What do you like about your occupation?

You get to use your creative energy to help people who are often forgotten.

What do you dislike about your occupation?

There will always be too much red tape and paperwork compliance.

What are the misconceptions about your profession?

That you just play games all day and it's not hard work.

On a scale of 1 to 10 (10 being great), how would you rate your occupation and why?

I give it an 8—it is fabulous if you are creative and empathetic and love moving around, doing new things, and helping people.

What factors or former positions led to this occupation?

I believe I chose this path in part because I grew up without grandmothers and always felt that lack in my life.

What career choices were most helpful?

Doing a practicum while still in school was huge in making sure this was something I could really do.

What type of education was needed for your position?

Currently most states require a college degree in a geriatric field and some type of national certification.

Do you have to update your career with ongoing training and certificates?

Yes, to keep certification you must complete 30 CEUs (continuing education units) every two years.

In a typical week, are your hours fixed or flexible? On what days do you tend to work overtime?

Flexible because you might have to cover evening or weekend activities or special events. Also, if you are the head, you must cover for your staff shortages.

What types of conflicts do you deal with?

Personality conflicts of the patients, especially those with any dementia; department conflicts when different needs come up at the same time.

What are your coworkers like?

Most people in this environment have chosen this setting because they enjoy it and are good to work with.

What is management like?

It varies; sometimes the head would be very corporate oriented and not realistic about what could actually be done, while others were more in tune with the real issues of running a facility.

What would be your next career move?

Working with higher-functioning patients in a day care setting, with less responsibility and fewer hours, to suit my family.

How much fulfillment do you get out of your career?

A great deal when you know that what you create and plan and do has such a direct impact on people's lives.

Do you feel that you are fairly compensated?

Not even close. This is not a high-paying field, unfortunately.

**Any comments or words of advice for
someone entering your field?**

Be realistic about what you can accomplish, and learn that you will
be dealing with death and dying, and you need to be able to work
with this aspect. Also, it is incredibly rewarding. I always felt like I
had a big group of surrogate grandparents and extended family.

MILITARY CAREER COUNSELOR

Name

Nick B.

Location

Central Texas

Education

Some college

Total years in profession

13

Brief occupation description/goal of occupation

Retain soldiers and counsel them on their career goals
and futures both in and out of the military.

Why did you choose this career path?

The future of our army is found in the quality of the current troops. It is my job to not only retain these troops, but also counsel them on how to make themselves, their unit, and their army better. What better job is there?

What do you dislike about your occupation?

Being away from my family for long periods of time.

What are the misconceptions about your profession?

Many people believe that I am a recruiter. I am not a recruiter. The soldiers that I counsel have already been recruited. It is my job to enhance their futures through counseling, mentoring, and leadership. My next priority is to retain them in the army, whether that be on active duty or in the reserve component.

On a scale of 1 to 10 (10 being great), how would you rate your occupation and why?

I give it a 10. Again, I can think of no occupation that is more important than retaining quality soldiers on active duty. The challenge of ensuring they have the most accurate information possible is awesome, and I look forward to it every day.

What factors or former positions led to this occupation?

I was an armor crewman for the first ten years of my military career. I watched many good soldiers leave the service because no one sat them down and gave them all the information they would need to plan their future. I was one of those soldiers early on.

What career choices were most helpful?

Joining the US Army.

Did you have a mentor? If so, how did you find them? Did they help?

I have had many mentors, and they came to me in any number of ways.

What type of education was needed for your position?

Much of what I have needed came from face-to-face life experience, but I have to say that studying subjects like psychology and sociology has helped me immensely. This is especially true in terms of dealing with different types of people from any number of backgrounds.

Was your formal education necessary for this position?

It wasn't a requirement, but it has certainly been necessary.

Do you have to update your career with ongoing training and certificates?

Absolutely. It is essential for my personal career development.

In a typical week, are your hours fixed or flexible? On what days do you tend to work overtime?

I am in the army, so we don't have a fixed schedule at all.

Is your work environment "hectic," "all work and no play," "serene," "laid back," or other? Briefly explain.

My work environment is usually pretty chaotic, but there are times when things are slower and I can focus on preparing training and other things.

What types of conflicts do you deal with?

I run across soldiers who aren't interested in continuing their service in the army. I also have to deal with commanders and senior personnel who feel as though they can better provide for their soldiers than I can.

Do you interface with coworkers, groups, or vendors, or do you work alone?

Counseling soldiers is a collaborative effort. The unit commands are required to track who is in need of counseling. I also have to work with other sections to ensure that a soldier's personnel data is accurate and fix any deficiencies.

Is input accepted, or do you fare better as a "yes man"?

I am by no means a "yes man." It is my responsibility to ensure that my reputation facilitates an environment where my leadership trusts my input and requests it.

How important is/was networking or connections in finding your current or other positions? Is it a factor in advancement once you're on the job?

Networking is a huge part of my job. There is always someone who knows something that I don't. At the same time, there are always people who may need to ask me about something they don't understand. There are many times when I may need to "pull strings" to get a soldier where he wants to be. Networking is crucial.

What would be your next career move?

My next career move, outside of the military and upon retirement, will be into the human resources field.

Do you relocate often? Are there travel requirements?

I haven't had to relocate in about six years, but yes, relocation is part of the military. As for travel, I have to travel quite often and sometimes for long periods of time.

How much fulfillment do you get out of your career?

I can't imagine being more fulfilled by the job that I do.

Do you feel that you are fairly compensated?

My compensation comes from knowing that I am defending my

country. Everyone would like to be better off financially, but I don't feel as though I am getting the "raw end of the deal" by any means.

Are the benefits and vacation schedule fair?
The benefits and vacation schedule in the military are unbeatable.

If you could choose again, how much would money be a factor?
It wouldn't, isn't, and hasn't ever been a factor in the military.

Would you choose the same career path?
Absolutely.

Any comments or words of advice for someone entering your field?
You have to care about people to take care of them. You have to care about their families if you want to be able to assist them with their futures.

ALUMNI CAREER SERVICES

Name

Angela L.

Location

Western Massachusetts

Education

Bachelor of Arts

Total years in profession

4

Brief occupation description/goal of occupation

My number one goal is to provide complete and up-to-date career development and job search strategies, networking opportunities, and resources for 220,000 alumni and 25,000 students. I accomplish this through regional events, live and on-demand webinars, our career blog and how-to videos, one-on-one career counseling sessions, workshops, and our mentoring program.

Why did you choose this career path?

I like helping people and I'm a good problem-solver.

What do you like about your occupation?

It's rewarding to see people stop feeling like a captive to their career and start taking control of it because of advice I gave them, or an event they attended that my department put together.

What do you dislike about your occupation?

Administrative work. A lot goes on behind the scenes in terms of paperwork, data entry, and organizing information. It's tedious.

What are the misconceptions about your profession?

That we have to know everything about every industry/profession. In truth, we just need to know the resources and make sure we give the right information out to each person.

On a scale of 1 to 10 (10 being great), how would you rate your occupation and why?

It's a 9. I think there are always ways to improve, but overall I am very happy.

What career choices were most helpful?

Starting my own business gave me the feeling of having ownership over something very important. It changed my work ethic forever.

What career choices were least helpful/detrimental?

Taking a job because I needed one and feeling compelled to stay because the company was such a disaster. I wanted to save the day but got burned out instead.

Did you have a mentor? If so, how did you find them? Did they help?

Yes, several. Some of them I worked with, others I met at networking events and felt they would be good advisors/mentors. The most important thing to remember when working with a mentor is to know exactly what you are looking for and know when you've found it. You don't want to waste anyone's time, and often a mentoring relationship doesn't need to last long to get what you need.

In a typical week, are your hours fixed or flexible? On what days do you tend to work overtime?

They are fixed, but often change because of workshops/webinars at night. I work overtime most often on Tuesday, Wednesday, and Thursday evenings. Occasional weekend hours are required as well.

Is your work environment "hectic," "all work and no play," "serene," "laid back," or other?

It goes from hectic (start/end of each semester) to laid back (summers, winter holidays). It's nice to have a change of pace every so often. Keeps things interesting.

What types of conflicts do you deal with?

Disappointed/frustrated alumni who don't know what they want to do with their lives.

Do you interface with coworkers, groups, or vendors, or do you work alone?

I partner with alumni volunteers, schools, and colleges on campus, career professionals, and hotel/event spaces.

How important is/was networking or connections in finding your current or other positions? Is it a factor in advancement once you're on the job?

Critical. I used networking to find the position. I am confident I would not have this job if I didn't know the right people.

Do you prefer going to work or leaving? Why?

I love going to work! I also love leaving. My life as a whole is great and I look forward to each minute of it.

How much fulfillment do you get out of your career?

A ton. I picked a job that allows me to help others excel. I can't think of anything better.

If you could choose again, how much would money be a factor?

Probably more, but I'm not unhappy. I didn't used to be focused on money at all, but I think that's because I didn't understand my value. Now that I realize I have a lot to offer, I feel adequate compensation is a fair trade.

Would you choose the same career path?

Yes.

Any comments or words of advice for someone entering your field?

Trust your instincts and know that you can't help everyone, but do your best with each person you meet.

PASTORAL MINISTER

Name

James P.

Location

Worcester, Massachusetts

Education

Bachelor of Divinity in Religious Studies

Total years in profession

5

Brief occupation description/goal of occupation

Prepare and deliver sermons and Bible studies. Visit the sick and regular members. Perform weddings, baptisms, and funerals, and provide counseling.

Why did you choose this career path?

I felt a call of God to serve Him and His people by ministering the Word and the Sacraments to the local church body and through personal outreach to the lost.

What do you like about your occupation?

Preaching and getting to know and understand about the lives, the hurts, and the ways I was able to offer help as a solution to their hurts and pains!

What do you dislike about your occupation?

The pay that was generally lower than that of the congregation. The criticism and back-biting. Petty problems blown out of proportion. Having to run business meetings.

What are the misconceptions about your profession?

That a minister only works on Sunday. Believed by many, since that is the one time when all the congregants see the pastor up front in a public service. People fail to realize the amount of personal study involved for preparing sermons and Bible lessons.

On a scale of 1 to 10 (10 being great), how would you rate your occupation and why?

It's a 10 because there is no "higher calling" than to serve the Creator and Sustainer of the Universe.

What career choices were most helpful?

Practical, prior experience in the local church with youth groups and Vacation Bible School that eventually led me in the direction of receiving the kind of education that helped prepare me for the Gospel Ministry.

Did you have a mentor? If so, how did you find them? Did they help?

Yes, sort of. New ministers were under the supervision of a group of seasoned pastors to whom they were accountable until they passed their period of probation and were ordained, first a deacon, and then an elder.

If you didn't have a mentor, would you have liked one?

Yes, because as a beginner in the ministry, other than this board of fellow pastors, you never had one particular person to whom you could go for help and assistance when needed. For the most part, you were pretty much on your own, being the only pastor in a church. Learning to sink or swim could be detrimental and even damaging in some cases!

What type of education was needed for your position?

College or seminary, or both, if possible.

Was your formal education necessary for this position?

Yes; there are many requirements listed in scripture for a pastor, but most of the formal training was under the category of academics, so that most people who enter the ministry have much learning to do regarding the practical aspects of dealing with people and handling crises.

When you were hired, did you receive professional training or was it basically "on-the-job training"?

If you entered the ministry having both a college and a seminary degree, you only had to attend two years of summer school of theology for two weeks, at the denomination's own camp, before Elder's Ordination, following the completion of prescribed courses and the submission of a thesis. If having only a college degree, then you were required to attend four years of summer training, take other courses during the year, and finally submit a thesis before being ordained an elder.

In a typical week, are your hours fixed or flexible?
On what days do you tend to work overtime?

Very flexible. Usually, the morning time was devoted to personal meditation and reflection, sermon preparation, and prayer. The afternoon could be spent visiting someone in a hospital or nursing home or at their residence, and the same in the evening. A mid-week prayer and Bible study hour was held at the church once a week. Sometimes business meetings were held which the pastor attended to have an idea of the inner workings of keeping a church going or to sometimes take charge.

Is your work environment "hectic," "all work and no play," "serene," "laid back," or other? Briefly explain.

Well, if you let it, it could consume all your time because there was always something unexpected happening that required your attention. Between all the duties and responsibilities of serving the congregation and community, much time could be spent that would normally go toward your time in the basic duties of a pastor. Monday is generally known as the "preacher's day off," but it all depended on the size of the church and the number of groups, activities, and ministries a church conducted.

What types of conflicts do you deal with?

People conflicts with parishioners: things like misunderstandings, perceived goals, decisions on building and parsonage improvements, and having different ideas about how a certain program should be run!

Do you interface with coworkers, groups, or vendors, or do you work alone?

As a pastor, you were all on your own when it came to studying Bible lessons and preparing sermons, visiting the sick, and counseling individuals. But, since ministry involves people, both you and they were always in the mix in one way or another, since what they did and said and what you did and said could affect the life of the congregation for good or ill.

What is management like?

For a pastor, it was often a lonely place to be because everyone looked at you as the do-all and be-all in the local church!

Is input accepted, or do you fare better as a "yes man"?

I think the fact that I was not always a "yes man" is a key point as to why I may have had more problems in the church.

What issues have prevented your advancement?

Matters pertaining to how much education and experience you had, etc., generally determined how large a church you served.

How important is/was networking or connections in finding your current or other positions? Is it a factor in advancement once you're on the job?

It was a friend of mine already serving in the denomination that I would eventually be serving in as well who, after I visited him while on my way to seeing my parents in another state, strongly suggested that I consider entering as a candidate. So I'd say that you never know how others, such as family, friends, or even strangers, can influence you to change direction and pursue another opportunity!

Do you relocate often? Are there travel requirements?

In the five years I pastored, I lived in three states, thus serving in three congregations! They were, in order: Wisconsin, Pennsylvania, and, finally, Massachusetts.

Do you prefer going to work or leaving? Why?

As a minister, I never, ever felt that I started or ended my work at a particular time, because I was on twenty-four-hour call, in between all the other things to get done!

How much fulfillment do you get out of your career?

On the one hand, whenever I could see good things happen as a result of my personal ministry, I felt fulfilled, but with all the turmoil, location moves, stress, undone work, etc., it is still quite frustrating looking back and seeing where I failed or in what way I could've handled a matter much better!

Do you feel that you are fairly compensated?

No—not that I am greedy, but it was rather difficult to try to serve others in ministry when the finances were always a daily issue and burden.

Are the benefits and vacation schedule fair?

Not if you are just starting out in the ministry! For the amount of work you do, one week off in a year is simply not enough. As was said already—the bigger the church, the more the money and vice versa!

If you could choose again, how much would money be a factor?

I don't think making more money would have kept me in the ministry. My health and family life, namely my relationship with my wife, had suffered. With that taken together with all the stress factors of church ministry, my only sane choice was to step back and move on in order to spare myself any further heartache!

Would you choose the same career path?

No, not in today's world of instant solutions, conflicts, and expectations put upon the average minister of a modern church!

Any comments or words of advice for someone entering your field?

Make sure you consider all other career possibilities! By all means do something else if that is what makes you happy in life. The pastoral ministry can be a joy in seeing positive change and growth in the lives of people! Yet, in the process, the burdens and responsibilities, especially if you're the one and only pastor in a church, can be career-ending, if you don't have the proper support and understanding of the people and you are not tough enough to overlook all the hurts, disappointments, struggles, frustrations, etc. that come with the territory!

HUMAN RESOURCES MANAGER

Name

Jim B.

Location

Atlanta, Georgia

Education

Master in Business Administration

Total years in profession

17

Brief occupation description/goal of occupation

Manage a human resources department: recruiting, benefits, compensation, performance management, policies, and employment practices.

Why did you choose this career path?

I received a psychology degree from college and decided I wanted to use it in a business environment.

What do you like about your occupation?

Variety. Being involved in important decisions affecting the company and its greatest assets—its people.

What do you dislike about your occupation?

It can be very administrative in nature. Often, my position doesn't get the respect and compensation that equivalent business partner positions do.

What are the misconceptions about your profession?

That we are the company police or that we are the touchy-feely department.

On a scale of 1 to 10 (10 being great), how would you rate your occupation and why?

I would say 9. I have thoroughly enjoyed it, and the opportunities are endless in terms of company type and size and specialization within the profession.

What factors or former positions led to this occupation?

None. I decided after getting my undergraduate degree that this was what I wanted to do.

What career choices were most helpful?

Doing an internship was integral to getting employed for me. Also, getting an MBA was helpful in building my business skills after an undergraduate degree in psychology.

What career choices were least helpful/detrimental?

Leaving a good job in 2001 for a start-up company and then getting laid off on 9/11.

Did you have a mentor? If so, how did you find them? Did they help?

Most importantly, I joined a professional organization while in school and was actively involved. The other members were a big help to me.

What type of education was needed for your position?

Either an undergraduate degree in human resources, or in my case, an MBA.

Do you have to update your career with ongoing training and certificates?

Yes, it's important to be involved with SHRM (Society for Human Resource Management), our professional organization, and also to get a professional designation, either PHR (Professional in Human Resources) or SPHR (Senior Professional in HR).

In a typical week, are your hours fixed or flexible? On what days do you tend to work overtime?

They are generally fixed, but throughout my career I have worked anywhere from forty to seventy hours per week depending upon the employer.

Is your work environment "hectic," "all work and no play," "serene," "laid back," or other? Briefly explain.

It's busy, but not overwhelming.

What types of conflicts do you deal with?

All types: employee issues, pay issues, job duties, workloads, policies, benefits.

Do you interface with coworkers, groups, or vendors, or do you work alone?

I interface with other employees and with vendors regularly.

What is management like?

Depends on the company, but in general, they expect good customer service and hard work and results.

Is input accepted, or do you fare better as a "yes man"?

Generally, in my career my input has been accepted, even solicited.

What issues have prevented your advancement?

Having children. Deciding that it was more important to spend time with my family than put in seventy hours per week at work.

Is your position secure, or are you frequently looking for the next opportunity?

It depends on the company, but I have been laid off four times in my career, so I don't feel that there is much security in this role these days.

How important is/was networking or connections in finding your current or other positions? Is it a factor in advancement once you're on the job?

I found two jobs through networking, two through my professional organization, and three through advertisements, so it has varied.

What would be your next career move?

I would prefer to stick with a small but growing company and see my position grow, but I'm not averse to taking a job at a larger company should the opportunity arise.

Do you relocate often? Are there travel requirements?

I have been in Atlanta for my entire career.

How much fulfillment do you get out of your career?

It has been fulfilling in several ways. One, through our professional organization and friendships there. Two, because our profession brings us into contact with many employees. Three, at some large companies I've worked for there has been great camaraderie within the HR department.

Do you feel that you are fairly compensated?

Fairly, yes. Well compensated, no. I still think HR is undervalued compared to some other departments.

If you could choose again, how much would money be a factor?

I think enjoying what you do is the most important factor. Of course, I also know employees who are good at what they do and enjoy their jobs but aren't well compensated. I think you need to understand the compensation for your field before you decide to devote a large part of your life to it.

Would you choose the same career path?

Definitely.

Any comments or words of advice for someone entering your field?

Get involved in SHRM. Get an internship. Get a mentor.

PRINCIPAL RECRUITER AND OWNER OF RECRUITING FIRM

Name

Chris S.

Location

Washington, DC

Education

Bachelor of Arts

Total years in profession

12

Brief occupation description/goal of occupation

Perform business development, bring in new clients, and fill executive, senior, and mid-level roles in professional services, sales, marketing, and R&D (research and development) in the IT industry across North America and Western Europe.

Why did you choose this career path?

I kind of fell into it while interviewing for a job; I thought I could do it. The challenge sounded like fun, and I love doing research. I gave it a shot working 100 percent commission and did pretty well my first year and just stuck with it. I also liked that I could learn about a lot of different cutting-edge technologies and was getting called by some pretty well-known executives in the industry. I felt like I fit in pretty quickly!

What do you like about your occupation?

I especially like the challenge of filling hard-to-fill positions. I like the flexibility my career offers me; even though I usually work twenty-four hours a day, I can work from anywhere in the world where I can get a cell signal and an internet connection—and at any time!

What do you dislike about your occupation?

Not much!

What are the misconceptions about your profession?

All recruiters are snakes. All recruiters don't know what they are talking about. You should never trust a recruiter.

On a scale of 1 to 10 (10 being great), how would you rate your occupation and why?

I would say 10—for me personally. I enjoy what I do. I don't pay attention to my competition much. I do a good job and my clients seem to respect that, and I have never had a down time where I've had trouble finding jobs to work on. Even during the market crash, we stayed really busy and worked on a number of retained and exclusive positions. I watched a lot of my friends lose their business or have to get out of the industry. I felt kind of lucky, but I know a big part of it was from my hard work.

What factors or former positions led to this occupation?

I'm a former competitive swimmer. I think that has a lot to do with my tenacity. I also was an archaeologist. I had to do a lot of research, and there was nothing like the feeling of finding that missing clue that led to the discovery of a great significant find!

What career choices were most helpful?

Jumping into recruiting in the first place was very significant. I was dating someone at the time who was re-evaluating his career choice. He was extremely encouraging toward me about jumping into a 100 percent commission position, and after a number of years of being successful, that gave me the courage to start my own business. Now both of us have our own businesses!

What career choices were least helpful/detrimental?

None, really—everything is trial and error. You live and learn from your mistakes.

Did you have a mentor? If so, how did you find them? Did they help?

Sort of. When I first got into recruiting, I was dating the person I mentioned before who helped guide me to the decision.

If you didn't have a mentor, would you have liked one?

Looking back, I wish I had a little bit more of a hands-on mentor in the beginning. I would have hit the ground running a bit faster. It took me eight months to really get started, and it was a bit scary at first.

What type of education was needed for your position?

None, really. I would recommend anyone in this industry have strong communication skills, be intelligent, be a problem-solver, be very analytical, and want to learn as much as they can about the industry they are in, so they understand their client's needs.

When you were hired, did you receive professional training or was it basically "on-the-job training"?

On-the-job training; however, I provide professional training to all my new hires. I think that anyone I'm investing time and money in should get every tool possible to succeed.

In a typical week, are your hours fixed or flexible? On what days do you tend to work overtime?

My hours are always flexible—but they are usually long. I work seven days a week and typically start around 6:30 a.m., and end around 10:00 p.m. with a couple of breaks throughout the day to eat, walk the dogs, and get some fresh air and clear my head.

Is your work environment "hectic," "all work and no play," "serene," "laid back," or other? Briefly explain.

It is what I make it. Some days it's hectic with deadlines, others it can be a little fun while I work.

What types of conflicts do you deal with?

Cocky candidates who think they are the best and are very hurt if they don't get the job. They can get extremely angry and lash out and blame everyone else for not getting the job. That is usually the most frequent problem we run into.

Do you interface with coworkers, groups, or vendors, or do you work alone?

I interface with coworkers and clients daily. About every quarter, I speak at a user group, or technology council meeting, and provide a class on how to apply for jobs and how to get jobs. I do have a home office and work out of there whenever I can.

What are your coworkers like?

Typically positive, type A, competitive in a friendly way, diligent, successful, fun, hardworking, play-hard types.

What is management like?

Since I am management, I'd like to think I'm pretty cool! I don't like to micromanage. I provide structured training and make myself available 24/7 for my team, and they take advantage of that! I let my recruiters make mistakes so they can learn on their own, but if I see them going too far in the wrong direction, I'll reel them back in and set them back on the right course.

Is input accepted, or do you fare better as a "yes man"?

Input is always accepted, but there are some things that are set in stone. We are a true recruiting firm, and our recruiters must be able to network, cold call, and recruit . . . they cannot surf job boards and get by.

What issues have prevented your advancement?

Nothing has stopped me—but possibly me—from moving to the next step, which would be growing bigger. I am starting to execute the plan to do this now (admittedly very slowly).

How important is/was networking or connections in finding your current or other positions? Is it a factor in advancement once you're on the job?

I would say it's probably very important. I have never had to apply for any job I've ever had, even when I was an archaeologist. I've always gotten my jobs through people I know.

What would be your next career move?

To grow my company bigger and diversify into different industries.

Do you relocate often? Are there travel requirements?

No, I don't relocate often. Occasional travel to conferences and tradeshows where we exhibit or attend as guest speakers takes place.

How much fulfillment do you get out of your career?

I love it! It gives me a lot of freedom to do all the things I love, like archaeology, animal rescue, travel, and working from home in my pajamas some days, and I can live anywhere in the world I want.

If you could choose again, how much would money be a factor?

It would be the same! The harder I work, the more money I make. My success is dependent on what I put into my career. Although it would be nice to take the easy way out, I like having the satisfaction that I've worked hard for everything I have.

Would you choose the same career path?

Probably. It's also a means to support my hobbies—like archaeology, travel, and animal rescue!

Any comments or words of advice for someone entering your field?

What you put into it is what you get out of it, and always remember recruiting is a numbers game. The more people you talk to, the more résumés you get; the more résumés, the more qualified résumés you get; the more qualified résumés, the more send-outs; the more send-outs, the more interviews, the more offers; the more offers, the more acceptances, and the more money you make!

CONTRACT TRAINER

Name

Penny H.

Location

Oklahoma City, Oklahoma

Education

Master of Human Relations

Total years in profession

10

Brief occupation description/goal of occupation

I work as a contract trainer providing training in soft skills with the goal of workforce development in job skills and interpersonal relationship-building in the workplace.

Why did you choose this career path?

I enjoy the challenge of helping participants to achieve the "aha!" in experiential and participatory learning opportunities. I want to make a positive difference in the quality of the workplace culture.

What do you like about your occupation?

I enjoy the needs assessments, working with clients, researching the topic, writing the curriculum, delivering the information, leading the learning sessions, and getting the feedback from participants.

What do you dislike about your occupation?

The inconstancy of doing contract work. Clients who expect me to work miracles "fixing" dysfunctional environments. The ups and downs of income based on contracts I secure.

What are the misconceptions about your profession?

That training or any professional educator's job is easy and that it doesn't take skill and dedication to actually bring learners to a higher level of cognitive understanding of information. The lack of understanding of the time necessary to prepare to facilitate a training session.

On a scale of 1 to 10 (10 being great), how would you rate your occupation and why?

It's a 10! I love it. I am energized by the entire process from initial interview to actual delivery of information and facilitation of the learning sessions. I get great satisfaction out of knowing workers are being more productive in their jobs, interacting in more positive ways, communicating better, and enjoying their jobs more and that I had a small part in helping that happen.

What factors or former positions led to this occupation?

I taught high school for fifteen years and wanted to move into adult education and participate in workforce development.

What career choices were most helpful?

Getting a master's degree and joining professional organizations that are opportunities to network with others in my field.

What career choices were least helpful/detrimental?

I didn't begin when I was younger.

**Did you have a mentor? If so, how did
you find them? Did they help?**

I have several. I found them or they found me as I networked in several professional organizations.

What type of education was needed for your position?

A master's degree and certifications of qualification as a corporate trainer.

Was your formal education necessary for this position?

Yes. It gives me the credentials I need to "sell" my services.

**Do you have to update your career with
ongoing training and certificates?**

Yes. I need to have current training listed on my résumé.

**When you were hired, did you receive professional
training or was it basically "on-the-job training"?**

Professional training. Having spent ten years in this field, I have a great deal of wisdom from "on-the-job" experiences.

**In a typical week, are your hours fixed or flexible?
On what days do you tend to work overtime?**

My hours are flexible and dependent on the contracted times with clients. I tend to train only three days a week for the client and work two days a week in my home office doing record-keeping, curriculum writing, research, etc.

What types of conflicts do you deal with?

Clients who expect miracles. Participants who are resistant to learning and to change.

Do you interface with coworkers, groups, or vendors, or do you work alone?

I interface with clients, training coordinators, support personnel, and participants.

Is input accepted, or do you fare better as a "yes man"?

I am expected to give input after each training session and administer evaluation sheets to the participants.

What issues have prevented your advancement?

I am not skilled at self-promotion and selling my services.

Is your position secure, or are you frequently looking for the next opportunity?

I am always looking for the next opportunity.

How important is/was networking or connections in finding your current or other positions? Is it a factor in advancement once you're on the job?

Networking is vital to contract work. It is word of mouth and repeat contracts that keep me working.

What would be your next career move?

A permanent position with one employer.

Do you relocate often? Are there travel requirements?

No. Travel is at my choice depending on the contract.

How much fulfillment do you get out of your career?

It is maximum. I love the process and the challenges.

Do you feel that you are fairly compensated?

Sometimes yes, sometimes no. Some contractors have a maximum fee that they are allowed to pay, so I have to determine the intrinsic rewards as a part of the payment.

If you could choose again, how much would money be a factor?

I might not opt to be self-employed in order to build a better retirement fund for myself.

Any comments or words of advice for someone entering your field?

Network, observe, take risks!

SOCIAL STUDIES TEACHER

Name

Matthew T.

Location

Long Island, New York

Education

Master of Arts

Total years in profession

10

Brief occupation description/goal of occupation

Teacher of social studies in a junior high and high school setting.

Why did you choose this career path?

I love to teach and inspire the passions of learning in others.

What do you like about your occupation?

The impact I have on the youth of today and helping them feel like they can impact our future.

What do you dislike about your occupation?

Too many standardized tests. Too much emphasis on teaching to the test and less emphasis on whether students can interpret and use their knowledge beyond the here and now.

What are the misconceptions about your profession?

Teachers only work 180(ish) days a year.

On a scale of 1 to 10 (10 being great), how would you rate your occupation and why?

I would say 9. The fruit of student learning makes all the preparation worth it. Teachers give much time and effort to planning, implementing, and evaluating their lessons and the impact that each lesson has on each student.

What factors or former positions led to this occupation?

Teachers of my past.

What career choices were most helpful?

Starting off as a substitute teacher helps with the basic foundation of classroom management skills.

What career choices were least helpful/detrimental?

Starting off teaching a grade level that, even though I was certified to teach, I was not prepared to teach. Teaching an elementary-level class takes a skill or tact that, in my case, I did not have. I have found that for me, teaching at the secondary level was better suited for my talents and skills.

Did you have a mentor? If so, how did you find them? Did they help?

My mentor, believe it or not, was one who let me go from my position. I had a rough patch of teaching before my latest teaching position. My teaching style may have been decent, but my planning was horrid. My supervisor was on top of me, checking my plans every week to ensure that my planning was going to be effective and structured. She instilled in me the work ethic needed to survive, and as a result of that planning technique . . . the art of teaching became easier and more rewarding.

What type of education was needed for your position?

In New York state, you need to at least obtain a bachelor's degree, pass a battery of state certification exams, and student teach (practice teaching in a real classroom with real students).

Do you have to update your career with ongoing training and certificates?

The teacher must have his/her master's degree within five years of starting to teach in a public school and pass another state exam for professional/permanent certification. And for every five-year term, the teacher must have a certain number of professional development hours to retain a valid certification (if it is a professional certification).

When you were hired, did you receive professional training or was it basically "on-the-job training"?

Yes, there were weekly department meetings, monthly building-wide meetings, and several district-wide meetings per year.

In a typical week, are your hours fixed or flexible? On what days do you tend to work overtime?

Fixed . . . overtime? What's that? Just kidding. Overtime is unlimited, just do not expect to be paid for it. There are other activities that are outside of the contractual work obligations, such as mentoring, coaching, or advising programs that a teacher can receive additional monetary compensation for.

What types of conflicts do you deal with?

Conflicts come from many angles: they can come from administration (to keep up with the state's testing requirements) or parents who believe that their children do no wrong and since they pay taxes, they own you; conflicts could arise in the time management of schoolwork that infiltrates the home life.

Do you interface with coworkers, groups, or vendors, or do you work alone?

Let's put it this way—if a teacher is doing it alone, they will not survive. They will burn out, not learn new ways of teaching (pedagogy) or even worse, be known as the weird teacher who mumbles to themselves. It sounds like I am making a joke about this, but all teachers, regardless of who they think they are or what academic background they have, will need to interface with other teachers, parents, or even book reps to get the job done completely and with efficiency.

What are your coworkers like?

They come from a varied background. Some had come from the business world and wanted to change careers, some were born teachers and followed through, some came from the political world and wanted to make an earlier impact on young minds, and, finally, there are those who did not know what they wanted to do with their lives while in college and ended up with their last-resort major, education.

What is management like?

Management is similar to any other management in any business. Their job is to promote efficiency, dedication, and high achievement for their teachers and, ultimately, the students.

Is input accepted, or do you fare better as a "yes man"?

Input is always accepted, but you must remember, in order to give input, you have to be willing to receive and accept critiques, because teachers work as a team for the betterment of their students.

What issues have prevented your advancement?

None, other than school budgets that fail, which cause positions to be let go.

Is your position secure, or are you frequently looking for the next opportunity?

After tenure, many teachers enjoy a lifelong career in the same school district. Mine was cut short due to that budget failure, and now I am looking for the next opportunity.

How important is/was networking or connections in finding your current or other positions? Is it a factor in advancement once you're on the job?

Networking and connections help quite a lot in finding a job. Advancement has little to do with networking or connections; it certainly won't hurt, but there is no guarantee.

What would be your next career move?

Possibly to teach collegiate-level education.

Do you relocate often? Are there travel requirements?

No relocation. The only travel requirements could be on the position that requires a teacher to teach in two buildings during the day.

How much fulfillment do you get out of your career?

Teachers teach for the love of teaching, not for the money.

Do you feel that you are fairly compensated?

When you look at the amount of time a teacher is in the classroom compared to the compensation, then yes, but when the teacher has to be not just an instructor, but a social worker, psychologist, in loco parentis, coach, referee, "babysitter," security guard, mandated state abuse reporter, and possibly the only adult students can trust, then no, we do not get fairly compensated.

If you could choose again, how much would money be a factor?

If someone really wanted to be a teacher, then the money should not be a major factor, but a little more wouldn't hurt.

Any comments or words of advice for someone entering your field?

Patience, caring, nurturing, passion, humility, perseverance, consistency, attentiveness, willingness to do more than coasting, and the desire to change and teach the minds of our future—if you don't have these, then maybe this job isn't for you.

ASSISTANT WITH ADULT LIVING

Name

Christy M.

Location

Northern West Virginia

Education

High school

Total years in profession

7

Brief occupation description/goal of occupation

I work in the homes of mostly adults with ID (intellectual disability) and assist them with their daily living.

Why did you choose this career path?

I have wanted to be in this field since I was in grade school. I wanted to help people who were not as fortunate as me and be their voice that the world needs to listen to.

What do you like about your occupation?

I love the people I work for.

What do you dislike about your occupation?

I don't like the way ID people are treated by the "outside." It makes me angry that people sitting behind a desk can be in charge of the lives of "my guys" and not even know them. The staff will try to speak up for "my guys," but the desk people always have the last say.

What are the misconceptions about your profession?

That it is a hard and bad career. If you give a little love, you are going to get it in return. Yes, there is some degree of difficulty working with some of "the guys." You have to learn to love where you can and help with what you know.

On a scale of 1 to 10 (10 being great), how would you rate your occupation and why?

It's a 10! My occupation is something that I have always wanted to do and is very fulfilling to me. If I have made one person smile and/or taught something they didn't know, my day is complete. That is the greatest reward.

What factors or former positions led to this occupation?

I volunteered with the Special Olympics and helped a few summers as an aide with Easterseals Camp. I also took care of a few girls who lived at home while their families were away.

What career choices were most helpful?

It was a choice on my part, but there wasn't anything that swayed my decision. In grade school, when I decided what I wanted to be "when I grow up," I had not come in contact with anyone who was ID. It was just a decision I made, and I'm glad I stuck with it.

Did you have a mentor? If so, how did you find them? Did they help?

I did not have a mentor. The best answer that I can give you is that while helping at the camp for several summers, there were adults there who had been in the field for a long time. They gave me their history of work. I listened and learned.

What type of education was needed for your position?

I am a high school graduate, and that is all you need education-wise for this position. If I wanted to be a teacher, case manager, etc., then I would have to go to college. I am happy with where I am.

Do you have to update your career with ongoing training and certificates?

We have CPR, first aid, AMAP (giving meds), and a class on what to do in protecting their dignity and preventing self-injury. We have to update these trainings every year.

When you were hired, did you receive professional training or was it basically "on-the-job training"?

We had in-the-office training and then were sent to the homes to "shadow" with staff that were already in the houses.

In a typical week, are your hours fixed or flexible? On what days do you tend to work overtime?

In a forty-hour week, I work one day, one afternoon, and three midnights. There is not a certain day for overtime. It is frowned upon, but sometimes necessary.

Is your work environment "hectic," "all work and no play," "serene," "laid back," or other? Briefly explain.

Work is never "all work and no play." It is sometimes very hectic and very demanding. You also have times when everything is serene and you have time to laugh, joke, and dance around. I try to make the house run like I would at home: get the work done (they have chores just like my house does) and then play around (we sing, dance, work on puzzles, go out in the community, etc.).

What types of conflicts do you deal with?

There are staff members who don't see eye to eye on subjects. If you have a staff member with one idea working and eight hours later get a staff member with a totally different way of thinking, it sometimes can be confusing to "our guys." The most annoying conflict is the office staff that make decisions (behind a desk) that the house staff know are wrong for "our guys"; then we have to butt heads with the bigwigs to explain why they made bad decisions.

Do you interface with coworkers, groups, or vendors, or do you work alone?

Some of the staff members work with other staff, and some work alone. Day shift and afternoon shift sometimes have more than one staff member in the house (if there is more than one "guy" in the house). Midnight shift usually works with one staff person. Different houses of people get together for events or socialization, so there are many staff members together at once. Pretty much living the same way I do at home.

What are your coworkers like?

Coworkers are great. They are caring people who want the same life for "our guys" as I do. There are some who care more than others, but, basically, we are on the same track.

What is management like?

For the most part, they are good. They have hearts and good feelings for their jobs. Sometimes, their ways of doing things are not in agreement with the staff or "our guys." Most of the time, they present things the way we like them, and sometimes we have to make them listen to us.

Is input accepted, or do you fare better as a "yes man"?

Believe you me, we give input! If I don't like what management has suggested, they hear me. I am the "loud" speaker of the staff I work with, and they have me start the input and the rest chime in. We have changed things in the past that way. Once in a great while, when you know you can't change things, you go along with the "yes."

What issues have prevented your advancement?

There is no advancement for me. If I went to college and got a degree, I would be working in the office and not "hands on" in the houses. I love working in the houses.

Is your position secure, or are you frequently looking for the next opportunity?

As far as I know, this position is secure. West Virginia has been whispering for a while that they can't afford individual housing and that they are considering reopening institutions to put all "our guys" in again. So far, it is just whispers.

How important is/was networking or connections in finding your current or other positions? Is it a factor in advancement once you're on the job?

The position I have now I found out about from a friend. She knew what I wanted to do, and she worked here and told me about it.

What would be your next career move?

This is my career, and there will be no move.

Do you relocate often? Are there travel requirements?

You can relocate if you want to. This company is all over the United States. I want to stay here, so I don't relocate. There are no travel requirements for me.

How much fulfillment do you get out of your career?

There is a lot of fulfillment in my work. It is a great joy when you know that you have helped someone with something that they have struggled with, or spoken up and told others how they feel (when they can't find the right words themselves). This work has made me a better person.

Do you feel that you are fairly compensated?

When management has you perform chores that they should be doing, then no, I don't feel that we are fairly compensated. When I get online and find out that the same company I work for pays higher in other states for the same thing I do here in West Virginia, then no, I am not fairly compensated.

If you could choose again, how much would money be a factor?

If I could choose again, I would choose for West Virginia not to be a poor state. No matter who you are, money is always a factor.

Would you choose the same career path?

I didn't want this career because of the money. So yes, I would choose the same career path. The only thing I would change is getting this career earlier in my life.

Any comments or words of advice for someone entering your field?

If you really want to make a difference for someone and work "hands on" with people that really need a helping hand, then this is the career for you. We need employees who will stand up for what they believe and give "our guys" every chance possible to live a normal life.

CHAPTER SIX

The Perfectionists

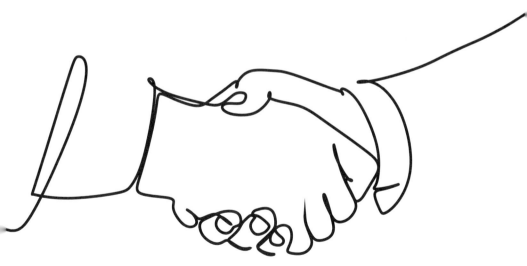

ACTUARY

Name

Paul C.

Location

Hartford, Connecticut

Education

Bachelor of Arts

Total years in profession

18

Brief occupation description/goal of occupation

Actuary—to provide financial and demographic analysis to the insurance and managed health care carrier industry.

Why did you choose this career path?

The opportunity to use my combined skills in mathematics, statistics, and finance.

What do you like about your occupation?

My occupation is intensely technical and challenging.

What do you dislike about your occupation?

My occupation is too tightly bound to a single industry: insurance.

What are the misconceptions about your profession?

That we can't communicate effectively with others.

On a scale of 1 to 10 (10 being great), how would you rate your occupation and why?

I would say 9. My occupation allows for a balance between work, technical, and personal interests.

What factors or former positions led to this occupation?

I read about the occupation at age twelve in a career book and it appealed to me right away.

What career choices were most helpful?

Getting a professional credential (fellowship in the Society of Actuaries) as quickly as possible was key.

What career choices were least helpful/detrimental?

A tendency to stick "close to home" limited opportunities geographically.

Did you have a mentor? If so, how did you find them? Did they help?

Establishing a reputation with a senior actuary while I was still early in my career opened many paths down the road as we both advanced through the corporation.

What type of education was needed for your position?

Solid grounding in mathematics and statistics was a door-opener; significant self-study was required for the next three to five years to pass exams of the Society of Actuaries.

Do you have to update your career with ongoing training and certificates?

Yes—twelve to twenty-four hours of continuing education per year is a must.

In a typical week, are your hours fixed or flexible? On what days do you tend to work overtime?

Fixed hours are the norm; some overtime is required if a project or presentation is nearing a milestone.

Is your work environment "hectic," "all work and no play," "serene," "laid back," or other? Briefly explain.

"Controlled chaos"—crazy at times, but all directed to a predetermined goal.

What types of conflicts do you deal with?

Dealing with others with conflicting agendas is an art that needs to be mastered—you can't offend them but must at the same time keep them on topic.

Do you interface with coworkers, groups, or vendors, or do you work alone?

I have lots of interface with coworkers and as a member of workgroups.

Is input accepted, or do you fare better as a "yes man"?

Being a "yes man" works in the short run but fails when the people you've been saying yes to fail and you're exposed.

What issues have prevented your advancement?

Once I had kids, I had a desire to balance work and family life, to the detriment of my career advancement.

Is your position secure, or are you frequently looking for the next opportunity?

My career is relatively secure (eighteen years and counting at one company), but the résumé is always handy.

How important is/was networking or connections in finding your current or other positions? Is it a factor in advancement once you're on the job?

Networking and connections are very important—80 percent of job openings are not published.

What would be your next career move?

I'm thinking of becoming a high school math teacher or a writer.

Do you relocate often? Are there travel requirements?

Little relocation and little travel in my job—I work in the home office.

How much fulfillment do you get out of your career?

My career is how I identify myself to relatives, friends, etc.; in other words, very central to my identity.

Are the benefits and vacation schedule fair?

Yes—generous pension and 401(k), flexible time off.

If you could choose again, how much would money be a factor?

There's no getting around the need to be paid well in today's world.

Would you choose the same career path?

Yes.

Any comments or words of advice for someone entering your field?

Get your credential ASAP—the clock is ticking; it's later than you think.

REGULATORY AFFAIRS, BIOTECH INDUSTRY

Name

Kent J.

Location

London, England

Education

Master of Science

Total years in profession

5

Brief occupation description/goal of occupation

Regulatory affairs departments in pharma (pharmaceutical) and biotech companies are responsible for all drug application filings with regulatory health authorities around the globe. In addition to seeking new drug licenses, we also file all necessary documentation to maintain our annual marketing authorization so we can keep our products on the market. It's a blend of science, business, and law.

Why did you choose this career path?

It's diverse—the work changes regularly. I get to work across multiple departments. I wanted to work in a cutting-edge technology-based industry rather than old-world business. I also liked biotech and pharma because I knew there was a good work-life balance and good income potential.

What do you like about your occupation?

I like working in biotech particularly because we see how the advances in the industry are driving innovation. I have been fortunate enough to work on both early- and late-stage development projects, and it's a completely different experience. Early stage is mostly with scientists, whereas late stage is mostly marketing folks and legal as we gear up for a new product launch. The people I work with are mostly bright and intelligent. I like the fact that I can make a decent living but am expected to work a very reasonable forty to forty-five hours a week and have good benefits.

What do you dislike about your occupation?

Sometimes some aspects of the work can be annoying because there is an element of compliance and no one likes that word. All in all, I can't complain about much at all, though sometimes we have big company bureaucracy.

What are the misconceptions about your profession?

I don't believe there are any because the only people who know specifically about regulatory affairs are people already in the industry, working in a pharma or biotech company, in some type of research and development—oriented role.

On a scale of 1 to 10 (10 being great), how would you rate your occupation and why?

It's a 9. Great benefits, interesting and intelligent coworkers, a good cause (we develop drugs for cancer and autoimmune disorders), very good pay, challenging work. It's not like being a photojournalist or making movies, but it's a very decent way to make a living in my estimation.

What factors or former positions led to this occupation?

Internships with Pfizer, Inc. in New York and California. Through those experiences, I learned about the important role regulatory played in the development process for new drugs. I also learned how bureaucratic large pharma companies can be and didn't want any part of that, so I made the decision for the bureaucracy reasons and the fact that most of the new products/science are coming from biotech to move in that direction.

What career choices were most helpful?

Getting a master's from USC School of Pharmacy in regulatory affairs. It opened doors—along with my internships with Pfizer—that otherwise likely would have been shut.

What career choices were least helpful/detrimental?

Going to law school for a year. I should have gone straight into regulatory in biotech after I finished my internship with Pfizer. But it all worked out in the end.

What type of education was needed for your position?

You need at least a bachelor's degree, and in reality, this would be career limiting. You really need a master's degree of some sort (scientific discipline), or a pharmacy degree, or a PhD/MD. But a master's really helps because most people working in corporate in biotech and pharma companies are pretty highly educated.

Do you have to update your career with ongoing training and certificates?

We attend training courses. It is not required but viewed as part of our professional development by the company.

When you were hired, did you receive professional training or was it basically "on-the-job training"?

On-the-job training. Once you get a couple years under your belt, it's very easy to move companies because there is a shortage of qualified regulatory professionals. This gives folks with experience a lot of flexibility to command higher salaries, titles, etc.

In a typical week, are your hours fixed or flexible? On what days do you tend to work overtime?

Fixed. Forty-hour week. Never weekends. Overtime would be extremely rare.

Is your work environment "hectic," "all work and no play," "serene," "laid back," or other? Briefly explain.

I would say serene. People work, but they also have time to chill. It's not what I would consider a high-stress profession. The work-life balance is excellent, there is excellent earning potential with regard to income, and you get to do interesting stuff.

Do you interface with coworkers, groups, or vendors, or do you work alone?

My only external communication is with government agencies, so dress is casual! I interface with nearly all departments inside the company, though—regulatory, commercial, marketing, legal, scientists, medical affairs, drug safety, quality, etc.

What are your coworkers like?

Pretty mellow. They tend to be mostly women as pharmacy is a good training ground for this profession and most pharmacists are women, though increasingly more men are getting pharmacy degrees.

What is management like?

Typical management of a NASDAQ 100 company. Smart but sometimes overly bureaucratic about our internal processes, in my opinion.

Is input accepted, or do you fare better as a "yes man"?

Input is accepted. However, you also need to know your time and place to speak up. Sometimes you get shot down.

What issues have prevented your advancement?

None thus far. My education is sufficient for the profession. Work experience is extremely important as there is no set educational training ground for the work of drug development.

Is your position secure, or are you frequently looking for the next opportunity?

Yes, the position is very secure. I could stay in my role many years. However, in reality I will likely move to another company in a few years' time because I will have been with my company for five-plus years and will want to advance in title, etc., and that's difficult in a big company.

How important is/was networking or connections in finding your current or other positions? Is it a factor in advancement once you're on the job?

It's always important. The more contacts you have, the easier it is to find jobs. You have to be political. I work in a corporate environment. If I am not known by anyone, it's hard to believe I would get promoted.

What would be your next career move?

To a manager of regulatory affairs position at another biotechnology company.

Do you relocate often? Are there travel requirements?

While in the US travel is very minimal—maybe just three to four trips to the East Coast a year. However, I am on international assignment right now, so I travel much more—in fact, all the time. Overall, I would say travel for US-based jobs is very minimal. But you still get out of the office for a business trip every few months, so it's a good mix.

While in Europe, I am always traveling. But that is more unusual for the profession.

How much fulfillment do you get out of your career?

Quite a bit. If I were independently wealthy, I would probably do something else—like travel photography—but I would say that I made a good career choice. I am very well taken care of by the profession and have a good balance between free time and work time. I also find the work I do to be interesting, and I work with smart, highly educated people. I like drug development, especially biological drug development, which is a completely different beast to traditional pill-based drug development. Everything we work on is for life-threatening illnesses, and the science is also much more interesting, new, and exciting.

Do you feel that you are fairly compensated?

Yes, probably too much so. Though don't tell the company that!

Are the benefits and vacation schedule fair?

Yes. In the US, I got three weeks paid first year, up to five after five years' service, plus the option to buy an additional week, plus thirteen paid holidays, full medical/dental/vision, and the company pays all. Also, 401(k) matches up to 6 percent with no cap. In Europe I get all this plus an additional two-week home leave each year, so right now I have six weeks' holiday plus two weeks' bank holidays for eight weeks off a year.

If you could choose again, how much would money be a factor?

It is an important factor. It costs a lot to live in the world today, and you need to be in a profession that lets you pay the bills and not just scrape by.

Would you choose the same career path?

Yes, without a doubt.

Any comments or words of advice for someone entering your field?

Network. Do an internship while in college so you know what regulatory is, the role they play in the company, and what the work is like. I would never have known without doing an internship. You'll know if it's right for you.

ACCOUNT CLERK

Name

Kathleen

Location

Jefferson City, Missouri

Education

High school

Total years in profession

15

Brief occupation description/goal of occupation

I am an account clerk for the state government. I enter purchase orders and ensure the funding availability and compliance of the equipment with state policy. The goal of this occupation is to waste tax dollars with bureaucratic bunk.

Why did you choose this career path?

I thought I could help my government and do something important.

What do you like about your occupation?

I like the fact that I earn vacation and sick leave monthly and my benefits are really good.

What do you dislike about your occupation?

I do not like the red tape one has to go through to get anything accomplished. I do not like that I make poverty wages.

What are the misconceptions about your profession?

That government employees are lazy and pampered. Only the managers and administrative employees are lazy and pampered.

On a scale of 1 to 10 (10 being great), how would you rate your occupation and why?

I would say 6. There are a lot of higher-paying career paths out there and the politics have caused many a sane person to turn to antidepressants. Getting anything to change for the sake of time takes more time than it's worth.

What factors or former positions led to this occupation?

It's easy to get in and stay in.

What career choices were most helpful?

Taking accounting in high school, typing, and a head for detail.

Did you have a mentor? If so, how did you find them? Did they help?

I haven't had a mentor. Politics do not allow for close relationships at work. If someone can do your job better or faster, you don't want to teach them how to do so. That is the mentality of my assigned area.

Was your formal education necessary for this position?

Not really. It's common sense, simple math.

In a typical week, are your hours fixed or flexible?
On what days do you tend to work overtime?

I work forty hours a week. We are pretty flexible. I haven't had to work overtime.

Is your work environment "hectic," "all work and no play," "serene," "laid back," or other? Briefly explain.

Hectic but with plenty of breathing space. I have many duties but enough time to complete them. For now, since it is the government, it changes every fiscal year and with every governor's election.

What types of conflicts do you deal with?

I work with a guy who resents women who are more successful than himself. He is rude and a real buffoon. Since it's the government and all politically correct, he is allowed to be a jerk.

What are your coworkers like?

Some are great; most are lazy and ineffective.

What is management like?

A joke. They don't have a clue as to what is going on most of the time, and have no control over their employees and what their employees do or do not do.

Is input accepted, or do you fare better as a "yes man"?

Input is accepted, then ignored.

What issues have prevented your advancement?

Lack of education, lack of tuition reimbursement, and cutbacks.

Is your position secure, or are you frequently looking for the next opportunity?

It's very secure. It takes an act of God to get fired. But I am always looking for a way to work from home.

How important is/was networking or connections in finding your current or other positions? Is it a factor in advancement once you're on the job?

I strive to make connections to help me advance. With the state, it's who you know, not what you can do.

How much fulfillment do you get out of your career?

Money, and that is it.

Are the benefits and vacation schedule fair?

Oh yeah, it's the state. I get ten hours of vacation and ten hours of sick leave every month. I get dental, vision, health, 401(k), and a pension plan.

If you could choose again, how much would money be a factor?

Money would be huge. If I knew then what I know now, I wouldn't have skipped college.

Would you choose the same career path?

NO!

Any comments or words of advice for someone entering your field?

Keep a positive outlook. Don't go into a government field thinking you are going to change the world. Eighty-five percent of government employees don't care about their jobs and resent you if you do.

REVENUE MANAGER

Name

James B.

Location

Los Angeles, California

Education

Bachelor of Business Administration

Total years in profession

6

Brief occupation description/goal of occupation

Analyze demand, set pricing strategy, forecast revenue, and maintain reservation system.

Why did you choose this career path?

I have been in the industry for over twenty years, so I was familiar with all aspects of it. The job suited my personality, and I have experienced relative success in this area of the industry.

What do you like about your occupation?

I manage systems, not people. It is routine oriented.

On a scale of 1 to 10 (10 being great), how would you rate your occupation and why?

I would say 9. The job rewards those who devote themselves to it. The closer you analyze the data, the better you become at making changes that will directly influence your hotel's top line financial performance. The revenue manager can have more impact in this area than any other single person in the hotel. To me that is very exciting.

What factors or former positions led to this occupation?

Previous to revenue management, I was in group sales in the industry. This introduced me to the pricing mix discipline, which dictates the top-line revenue success of a hotel. Achieving the optimal pricing mix defines the level of financial success the hotel will experience. Revenue management is all about achieving this optimal mix, and the challenge of that attracted me to this area of our industry.

What career choices were most helpful?

While working as a bartender in a hotel during college, I was promoted into my first manager's job. This worked as an introduction to the industry, which was similar to test-driving a car before purchasing it.

What career choices were least helpful/detrimental?

I stayed in one employment market for too long, fifteen years, so my earning potential was stunted by that. Then I turned it around by relocating for new jobs and nearly doubled my income in less than five years.

Did you have a mentor? If so, how did you find them? Did they help?

Yes, he was the director of sales and marketing that I first worked under as a group sales manager.

Was your formal education necessary for this position?

Typically required by the industry.

Do you have to update your career with ongoing training and certificates?

This job evolves with technology, which tends to keep you in a learning mode as the technology advances.

In a typical week, are your hours fixed or flexible? On what days do you tend to work overtime?

Flexible; however, I typically work at least fifty hours per week, Monday to Friday. Overtime tends to be seasonal, such as during budget season.

Is your work environment "hectic," "all work and no play," "serene," "laid back," or other? Briefly explain.

I operate from a home office, handling the revenue management responsibilities for four hotels. My work environment is laid back.

What types of conflicts do you deal with?

Not many. It is my job to "police" the group sales managers to be sure they are not holding rooms for group clients to the detriment of the overall financial goals of the hotel. This can occasionally lead to conflict, but not often.

Do you interface with coworkers, groups, or vendors, or do you work alone?

I work alone; however, I hold conference-call meetings with each of my hotels weekly.

What are your coworkers like?

Most are relatively easy to get along with, but since I do not interact with them daily, there is less opportunity for conflict.

Is input accepted, or do you fare better as a "yes man"?

My input is typically solicited since I am considered the "expert" in my area with each of my hotels.

Is your position secure, or are you frequently looking for the next opportunity?

I always try to stay abreast of opportunity in our industry, as the future is never certain; however, I feel very secure in my current situation.

How important is/was networking or connections in finding your current or other positions? Is it a factor in advancement once you're on the job?

Paramount. I think it is always important. Networking gives others a broader base from which to evaluate you for future opportunity.

What would be your next career move?

As a regional or corporate director of revenue management.

Do you relocate often? Are there travel requirements?

I have relocated two times in the past five years and plan to do so again in the next year.

Do you prefer going to work or leaving? Why?

Going. Each day represents a new challenge.

How much fulfillment do you get out of your career?

Considerable.

If you could choose again, how much would money be a factor?

It is secondary to finding a career that you love. Once you do that, the money will come.

Would you choose the same career path?

That depends on the situation. If my situation were the same leading to my career, then I believe I would choose the same. Where I might have made a change is in my college major, which would have likely resulted in a different career.

Any comments or words of advice for someone entering your field?

This is a career for someone who is self-motivated, who enjoys working with numbers.

SECRETARY/ ADMINISTRATIVE ASSISTANT

Name

Ellen D.

Location

Northern Maryland

Education

Some college

Total years in profession

20

Brief occupation description/goal of occupation

Secretary and administrative assistant means working in an office environment, handling bureaucratic functions, and generally assisting in the flow of information.

Why did you choose this career path?

I couldn't pass the eye exam to become a paramedic, so I learned to type.

What do you like about your occupation?

Absolutely nothing.

What do you dislike about your occupation?

Long hours, minimal pay, high expectations. Working for individuals who get paid way more than you do, but who have the average IQ of a pencil eraser. Working for individuals who don't care that you have a life and want you to work evenings and weekends so they can go home early. Spending hours fixing spelling and grammar so someone else's reports look good and they get the raise.

What are the misconceptions about your profession?

That it's somehow glamorous, that it's a "stepping-stone" profession. That there's camaraderie among "the girls." That we want to be called "the girls."

What factors or former positions led to this occupation?

I originally trained as a firefighter/paramedic. Then I failed the eye exam. I didn't know what else to do, but I could file and answer the phone. Then I learned to type, and the rest, sadly, is history.

What career choices were most helpful?

Quitting the jobs that wanted me to lie to: the IRS (Internal Revenue Service), the FDA (Federal Drug Administration), wives, girlfriends, boyfriends, etc. Quitting the jobs that thought it was appropriate to lie to clients to maximize profit.

What career choices were least helpful/detrimental?

Taking those jobs in the first place. Unfortunately, you never really know what you're going to get until you've signed on.

If you didn't have a mentor, would you have liked one?

There aren't many secretarial mentors. Probably because they'd all tell newcomers to go back to school and get a real job.

Was your formal education necessary for this position?

No. All that was really required was the ability to type, lie, kiss arse, and bullshit.

In a typical week, are your hours fixed or flexible? On what days do you tend to work overtime?

Hours are supposed to be fixed, but generally turn out to be flexible. Overtime seems to happen anytime the boss wants to play golf, leave early, or host a function, or forgets to notice that there's an impending deadline that requires his/her input.

Is your work environment "hectic," "all work and no play," "serene," "laid back," or other? Briefly explain.

Hectic, all work and no play, generally sexist, frequently repressive, always depressing.

What types of conflicts do you deal with?

Working with bosses who don't understand the limitations of hardware/software. Coworkers who don't understand the abilities of hardware/software. Clients who have had goods or services misrepresented to them by supervisors.

What are your coworkers like?

Generally sad, tired, and overworked. Frequently frazzled, often harried.

What is management like?

Horrid. You generally wind up working for some git that skimped through business school on a D and is now power-tripping but can't spell his own name without looking at his shiny new business cards. He can't write a sentence in English but gets offended when you correct his grammar.

Is input accepted, or do you fare better as a "yes man"?

Generally, input is not accepted. However, when it's needed, I'll give it regardless. I'm not inclined to let the department look inept because the boss is inept.

What issues have prevented your advancement?

Um, I have this little attitude problem . . .

How important is/was networking or connections in finding your current or other positions? Is it a factor in advancement once you're on the job?

Networking is not generally a part of finding or keeping a secretarial job. Generally, there is no advancement, unless you retrain and get a degree.

Do you feel that you are fairly compensated?

No. Secretaries do most all the work, while the boss gets most all the pay.

Are the benefits and vacation schedule fair?

Benefits and vacation are generally set on a corporate level. Taking that vacation, though, means scheduling it around the bosses' vacation choices. That means whatever is left over.

If you could choose again, how much would money be a factor?

Not at all. If I could choose again, I'd do anything else.

Would you choose the same career path?

No. Over the years I've filled in on some gigs like scrubbing urinals, mucking stalls, and being an aide in a nursing home. On reflection, I'd take any of those jobs over secretarial work.

Any comments or words of advice for someone entering your field?

Don't.

MEDICAL TRANSCRIPTIONIST

Name

Melisa G.

Location

Western Massachusetts

Education

High school

Total years in profession

6

Brief occupation description/goal of occupation

Provide quality reports to health care clients in a timely fashion.

Why did you choose this career path?

I have done a personality profile and medical/clerical were my strong suits. I also checked out a seminar on this occupation and liked it very much.

What do you like about your occupation?

The medical terminology aspect of the occupation.

What do you dislike about your occupation?

Having to advertise for clients and dealing with clients who do not pay on time—especially the administrators, not the doctors—and do not appreciate the work that is involved in this occupation.

What are the misconceptions about your profession?

That you can do a little work and make a lot of money. But if you have your own clients and do not work for a transcription company, you do a lot more than just transcribe dictation for health care professionals.

On a scale of 1 to 10 (10 being great), how would you rate your occupation and why?

It's a 9 because you can set your own rate for the jobs and I enjoyed the doctors because they were all very nice and appreciative of my diligence with the job.

What factors or former positions led to this occupation?

In addition to my personality profile and seminar, I was in clerical work previously for an insurance company, and I wanted to work from home so I could be there for whatever my children needed.

What career choices were most helpful?

Clerical and medical transcription. I worked for an insurance company for many years, and that improved my typing skills.

What type of education was needed for your position?

I had to learn medical terminology, medical formats, medical rules, and medical drugs and doses. I also had to brush up on my English language skills.

Do you have to update your career with ongoing training and certificates?

No, but it is a good idea to refresh one's memory on other disciplines if you only do one discipline for a long time.

In a typical week, are your hours fixed or flexible? On what days do you tend to work overtime?

Flexible and two weeknights and Saturday and Sunday, but my occupation hours have changed considerably since I do not have as many clients as I did before. I used to have over ten clients; now I have only two or three.

Is your work environment "hectic," "all work and no play," "serene," "laid back," or other? Briefly explain.

Hectic. Some of the doctors request rushed reports, which puts other work aside that will have you playing catch-up. Also, you have to do everything when you are the owner. Even if you have hired other people, you have to train them while you still do your own work, which can be a lot. You also have to be the billing person, office organizer, delivery person, etc., so that requires time. When the doctor is behind in his reports then you have to get them done as soon as possible, and sometimes that can involve anywhere from twenty-five to fifty reports in one week's time or less.

What types of conflicts do you deal with?

Not being paid on time. Having to call for my check and then getting yelled at for doing so. If the machine that records the dictation malfunctions, I have to inform the doctors and they either have to redo the dictation or forget it, which causes me to lose money. If someone does not sign the contract that was issued, then that poses a problem if they do not continue to give you work. If the doctor does not dictate properly, they think it is your fault that the dictation did not come through.

Do you interface with coworkers, groups, or vendors, or do you work alone?

I interface with the doctors, their receptionists, and administration, but not every day, unless the doctor needs something every day.

Is input accepted, or do you fare better as a "yes man"?

Input is necessary for the doctors to get reports that are not questionable.

Is your position secure, or are you frequently looking for the next opportunity?

It is not secure, because of the nature of the job. You get paid by how much dictation they give you, and recently a client violated the contract and stopped using my service and did not even give me a chance to lower my price so that I could keep transcribing for them. The money keeps coming so long as the doctors dictate.

How important is/was networking or connections in finding your current or other positions? Is it a factor in advancement once you're on the job?

The connection is important if they work for the company you have as a client, which I did. That is why I received ten clients.

What would be your next career move?

I am trying to apply for a company that hires medical transcriptionists or quality assurance specialists since I have had over six years of experience in this field.

How much fulfillment do you get out of your career?

If everything goes well, a lot of fulfillment.

Do you feel that you are fairly compensated?

When I had ten clients, yes. Now that I only have three, no.

If you could choose again, how much would money be a factor?

Not much. I really do not want to work as much as I did, so my monthly income does not have to be as much anymore.

Would you choose the same career path?

Yes.

Any comments or words of advice for someone entering your field?

Take a personality profile, as not everyone is suited for this occupation. Make sure you get good training; some colleges offer this training but are not very good. Realize that you will have to work full time if you work for yourself. If you join a company, you will not make as much money. It takes time to get clients, and you have to advertise and do the work to get your own clients. Also, if you have never met the person who signs your check, make the effort to meet them, because that can make the difference between keeping or losing a client if things change in that company. This is not necessary if you work for a transcriptionist company.

INFORMATION SECURITY CONSULTANT

Name

David N.

Location

Los Angeles, California

Education

Bachelor of Arts

Total years in profession

11

Brief occupation description/goal of occupation

I provide network security assessments and computer forensic investigation services. My goal is to help organizations secure their information and better prepare for the threats that they may face.

Why did you choose this career path?

Technology has always been of interest to me. Security is becoming an exciting field that provides many opportunities to always be challenged.

What do you like about your occupation?

Constant change and the requirement to always be learning more.

What do you dislike about your occupation?

Due to the constant change, there never seems to be enough time in the day to do all I want.

What are the misconceptions about your profession?

In regard to security, many people look to technology to solve many of the problems when they could be better solved with better policies and management.

On a scale of 1 to 10 (10 being great), how would you rate your occupation and why?

I give it a 10 because I love doing it every day. If I were independently wealthy, I would still be doing it because it is so much fun.

What factors or former positions led to this occupation?

Desktop engineer, server engineer, network engineer, IT management.

What career choices were most helpful?

I would suggest that anyone who wants to learn more about technology get involved with as many outside organizations or groups as possible—the more you are exposed to the better.

If you didn't have a mentor, would you have liked one?

Yes, one that I could trust.

What type of education was needed for your position?

A bachelor's degree helps, with IT certifications.

Do you have to update your career with ongoing training and certificates?

Yes, always.

In a typical week, are your hours fixed or flexible? On what days do you tend to work overtime?

Flexible. I work every day.

Is your work environment "hectic," "all work and no play," "serene," "laid back," or other? Briefly explain.

Hectic. Since I work for myself, I am thinking about work all the time.

Do you interface with coworkers, groups, or vendors, or do you work alone?

I interface with vendors, customers, coworkers, etc.

What are your coworkers like?

Most of my coworkers are contractors unless they are the customer, so I usually get to know them before I work with them.

What is management like?

Management is either me or the customer.

Is input accepted, or do you fare better as a "yes man"?

I am definitely not a yes man. I get paid to give my opinion on the state of an organization's security. I tell it exactly how it is.

What issues have prevented your advancement?

Mismanagement of my own time or resources.

Is your position secure, or are you frequently looking for the next opportunity?

I am always looking for more work since I run my own business.

How important is/was networking or connections in finding your current or other positions? Is it a factor in advancement once you're on the job?

Extremely important—even if you work for a company, you should always be networking, because you never know when you may be out on the street.

What would be your next career move?

Hopefully to stay where I am, maybe hire more employees.

Do you relocate often? Are there travel requirements?

I do not relocate, but I do travel a few times a year.

Are the benefits and vacation schedule fair?

Vacation? What vacation? It all falls on my back, so I have to plan out vacation and everything else. Currently things are too busy to think about time off.

If you could choose again, how much would money be a factor?

Money has to be a large factor because it is how we pay our bills. But you have to be happy in what you are doing, or eventually you will fail.

Would you choose the same career path?

Yes.

Any comments or words of advice for someone entering your field?

Get involved with networking and associations, and be sure to learn as much as you can on your own.

MERCHANT MARINE

Name

Ross B.

Location

Western Washington

Education

Bachelor of Arts

Total years in profession

18

Brief occupation description/goal of occupation

I work on a ship. I am a junior engineer in the engine room of a ship. I do some maintenance and take gauge readings and operate equipment. It means I must know what to do to operate turbine generators, air compressors, pumps, evaporators, boilers, etc. I am part of a team that serves as central power and light and propulsion for a ship. We take care of the air conditioning and every other mechanical piece of equipment on the ship.

Why did you choose this career path?

I have an education, but the navy provided me with something I just liked doing. I have a teaching certificate and two degrees, but this job is just fun and pays more than anything I have ever done.

What do you like about your occupation?

I get to travel all over the world and meet new people. If you like time off, you can take off months at a time.

What do you dislike about your occupation?

There is always some politics that I disdain. The union tends to cause more problems than solving them. It takes you away from home for months at a time.

What are the misconceptions about your profession?

You have to be a drunk to be a sailor.

On a scale of 1 to 10 (10 being great), how would you rate your occupation and why?

It's a 10 because I am highly paid and get to travel everywhere.

What factors or former positions led to this occupation?

I was a machinist's mate first class in the navy. I was trained in the navy. I took my knowledge and experience and took tests with the coast guard to get my Merchant Mariner's Document.

What career choices were most helpful?

I went to work for Military Sealift Command, which is a US government position. They give you every opportunity to advance and provide the training and experience you need to do what you set your mind on doing. This is especially true if you were not in the navy.

What career choices were least helpful/detrimental?

I wish I had stayed with one profession for all the years. I kept changing jobs, from bridge inspector, to math teacher, to mechanic, to production controller. Finally merchant mariner.

If you didn't have a mentor, would you have liked one?

Yes, I would like to have found out exactly what I needed to do and to have been aided in my efforts.

What type of education was needed for your position?

I went to a US Navy machinist's mate A school. I went to the US Navy nuclear power training (two years). Experience in the navy was the education that I needed. You can go to several different mariner training schools to get the endorsements on your Merchant Mariner's Document. Just google coast guard licensing requirements or some such and your education will begin.

Do you have to update your career with ongoing training and certificates?

Absolutely. It is necessary to renew your Merchant Mariner's Document periodically, and if you get a license, it must be renewed. Training is ongoing all the time.

When you were hired, did you receive professional training or was it basically "on-the-job training"?

There was a considerable amount of professional training and then years of on-the-job training.

In a typical week, are your hours fixed or flexible? On what days do you tend to work overtime?

Flexible hours. Twelve hours a day, seven days a week or more. You are not home and have no place to go when you are at sea, so why not rack up sixty or more hours of overtime?

Is your work environment "hectic," "all work and no play," "serene," "laid back," or other? Briefly explain.

Work will help you to fill the time. The work is mostly easy but sometimes dirty. Because of the travel, the crew, and friends, the job is worth it because of the fun times ashore.

What types of conflicts do you deal with?

There are no conflicts if you don't worry about what other people are doing. If you work hard, you will shine, and some lazy folks will be upset with you. The union can be a deterrent to getting any work done.

Do you interface with coworkers, groups, or vendors, or do you work alone?

Always work as a team. There are some rugged individualists, but coworkers depend on you to do your job.

What are your coworkers like?

Older, experienced men who are willing to help you if you are doing your job.

What is management like?

Managers look for input from the workers when the big jobs are done and appreciate initiative from the workers but want to know exactly what you are doing before you do it. They need to be informed and in control, especially when there is very expensive machinery and dangers involved.

How important is/was networking or connections in finding your current or other positions? Is it a factor in advancement once you're on the job?

Networking is okay because you need someone to lead you through the process. Ask for help to advance and you will be told how to do it. It is good evaluations that help you. Time, hard work, and experience are key to advancement.

What would be your next career move?

To get my license as a third assistant engineer.

Do you relocate often? Are there travel requirements?

You can have a house anywhere in the US. You are rarely home anyway if you want to make the big bucks. You commute to work and home a few times a year. They fly you to the ship and home.

Do you prefer going to work or leaving? Why?

Going to work. It is fun. I make big bucks.

How much fulfillment do you get out of your career?

I get my name on my stateroom door and the respect of my coworkers.

Do you feel that you are fairly compensated?

I make entirely too much money for what I do.

Are the benefits and vacation schedule fair?

With Military Sealift Command, it is hard to get home. The benefits are great. Thirty days a year vacation.

If you could choose again, how much would money be a factor?

I would have started this much sooner. Money is a huge factor.

Would you choose the same career path?

Yes, only sooner and stick with it.

Any comments or words of advice for someone entering your field?

Whatever you enjoy doing, find a job doing it, and stick with it until you are the best person doing it.

CERTIFIED PHARMACY TECHNICIAN

Name

Lisa H.

Location

Birmingham, Alabama

Education

Some college

Total years in profession

5

Brief occupation description/goal of occupation

Make IVs (intravenous) for patients, perform compounding, credit patient medication, field phone calls, and assist pharmacist in every aspect of patient care and delivery of medications.

Why did you choose this career path?

I do not have a college degree, and this career gave me the income I needed to raise my children without going back to school.

What do you like about your occupation?

I love working in the health field. It's an honorable position and gives you self-gratification that you have done all you can for the patients.

What do you dislike about your occupation?

The stress level! It is high, but the rewards are wonderful.

On a scale of 1 to 10 (10 being great), how would you rate your occupation and why?

I would say 7. The pay is not that great for most pharmacy techs. You do a lot of work for the wages you receive.

What career choices were most helpful?

Probably waiting tables. That gives you a little more patience in working with the public.

What career choices were least helpful/detrimental?

Commercial fishing. You don't deal with the public too much, and when you do you are arguing over prices!

Did you have a mentor? If so, how did you find them? Did they help?

Yes, my mentor would have to be a third-shift pharmacist at the hospital where I work. He is my inspiration to achieve the goals I am after. He is always answering my ten thousand questions, and he gives me insight on why this drug will work, and why this one will not.

What type of education was needed for your position?

You do not have to go to college to be a pharmacy technician. Most places offer on-the-job training, and you will probably learn more on the job than in a classroom. Plus, you earn as you learn.

Do you have to update your career with ongoing training and certificates?

Yes—three hours of continuing education for registered techs, one of which must be live. Certified, you must have twenty hours and must be on pharmacy law. You are required to have three hours of continuing education each year.

When you were hired, did you receive professional training or was it basically "on-the-job training"?

On-the-job training. For each job in the pharmacy department (and there are a lot!), you are trained for a week, and you work that job for a week.

In a typical week, are your hours fixed or flexible? On what days do you tend to work overtime?

Forty hours' fixed schedule, no overtime unless authorized.

Is your work environment "hectic," "all work and no play," "serene," "laid back," or other? Briefly explain.

Mostly hectic, but depending on the season, sometimes it's laid back. During cold and flu months, you are busier because of the amount of patients in the hospital.

What types of conflicts do you deal with?

Nurses trying to get medications to the floor for their patients. Due to a variety of factors, they usually aren't too nice to deal with.

Do you interface with coworkers, groups, or vendors, or do you work alone?

You will typically work with a lot of people in the department, and you will work with other departments as well.

What are your coworkers like?

They are the best group of people I have ever met!

What is management like?

Helpful, not too overbearing, usually will always try to meet the needs of a particular problem you may be having and try to resolve it.

Is input accepted, or do you fare better as a "yes man"?

Input is always accepted. The goal of the hospital pharmacy is to get the patients' medications to the floor as quickly as possible. Sometimes suggestions are used to decrease the order entry time to delivery time.

Is your position secure, or are you frequently looking for the next opportunity?

Very secure.

How important is/was networking or connections in finding your current or other positions? Is it a factor in advancement once you're on the job?

Not too important. If you work hard, your job performance will speak for itself.

What would be your next career move?

Going back to college and becoming a pharmacist.

Do you relocate often? Are there travel requirements?

No relocation, and no travel requirements.

How much fulfillment do you get out of your career?

I get a lot of fulfillment out of my career. I feel pretty good about myself when I know there is a patient on the floor and they are rushing him to an emergency open heart surgery and I have made all the IV fluids in a timely manner. I hold his life in my hands. The greatest doctors in the world cannot start surgery without the IV fluids.

Do you feel that you are fairly compensated?

No, not really. Technicians should probably make half of what a pharmacist makes, because we do all the work. However, that's not the case. Hopefully, as we move forward to better trained techs and knowledge-based technology, we will get the credit we deserve.

If you could choose again, how much would money be a factor?

Not much.

Would you choose the same career path?

Yes.

Any comments or words of advice for someone entering your field?

Learn how to become a team player. In this profession, you will work with a lot of people from a variety of professions. To get all the work done during your shift, you have to help each other. Also, learn patience. Patient care is a self-rewarding job. It is also a high-stress job. You will not save every person, but the ones you do save are worth every moment.

TECHNOLOGY SALES

Name

Susan K.

Location

San Diego, California

Education

Bachelor of Arts

Total years in profession

32

Brief occupation description/goal of occupation

I am a sales professional in the high tech industry.

Why did you choose this career path?

I was hired by a large technology manufacturer right out of college.

What do you like about your occupation?

Variety, interesting people, and seeing lots of industries.

What do you dislike about your occupation?

Up and down cycles in the economy and businesses that crash and burn.

What are the misconceptions about your profession?

That it is a dog-eat-dog world.

On a scale of 1 to 10 (10 being great), how would you rate your occupation and why?

It's a 9, because it is fun, but not perfect. There are stresses.

What career choices were most helpful?

It was more about knowing great people and being able to be competent so that people were always ready to hire me when I was available.

What career choices were least helpful/detrimental?

Whenever I decided that I must get in on some wild, unproven technology (like robotics early on), I found I was always too early.

What type of education was needed for your position?

General college degree.

Do you have to update your career with ongoing training and certificates?

Yes. I am always looking for ways to improve how I do my job.

When you were hired, did you receive professional training or was it basically "on-the-job training"?

Yes, my first job trained us very well—technically, as well as in sales techniques.

In a typical week, are your hours fixed or flexible? On what days do you tend to work overtime?

Flexible—I can work any seventy hours I want!

What types of conflicts do you deal with?

Making quota, finding customers, selling, accepting rejection, losing sales, fighting with suppliers.

Do you interface with coworkers, groups, or vendors, or do you work alone?

I work with everyone in my company, with our business partners and with customers.

What are your coworkers like?

My coworkers are all very senior people, mostly very funny and always intelligent.

What is management like?

I have a great management team: one brilliant strategist, one wonderful humanist.

Is input accepted, or do you fare better as a "yes man"?

Input is accepted, fought over, reformulated, molded, ignored, repeated, buried, laughed at, used, repeated, and honed.

What issues have prevented your advancement?

I am nowhere near a good strategist or big thinker. I am also unwilling to work 150 hours per week.

Is your position secure, or are you frequently looking for the next opportunity?

I think my position is fairly secure. I think. Probably. Maybe.

How important is/was networking or connections in finding your current or other positions? Is it a factor in advancement once you're on the job?

I am finally realizing how important networking is. It sounds corny, but it is important.

Do you relocate often? Are there travel requirements?

I have only relocated five times in my career. Now, I am almost all about a driving territory, which I love.

How much fulfillment do you get out of your career?

I get some fulfillment—lots of anxiety.

If you could choose again, how much would money be a factor?

I would settle for something easier. I wanted to be a pioneer in careers for women. It was hard.

Any comments or words of advice for someone entering your field?

It is interesting and fun, but everyone has to find their own way of working out the kinks.

CLIENT SERVICE OFFICER

Name

Amy M.

Location

San Francisco, California

Education

Bachelor of Science

Total years in profession

4

Brief occupation description/goal of occupation

Assist with middle market wholesale businesses' banking needs—especially online services. All service aspects included.

Why did you choose this career path?

I love to work with people and develop relationships.

What do you like about your occupation?

I have a dedicated portfolio of customers who I have gotten to know. I like the personal aspect of my job in the banking industry.

What do you dislike about your occupation?

Some of the customers are not happy and can be very demanding in their requests.

What are the misconceptions about your profession?

Many people only look at direct sales as a measurement of success. My department is not revenue-generating, but service does affect the bottom line: without great service, there would be no future sales. Many times, my position is undervalued.

On a scale of 1 to 10 (10 being great), how would you rate your occupation and why?

An 8. I love my job. I like the way my managers do not micromanage me. Once I've established the relationships with the customers, they believe in me.

What factors or former positions led to this occupation?

I started out in banking as a personal banker, which was not the position for me. I learned that I like service but am not good at sales. My company saw the value of my service skills and found a position for me focusing on sales.

What career choices were most helpful?

My company's HR (human resources) person directed me to my current department. I applied for my current job for over a year. My current manager told me she finally called me in for an interview so she could either hire me or get me to stop calling her. The persistence I showed paid off.

Did you have a mentor? If so, how did you find them? Did they help?

I do not have a direct mentor, but I work with a team of eighteen people who readily share job knowledge.

What type of education was needed for your position?

High school.

Do you have to update your career with ongoing training and certificates?

My company has ongoing training for new products and refreshers for existing products. We go to about three trainings a month.

When you were hired, did you receive professional training or was it basically "on-the-job training"?

I received professional training that was based on product knowledge. Because I do customer service, many of the situations required on-the-job training because it would have taken too long to discuss every possible scenario.

In a typical week, are your hours fixed or flexible? On what days do you tend to work overtime?

My hours are fixed. I am exempt, so I don't get paid overtime. In a typical week, I probably work three to five hours outside of my scheduled hours.

Is your work environment "hectic," "all work and no play," "serene," "laid back," or other? Briefly explain.

We are all about customer service, but because it is a call center environment, we do not see our customers, so the environment is laid back. It can be hectic based on system issues or time of the month or year, but we try to keep each other grounded.

What types of conflicts do you deal with?

Customers call when there has been some kind of problem with their banking. Sometimes they start out hostile and it is my job to resolve the issue as well as not be "baited" by them.

Do you interface with coworkers, groups, or vendors, or do you work alone?

I work in a call center, so I am either on the phone or emailing customers all day. I work face to face with my coworkers and our research teams.

What is management like?

My direct manager has a way of building you up even when she is coaching. This makes it a safe environment. Her boss takes an interest in us personally, which makes her approachable.

Is input accepted, or do you fare better as a "yes man"?

Input is accepted, but if you criticize, have a suggestion or a solution. You have to know when to say yes because some things are not negotiable.

What issues have prevented your advancement?

I was not doing enough "extra projects." I was doing my job but needed to step up to be a role model for my team. I've just started doing more and hope this shows on my next review.

Is your position secure, or are you frequently looking for the next opportunity?

I don't think you should ever feel your position is totally secure because we can all be replaced, but I don't feel that pressure on a daily basis. I've been in my current position for two years and am not ready to look for something else.

How important is/was networking or connections in finding your current or other positions? Is it a factor in advancement once you're on the job?

My customer service history and persistence got me my job, not networking.

What would be your next career move?

I would like to be a team leader for my current team members within the next two years.

How much fulfillment do you get out of your career?

Most of my fulfillment actually comes from my customers. They seem to appreciate the work that I do. We do have recognitions at work that help.

If you could choose again, how much would money be a factor?

When I think about changing jobs to increase my salary, it makes me nervous because I feel I finally found a job I like. I have thought about it because I would like to make more money, but the fear of not liking my new job keeps me where I am for now.

Would you choose the same career path?

No. I ended up in banking by circumstance, so if I had to do it over, I would not choose this path.

Any comments or words of advice for someone entering your field?

You really have to understand that customer service is the bottom line. You may have to apologize and "suck it up," but it's not about you personally. You represent your company, and your job is to keep the customer happy. If you're not into that, this job would not be for you.

MORTGAGE BROKER

Name

Bruce D.

Location

Orange County, California

Education

Master of Business Administration

Total years in profession

10

Brief occupation description/goal of occupation

Mortgage broker/real estate sales. Goal: complete financial independence and control over my own time.

Why did you choose this career path?

I chose sales on the advice of a college professor. I chose mortgage brokering because I was having difficulty finding a job that paid a salary.

What do you like about your occupation?

I am completely independent and work for myself.

What do you dislike about your occupation?

Income can be sporadic. I never know if the money will stop.

What are the misconceptions about your profession?

I think the misconception is that my business is too highly competitive to make a living doing it. I compete with dozens of companies that advertise on billboards, radio, and TV. However, hard work will still prevail.

On a scale of 1 to 10 (10 being great), how would you rate your occupation and why?

I would rate it as an 8. I enjoy doing it, but there is a certain amount of stress in not knowing if the money will stop or I will hit a dry spell. However, a year from now I might rate it as a 10 once the uncertainty is gone.

What factors or former positions led to this occupation?

A downturn in the tech market made it difficult to find work selling software. A friend introduced me to someone in the mortgage business, and I immediately started making money. I worked longer hours but enjoyed the freedom.

What career choices were least helpful/detrimental?

Initially, leaving management and going into sales seemed detrimental. I went from making what I thought was a good salary to making very little on commission-only sales. My level of education had gone up, but my income had gone down.

Did you have a mentor? If so, how did you find them? Did they help?

Yes, I have had several mentors. My most recent one was introduced to me through a friend. He had made money for years in my current profession. I wouldn't have had the confidence to go into this profession if I hadn't known someone who was successful at it.

What type of education was needed for your position?

A formal education was not needed. What was needed were good communication skills, good sales skills, the ability to make cold calls, and determination.

Was your formal education necessary for this position?

No, not at all. Although the education is not necessary, the skills that come from the education are necessary.

Do you have to update your career with ongoing training and certificates?

Ongoing education is necessary if I want my career to evolve into something different. For example, I can get a banking license, which would give me more income-making potential. Otherwise, I could stay where I am without any additional training.

When you were hired, did you receive professional training or was it basically "on-the-job training"?

No training at all. I was shown where my desk was and told to press "9" to make an outside call.

In a typical week, are your hours fixed or flexible? On what days do you tend to work overtime?

Flexible. I generally work every day. I sometimes take Sundays off.

Is your work environment "hectic," "all work and no play," "serene," "laid back," or other? Briefly explain.

Hectic! There aren't enough hours in the day, so I never take lunch and I never finish everything I plan to do for the day. There is no room for play, unfortunately.

What types of conflicts do you deal with?

Lenders who change loan terms, making it impossible for a client to get a loan or buy a house. Potential lawsuits on real estate transactions caused by sellers not providing full disclosure. Clients who want to negotiate a better deal for themselves by reducing my income. The list is really quite long.

Do you interface with coworkers, groups, or vendors, or do you work alone?

I mostly work alone, which has its pluses and minuses. I am a social person, so I miss the interaction with other people, but I have limited time to socialize anyway.

What are your coworkers like?

Generally very good people, but I don't have much time to talk with them.

What is management like?

Management is almost nonexistent. I have a boss I can call with a question, but as time goes on, I call him less and less.

Is input accepted, or do you fare better as a "yes man"?

My manager will allow me to say anything to him.

What issues have prevented your advancement?

Nothing has prevented my advance. My advance is all about making money and my income is on the rise.

Is your position secure, or are you frequently looking for the next opportunity?

My position is secure, but I never know where my next sale will come from. That is the uncertainty.

How important is/was networking or connections in finding your current or other positions? Is it a factor in advancement once you're on the job?

Yes, networking is important to find business. This is a relationship-driven business.

What would be your next career move?

Mortgage banker!

How much fulfillment do you get out of your career?

A lot because I am doing it solo, making money with my wits and not relying on someone else to pay my salary.

Do you feel that you are fairly compensated?

Sure. The harder I work, the more money I make.

If you could choose again, how much would money be a factor?

Money is imperative. If I could find a job that paid more and still gave me the freedom, I would change tomorrow.

Would you choose the same career path?

I would probably study a different profession in school and go into architectural design, but that might just be a dream profession.

Any comments or words of advice for someone entering your field?

Network as much as possible. The more people you know, the better you will do in this profession or any other.

FLIGHT ATTENDANT

Name

Kristin B.

Location

Phoenix, Arizona

Education

Junior college

Total years in profession

14

Brief occupation description/goal of occupation

Safety and security of flight and all operations regarding flight/airport safety.

Why did you choose this career path?

At the time, for the travel and the benefits.

What do you like about your occupation?

I like the flexibility.

What do you dislike about your occupation?

The general public.

What are the misconceptions about your profession?

That it is glamorous.

On a scale of 1 to 10 (10 being great), how would you rate your occupation and why?

I would say 7 to 8. It goes in phases. Everyone has burnout. It is very tiring and physical. Dealing with the public is hard, but the flexibility and the growth in seniority are priceless. Naturally the money and schedules get better with time, but the public gets worse every year.

What factors or former positions led to this occupation?

I studied travel and hospitality in college. A neighbor of mine was a flight attendant and she shared her experiences with me. At the time, I too thought it would be glamorous. I was very young then.

Did you have a mentor? If so, how did you find them? Did they help?

I don't know that I'd call them mentors. They were individuals who answered questions when I had them. Ultimately, I made my own decision to fly.

What type of education was needed for your position?

I needed to be a graduate of high school. There was a minimum age requirement of twenty (most large carriers).

Do you have to update your career with ongoing training and certificates?

Yes, yearly.

When you were hired, did you receive professional training or was it basically "on-the-job training"?

Four-week professional training.

In a typical week, are your hours fixed or flexible? On what days do you tend to work overtime?

Flexible. Overtime happens often. It is very random. It could be daily on the days I fly or not.

Is your work environment "hectic," "all work and no play," "serene," "laid back," or other? Briefly explain.

Almost always hectic. Always busy and fast paced. We definitely make it playful. At times it has been chaotic, fearful, peaceful, and tremendously bonding.

What types of conflicts do you deal with?

Where do I start? No one wants to check their luggage; they can't find a seat and/or someone took their seat. They get up when the seatbelt sign is on and then argue about it. They trip you as you walk up and down the aisle. They tell you they think you should be a brunette instead of a blonde, that your company is the worst, that they are never flying with you again. You are blamed for everything regardless of whether you even know about it or not. No "please" and "thank you" ever! Too hot, too cold, no pillows, no blankets. Chewing gum, snotty tissues, hearing about their personal prostate/gastrointestinal/foot fungus problems and bad breath! I could keep going . . .

What are your coworkers like?

Flight attendants—primarily way cool.

What is management like?

Please don't get me started.

Is input accepted, or do you fare better as a "yes man"?

I am not a "yes man" type of person. However, input is not accepted either.

What issues have prevented your advancement?

I don't want advancement. I like being a flight attendant. Several people become in-flight supervisors, but most of us look at that as a "downgrade" and make fun of them.

How important is/was networking or connections in finding your current or other positions? Is it a factor in advancement once you're on the job?

Networking played a small role in getting me an initial interview. Beyond that, I was on my own. To a certain degree it can be a factor in advancement, depending on the division—but I have no desire to change where I currently am.

What would be your next career move?

I'm a lifer. I could possibly do some personal venture on my own outside of that entirely in addition, but ultimately, I'm a lifer.

How much fulfillment do you get out of your career?

I feel pretty fulfilled. Bad days are exhausting, but I've learned not to take them too personally. I also am at the point in my career where I can choose to fly with whom I want, so my friend and I "buddy bid" every month together. That helps.

If you could choose again, how much would money be a factor?

It would play a fairly large factor. Hindsight is twenty-twenty. If I only knew then what I know now.

Would you choose the same career path?

Possibly.

Any comments or words of advice for someone entering your field?

Talk to someone who is actually doing the job and has been for over five years. They have a more realistic outlook and the honeymoon phase is over. Be prepared for the good and the bad, and for heaven's sake make a budget early on and stick to it. Give up on the idea of ever being home for another holiday, but be prepared to make the best friends of your life!

NETWORK SECURITY

Name

Derrick S.

Location

Los Angeles, California

Education

Bachelor of Science

Total years in profession

7

Brief occupation description/goal of occupation

Implementation, monitoring, and maintenance of computer networks and security.

Why did you choose this career path?

I happened into it. My family moved back east and I needed a job to pay the bills. I had some experience with computers and was able to get my first job working in the computer field because I had a security clearance.

What do you like about your occupation?

I like the pay (usually), freedom/travel (depending on the boss), and the opportunity to work with new technology.

What do you dislike about your occupation?

That I can be split between two things, bad bosses/supervisors, and too much time working.

What are the misconceptions about your profession?

That all computer people are nerds. Most of the people that I have worked with and known were actually normal and had interests other than computers.

On a scale of 1 to 10 (10 being great), how would you rate your occupation and why?

I would say 3. In the beginning (when I was getting raises more often and the lure of money was there) I would have rated working in the IT field higher. But now I have sort of topped out on the pay charts for a worker bee and the only choice is to go into management or development.

What factors or former positions led to this occupation?

The need to pay my bills. I got into networking and security because you rarely have to deal directly with end users.

What career choices were most helpful?

Specializing has helped me to earn more money, but there are fewer opportunities for advancement and work at other companies because of my specialization.

What career choices were least helpful/detrimental?

I should have stayed true to myself and gone into a career that I would have been happier doing. I cannot say that I have been happiest working in the computer field.

Did you have a mentor? If so, how did you find them? Did they help?

I have had some good mentors at various times. If you find one, hang onto them and learn everything you can. Their knowledge and experience will last your entire career.

What type of education was needed for your position?

I have a certain number of certifications now, and the work experience to go along with it.

Was your formal education necessary for this position?

Not really. Professional certifications are almost always valued higher.

Do you have to update your career with ongoing training and certificates?

You will need to constantly learn and update your skills and knowledge; technology is an ever-changing field.

When you were hired, did you receive professional training or was it basically "on-the-job training"?

Most employers usually will only send you to a minimum of training and expect that you come to their company already trained.

In a typical week, are your hours fixed or flexible? On what days do you tend to work overtime?

The hours are always flexible. I have worked over eighty hours in a week before.

Is your work environment "hectic," "all work and no play," "serene," "laid back," or other? Briefly explain.

It is usually hectic, especially if someone cannot get their email.

What types of conflicts do you deal with?

Interpersonal ones between management and coworkers, and sometimes with customers and their expectations.

What is management like?

Sketchy at best. Most people whom I have worked for have gotten the position even though they have no ability to lead or motivate their employees.

Is input accepted, or do you fare better as a "yes man"?

Depends upon the boss. Some only want you to go along with their program (like my last one) while others know and appreciate your input.

What issues have prevented your advancement?

My specialization. The more you know, the less likely you are to move up.

Is your position secure, or are you frequently looking for the next opportunity?

In computers you will always need to keep an eye out for the next opportunity.

How important is/was networking or connections in finding your current or other positions? Is it a factor in advancement once you're on the job?

This is one of the few things that I have to strongly recommend. Your network will always help you more than you can help yourself.

What would be your next career move?

I am planning on getting my MBA in finance and an MS in computer science.

Do you relocate often? Are there travel requirements?

Travel of one sort or another is typical these days, but relocation is not really necessary because I live in LA.

How much fulfillment do you get out of your career?

Early on, it was an awesome experience, but now after having been through a bunch of dud bosses, I don't like it as much anymore.

Do you feel that you are fairly compensated?

Sometimes yes, but a bad boss or work environment can make you think that you can never be paid enough for their abuse!

If you could choose again, how much would money be a factor?

If I stayed in this career, money would be the only factor.

Would you choose the same career path?

No, I can only recommend that you find something that you truly enjoy, not something that pays well.

Any comments or words of advice for someone entering your field?

Learn as much as you can, get certifications, and definitely get a degree!

LIFE INSURANCE SPECIALIST

Name

Pamela K.

Location

Omaha, Nebraska

Education

Some college as well as insurance industry professional designations.

Total years in profession

18

Brief occupation description/goal of occupation

Handle customer complaints and questions on existing life insurance policies. Responsibilities also included processing of verification of coverage, running illustrations, and handling variable transfers.

Why did you choose this career path?

There are two things that are very important . . . life and money. Working in the life insurance industry, I have the responsibility to my customers of explaining how their policies work, showing sensitivity to people who have recently lost someone and providing them efficient servicing at a critical time in their lives. I also have the responsibility of managing variable transactions of separate sub-accounts of policies, which is very important. When you work in financial service, one mistake can cost millions.

What do you like about your occupation?

Being able to help people.

What do you dislike about your occupation?

Paperwork.

What are the misconceptions about your profession?

Some people believe that life insurance companies are out to "get" the average person; but in fact, my job is to educate people about how their policies work and be a liaison between the customer and my company.

On a scale of 1 to 10 (10 being great), how would you rate your occupation and why?

I would say 8. Overall, I love feeling that I helped someone, but like any profession, you have good and bad days.

What factors or former positions led to this occupation?

I started working in sales, then was brought into insurance through a call center customer service position handling life, health, critical care, and med supplement policies. I furthered my education through industry education. I felt I helped the most in life insurance. I was then offered the position I currently have and had to pass licensing for Securities and Exchange Commission purposes.

This opened the door to the financial aspects and further industry training.

What career choices were most helpful?

Education.

Did you have a mentor? If so, how did you find them? Did they help?

Call center managers at one position encouraged me and put in recommendations for my promotion. Also, a senator who was involved in an insurance society that I belonged to put in a good word to further my career.

What type of education was needed for your position?

Education is a continual process within the insurance industry.

Was your formal education necessary for this position?

Yes. Associate's degree or higher for entry level.

Do you have to update your career with ongoing training and certificates?

Yes. Series 6 (investment certifications).

When you were hired, did you receive professional training or was it basically "on-the-job training"?

Professional training.

In a typical week, are your hours fixed or flexible? On what days do you tend to work overtime?

Rotating: two months from 7:00 a.m. to 3:30 p.m., two months from 8:00 a.m. to 4:00 p.m., two months from 8:30 a.m. to 5:00 p.m.

What types of conflicts do you deal with?

People calling to advise of death of family members, fraud on part of policy owners, complaints.

What are your coworkers like?

Compassionate, hardworking, intelligent people.

What is management like?

Laid back, friendly, allows us to use our knowledge without "standing over us."

Is input accepted, or do you fare better as a "yes man"?

Very much so. Weekly team meetings encourage it.

Is your position secure, or are you frequently looking for the next opportunity?

Secure.

How important is/was networking or connections in finding your current or other positions? Is it a factor in advancement once you're on the job?

Very important, yes.

What would be your next career move?

Bachelor's degree completion (short-term goal), trainer position (short-term goal), then management opportunities (long-term goal).

How much fulfillment do you get out of your career?

A lot.

Do you feel that you are fairly compensated?

Yes, but I want more.

If you could choose again, how much would money be a factor?

A lot.

DATA OPERATOR

Name

Janet C.

Location

Southern Georgia

Education

Two-year computer science degree

Total years in profession

11 years

Brief occupation description/goal of occupation

Worked as a civilian computer/data operator/supply clerk (among other positions) at a military base for eleven years.

Why did you choose this career path?

I wanted to make my own living, to be able to support myself, and to prove to myself that I could support myself and be independent, even though I was/am handicapped and have been since birth.

What do you like about your occupation?

When I was working, I mostly liked all aspects of my work and most of the people I worked with and worked for every day.

What do you dislike about your occupation?

The hassles of dealing with certain people who can be unwilling to compromise and/or let you do your work to the best of your ability without constant criticism and ridicule—to the point that you even hate to go to work every day.

On a scale of 1 to 10 (10 being great), how would you rate your occupation and why?

For the first six to eight years that I worked at the base, I would have rated it around an 8, but toward the last two or three years—I would have rated it a 5 to 1.

What factors or former positions led to this occupation?

That is what I wanted to do, and that is what I went to college and acquired an associate's degree in computer science to do.

What career choices were most helpful?

The fact that I was able to prove myself worthy and reliable to the people I worked for during the many years that I worked for certain divisions and sections on the base.

What career choices were least helpful/detrimental?

Finding out that not everyone is out to help you get ahead in your career.

Did you have a mentor? If so, how did you find them? Did they help?

Yes. On my first job, the lady I worked closely with and who trained me was—and is—a dear friend of mine—one of the few people I could count on and trust.

What type of education was needed for your position?

A college background and hands-on experience in the computer field at that time.

Do you have to update your career with ongoing training and certificates?

I am retired now, but I still need refresher/newer courses in computer operations.

In a typical week, are your hours fixed or flexible? On what days do you tend to work overtime?

When I worked at the base, it was an eight-hour day, five days a week most of the time. If I could get back into the workforce, I would spend at least six hours per day, six days a week.

Is your work environment "hectic," "all work and no play," "serene," "laid back," or other? Briefly explain.

While I was working at the base, mostly hectic 80–90 percent of the time.

What would be your next career move?

My own home-based business—one that I could/would be successful at doing for the rest of my life and make a good living at.

If you could choose again, how much would money be a factor?

Money would be a factor a whole lot—to pay my bills, live my life without worrying where money was coming from or how my next bill would get paid, and still have enough money for food, clothes, rent, medicine, insurance, etc.

Would you choose the same career path?

Yes, I believe that I would.

Any comments or words of advice for someone entering your field?

Be careful, choose your career wisely, and make sure that it will be "the right choice for you," that you will be able to live off the benefits for the rest of your life without worrying about mounds of bills that you won't be able to pay—if it is possible!

PARALEGAL

Name
M. S.

Location
Springfield, Missouri

Education
Some college, plus specific paralegal training, in-house and mentoring.

Total years in profession
20+

Brief occupation description/goal of occupation
Provide assistance to attorney through legal research and writing, assistance at trial, data gathering, interviewing and witness preparation, and investigation of facts.

What do you dislike about your occupation?

Low pay and lack of respect for qualifications to perform tasks generally assigned to newly licensed associate attorneys. Always having to "prove" oneself.

What are the misconceptions about your profession?

That a paralegal can be "independent." A second misconception would be that paralegals are either disbarred attorneys or glorified secretaries.

On a scale of 1 to 10 (10 being great), how would you rate your occupation and why?

I would say 9. I have the satisfaction of knowing I've done my very best and, even though someone else is there to take the glory, the matter has been completed!

What factors or former positions led to this occupation?

Enactment of the Equal Employment Opportunity Act, love of research and attention to detail, and having found a niche in which I could utilize nearly every marketable skill I had.

What career choices were most helpful?

Human resources training, accounting, psychology, and teaching.

Did you have a mentor? If so, how did you find them? Did they help?

Yes. Judges and attorneys. Contacts through cases. A couple of the judges by whom I was mentored were instrumental in the writing of much of the legislation passed in the various areas of the law, so I had firsthand knowledge regarding the history of the reasons for enactment of many of our state statutes.

What type of education was needed for your position?

At that time, very little formal education was available unless one planned to attend law school and took pre-law, or as many criminal justice classes as possible.

Was your formal education necessary for this position?

In the early years, formal education in the paralegal field was not available.

Do you have to update your career with ongoing training and certificates?

Yes!

In a typical week, are your hours fixed or flexible? On what days do you tend to work overtime?

Flexible. Overtime depends upon caseload.

Is your work environment "hectic," "all work and no play," "serene," "laid back," or other? Briefly explain.

Any and all of the above.

What types of conflicts do you deal with?

Domestic relations; difficult heirs; people generally just wanting their day in court.

Do you interface with coworkers, groups, or vendors, or do you work alone?

Both/either. It depends upon the type of case.

What are your coworkers like?

Primarily "type A."

What is management like?

It depends upon the personality of the attorney.

Is input accepted, or do you fare better as a "yes man"?

It depends upon the personality of the attorney.

What issues have prevented your advancement?

Licensing.

How important is/was networking or connections in finding your current or other positions? Is it a factor in advancement once you're on the job?

Very important. Yes, it can definitely be a factor in advancement.

What would be your next career move?

Retirement.

Do you relocate often? Are there travel requirements?

It depends on the size of the firm and opportunities presented by the type of cases involved.

Do you prefer going to work or leaving? Why?

I always loved going to work. I like the excitement of discovery just around the corner, meeting and working with people, and helping people through difficult situations.

How much fulfillment do you get out of your career?

It depends. When we were up, we were way, way up. When we were down, we tried to be sure to put the skids on quickly and move on to other matters.

Do you feel that you are fairly compensated?

In the beginning, the work was done primarily for the experience. There was very little pay, very long hours, and no glory for the paralegal. As those in the legal field became more aware of the benefits of having a paralegal as a member of the delivery of legal services team, life and money became better.

Are the benefits and vacation schedule fair?

More and more attorneys are discovering the tax and other advantages of setting up retirement funds (401(k), SIMPLE, SEP, etc.) and discovering that the better the benefits offered, the easier it is to attract (and keep) highly qualified paralegals who remain loyal, thus avoiding costly high turnover rates and training costs.

If you could choose again, how much would money be a factor?

Probably not as much as I would like to think.

Would you choose the same career path?

Yes!

Any comments or words of advice for someone entering your field?

Be prepared to be constantly learning new things, to be required to maintain a level of continuing education, to be willing to labor very hard and stand back to let someone else take the credit. (The rule is that the paralegal's work must meld into the attorney's work product in such a manner as to be indistinguishable from the attorney's work product.) Until such time as there is some form of legislated regulation regarding the paralegal profession (such as has been enacted regarding nurse practitioners), the profession will be stymied as to how high its participants can fly.

NETWORK SECURITY CHANNEL SALES MANAGER

Name

Christopher H.

Location

San Diego, California

Education

Bachelor of Arts

Total years in profession

12

Brief occupation description/goal of occupation

Work with computer network security value-added resellers (VARs) and system integrators throughout the United States and Canada. Prospect, research, qualify, recruit, and train VARs to sell company's network security products. Help create successful VAR business plans, negotiate partnership terms and conditions, and sign VARs to premier reseller program. Conduct joint on-site end-user sales calls with partner to ensure timely closure. Work closely with VAR management on-site or via Webex to train and continually educate respective sales teams on how to effectively sell the company, products, and services. Represent company, often at regional and national trade shows. Achieve quarterly revenue goals with forty premier VAR accounts and distribution partners. Manage a pipeline and forecasts with VARs and territory sales representatives. Assist in the creation and delivery of VAR marketing campaigns. Deliver updated on-site VAR sales training presentations as new products and new product features are developed. Track leads provided by the company to the VARs and follow up to closure.

Why did you choose this career path?

I kind of fell into it by accident; I like technology, love relational selling, and like working with people.

What do you like about your occupation?

Development of longer-term relationships.

What do you dislike about your occupation?

Constant pressure to do more than the previous year.

What are the misconceptions about your profession?

That technology is always exciting and that business travel is glamorous.

On a scale of 1 to 10 (10 being great), how would you rate your occupation and why?

An 8. I like being in a field that involves many smart people.

What factors or former positions led to this occupation?

Reseller sales positions.

What career choices were most helpful?

Going from general networking to network security.

What career choices were least helpful/detrimental?

None . . . they all have prepared me for my role today and have helped shape the person who is typing right now.

Did you have a mentor? If so, how did you find them? Did they help?

I have an excellent mentor who has taught me many things about channel sales. I worked for her for a while until she decided to get out of the rat race, but we still chat often.

What type of education was needed for your position?

Technical training, network configuration and architecture, general technology terms.

Was your formal education necessary for this position?

No, but it helps.

Do you have to update your career with ongoing training and certificates?

I'm always trying to improve my skill set to make me more marketable as I grow older.

When you were hired, did you receive professional training or was it basically "on-the-job training"?

On the job all the way, baby . . . very little professional training.

In a typical week, are your hours fixed or flexible? On what days do you tend to work overtime?

Flexible. Mondays truly live up to their reputation.

Is your work environment "hectic," "all work and no play," "serene," "laid back," or other? Briefly explain.

Hectic . . . juggling many tasks at once, always trying to prioritize my day, having to shift things on the fly.

What types of conflicts do you deal with?

Corporate politics, idiotic policies/procedures, sales team competition.

What are your coworkers like?

Driven and dedicated, sometimes to a fault.

What is management like?

Shortsighted, uncaring at times.

Is input accepted, or do you fare better as a "yes man"?

Input is accepted until the point that management doesn't want to hear it anymore. The open-door policy that most management teams tout is a figment of their own imagination.

What issues have prevented your advancement?

My uncanny knack for speaking the truth that people sometimes don't want to hear. My own reluctance to venture into management because sales is in my blood.

Is your position secure, or are you frequently looking for the next opportunity?

My position is secure, but job security is dying out with my father's generation.

How important is/was networking or connections in finding your current or other positions? Is it a factor in advancement once you're on the job?

Networking is probably the single most important factor in finding my current and past jobs. It can also be a factor on the job.

What would be your next career move?

Starting my own company, calling my own shots . . . you know, Chris Inc.

Do you relocate often? Are there travel requirements?

I have relocated twice because I like new cities. The travel requirements can be strenuous at times, and other times a true joy.

How much fulfillment do you get out of your career?

My career is very fulfilling. I derive a good amount of self-worth from my work.

Do you feel that you are fairly compensated?

No, not compared to the going market rate.

If you could choose again, how much would money be a factor?

Money is not the be-all and end-all.

Would you choose the same career path?

Maybe, maybe not . . . I would love to go to law school.

Any comments or words of advice for someone entering your field?

Max your 401(k) out at the beginning of each calendar year and build up a reserve of six months' salary . . . you never know when you are going to be laid off.

CONCLUSION

The Keys to the Corporate Kingdom

"Go West, young man." —Horace Greeley

Career choice is not something to take frivolously. It will affect half of your life, or around forty years. With early preparation, maybe those forty years can be enjoyable. They don't have to be a daily grind—if you do the groundwork and determine what is best for you. And it doesn't even have to be forty years. Maybe you'll open your own business and sell it when you're fifty and make enough money to retire to an island. My hope is that from reading about the 101 different jobs and what people in those occupations have to say about them, you have gleaned some information about yourself and what may be the right occupation for you. What inspires you? What motivates you? What challenges you?

To help you in your pursuit of the best career for you, let's look at a few tools that will help any job hunter find success.

"The quality, not the longevity, of one's life is what is important." —Martin Luther King Jr.

Silence, Simplicity, and Sincerity

1. Listen more than you talk. Remember the old saying, "You have two ears and one mouth." I once interviewed with an obnoxious, verbose, stereotypical sales manager. During the interview, he babbled excessively, like society's jackass, for an hour. He was exceptionally proud of the "twelve selling traits" that all of his sales team had to know and learn verbatim. To him, these were the keys

535

to the kingdom, his Ten Commandments, his Bill of Rights, and the rules every salesperson should live by to acquire business.

He asked me to name what I'm finest at in sales, and I said, "listening." That was not on his list. It wasn't one of his selling traits, and he immediately knew it was a flaw in his childlike program. This decimated his world. He sat back with a baffled look and almost whimpered. It was hysterical. With all that prattling, he never listened to anyone but himself. He was Oz behind the curtain; his Achilles's heel was exposed. He begged me to work for him, but I declined. (A guy like that will say "work for" and not "with." When you hear that, walk.) In the end, after some digging, I found out he was less than honorable and, as you have just read, an utter buffoon.

This brings me to my next point.

2. The simple life is the easy life. You can only carry so much water. The more complications in your world, the less focused you'll be. Be ethical and don't take cheap shortcuts to debase people or the system—it will come back to haunt you. And if you end up in a new place and don't know anyone, take it from Harry Truman, who once quipped, "If you need a friend, get a dog."

A year after college I was meandering through life. I had a stable job, so I lived at home for a year to save money. During that time, I would hear others talk about the housing market and real estate. It was considered a good way to make a few bucks instead of renting. I believed the hype. Everyone was making a killing on real estate, so why not jump in? A buddy I grew up with bought into the idea, and we split a condo in a town a few miles away from where we grew up. So, at twenty-three I was settled down with a thirty-year mortgage. Not a great idea. Soon, I was bored at my job and wanted to make the big bucks, plus the real estate market was tanking—not a great combo. I tried to sell life insurance and lasted six months. Along with the real estate market, the economy wasn't doing great either and jobs were scarce. So, for the next few years I bounced around jobs while dealing with the condo and being the condo association president. My roommate was preparing to get married, and I was thinking of moving to California. We decided to rent the condo. We rented to people who knew the ins and outs of rental laws (professional renters), and soon they stopped paying the rent. At this point, I was in California, working two jobs to cover the bills, and my old roommate had to go to court and fight with judges to evict them. Is this the best way to spend your twenties? It may be best to put off such adult decisions until you're ready. For me, maybe graduate school would have been a better choice. For others, early marriages and children at twenty-two might be overwhelming. Life is going to be challenging you, so if you can choose the proper profession earlier, maybe you will be more prepared for the big decisions later, like real estate, marriage, children and other domestic issues. You don't have to grow up so fast. One day you will be old and you will want to be young again.

"If you build it, they will come." —Field of Dreams

3. Network. It sounds tacky and clichéd and shares more than one thing in common with speed dating—and yet, it's essential in almost every profession and should be leveraged as you begin exploring careers. Pleasant people will talk about their professions if you ask kindly, and the fascinating ones will tell you about their occupations. It's astounding how many people you meet who will help you out years later. The other day I got a message on LinkedIn from a business associate I've known for years—a good guy and doing well. He thanked me for inviting him to some tech event that increased his visibility, knowledge, and network. I don't recall the event, but it was nice to hear about his successes two decades later.

My last interview, in Massachusetts, was for a job with the state. It was the perfect opportunity for me, but I came in second to someone who was better connected. My brother, who worked for the state and had reason to interact with the new associate, said that at best she was a dolt—but a connected one.

A job hunter's single best resource is also the most obvious: people already in that area. But networking can be a hard thing to do, especially for people who want to check out a number of different fields before taking the plunge. For the majority of us who are not "connected," we must network with skill and perseverance. Ask someone about their career. Maybe you have an uncle Vito or you know someone who knows someone. If not, go to association events, call offices and ask for fifteen minutes of a person's time, and find people in the professions that interest you—maybe family friends, neighbors, anyone with a pulse and clean breath. Take advantage of meetings to talk with people about their career paths. Meetings are best so you can get them to open up and share their career notes. Talking to people, genuinely and with interest, will get you years ahead of the competition. Explain to them that you're trying to find the best career choice for yourself.

Networking to find the right career will take quite a while, so I recommend dedicating a year to talking to as many people as possible about their professions. Do it one on one. Why? When in a group, they will say, "I enjoy my work. It's interesting." Alone, however, they may be more honest. For many, it's hard to admit failure, even if failure is a legitimate way to learn—I have a PhD in it, and Christopher Cross could have written a song about it. Be prepared for it, as well as for politics and nonsense, and keep the goal as to what interests you and how you can acquire it in mind. Pick up the phone, make a call, and get an appointment.

Eye of the tiger, Rock. Eye of the tiger!

The Goldmine: Internships, Volunteering, and Entry-Level Jobs

Internships are often a second thought, but they're the career deep-dive goldmine. You can always listen to someone bloviate ad nauseam in a social setting about how spectacular their profession is, but when you actually labor with them and see what a day in their real life is, as the sweat drips and the disappointment builds from years of simmering apathy, you might have saved yourself from a toxic situation of stress and anxiety. This will make it much easier to discard professions that aren't relevant to your interests after you've had direct experience in them.

Some time ago, I attended physical therapy for back issues, and the receptionist at the office was a young intern. From the information I gathered, he had recently finished college and was in the midst of determining the best career vertical (health care, IT, law, and so on). To do so, he was interning for three months within each profession that interested him. If I recall, he had four industries that intrigued him. This kid was living the book! I don't know where or how he ended up, but his strategy was brilliant. He spent a year learning about four industries. I have no doubt that those who interviewed him were impressed by his preparation.

Draw inspiration from this man. Once you've narrowed down your interests to three or four professions, do some internships over the period of one year and go from there. Internships are an investment in your future. Some offer stipends, but if not, look at it as résumé building and commit to maybe one day a week. Some colleges offer co-op programs (Northeastern University is one) where students get six months of real-world experience, which usually lands them excellent opportunities after college. What an outstanding idea!

Also, associations are goldmines of info. I got hundreds of people to answer questionnaires that took up to thirty minutes to do. It's funny—close friends didn't fill them out, but when I connected with associations, I always got a few members to talk about their careers. This shows that if you are in an association, you usually love your career choice, whereas some of my close friends were either too lazy or too embarrassed by their occupational decision to want to answer questions about it.

When you connect with associations, ask about local companies that offer internships or assistance programs—aka, volunteering. Mirror a lawyer for a week and you'll get a better understanding of what an attorney does than anyone in law school. Bring them coffee and supplies, and just observe what they do. Maybe every Friday, you can volunteer to assist in their office in some manner. People want to help the next generation succeed. Usually, they want their profession to succeed too.

Entry-level jobs are your pre-graduate school or your entry into the adult world. It's where the clock on your forty years starts. Not only will you learn the basic tasks of said job, but you will also learn office politics, operations, and how a business runs. Maybe you will gain some specialty knowledge that will help boost your career or bore you to tears, which could also help you focus more on what you want to do. Is this the place for you? Watch and learn from seasoned associates. Ask them questions. Plus, you will meet so many people from different backgrounds and educational levels that your daily interactions will be the opposite of college. It's a potpourri of ages and views. You might meet an Ivy League MBA working with a seasoned veteran who made his way up the ranks via the mailroom with a GED. Take this as a challenge to learn how the real world works. Also, it's your first opportunity, so the company will task you with basic entry-level activities until you make the grade. This will happen almost everywhere, so hopefully you choose a career that interests you. As time meanders on, your college affiliation will become less important. No one will really care where you went to school or what your grades were. They'll just want to know, can this kid hustle? Also, check out Gorick Ng's book *Unspoken Rules*. Ng breaks down the glass walls and gives you insight into corporate thought. It's a great read on day 2 after graduation—on day 1 relax, you've earned it.

I read a poignant article by the former labor secretary Robert Reich called "Get a Job!" The secretary said to take "go for" jobs (as in "go for coffee") in an industry of interest. He suggested doing so in an inexpensive city, as it would be an entry-level position and the pay would be the same in most places. (Companies in less popular cities might offer a chance for more responsibilities as well.) He also agreed with the volunteering objective. Reich recommended putting off or skipping graduate school to determine where to work or what to do first. Sounds like he's already a fan of *Careers By the People*!

Three Lessons from the Thirty-Year Grind

> *"Three o'clock is always too early or too late for anything you want to do."* —Jean-Paul Sartre

"The Rule of Three" is a writing principle that suggests a trio of events or characters is more humorous, satisfying, or effective than other numbers. Three of the most important principles in the Declaration of Independence are written by Thomas Jefferson: life, liberty, and the pursuit of happiness. In 1962, while dining with the Western hemisphere's Nobel laureates, John F. Kennedy quipped, "I think this is the most extraordinary collection of talent, of human knowledge, that has ever been gathered at the White House—with the possible exception of when Thomas Jefferson dined alone." So why not follow one of the most prominent thinkers of all time? Here's the *Careers By the People*'s take on the Rule of Three. Enjoy.

1. **Pursue your passion.** Discovering your passion is a difficult process. You will have to dig for it, but once you find it, it'll be your gold.

From the questionnaires, I hope you can see who landed on their passion, who didn't, and how/why. What made them passionate about their choices? What made them indifferent?

My passion has been writing this book. To get this done, my obstacle was working full time in sales. My days were and are filled with eking out opportunities in tech. I search for projects day in and day out—as they say, "smiling and dialing"—to acquire business. The process doesn't end. It keeps going and the goal line continues moving. Months and months pass, as well as years, and it never stops . . . dig deeper, find more, repeat. It's never enough. The sales joke for the quarter, month, or year is always "Rinse and repeat." A generation may have passed, but, like my father did in painting hospitals, I do the same relentless activity, only with a different name. It's not physical labor, but it's a similar process, just behind a computer.

So, what drives you? What interests you? What do you read about that challenges you and makes you want to learn more? What did you read about here that amazed you? Your goal should be to pursue two or three topics that capture—and deeply hold—your attention. What is your favorite class? Which one appeals to you most and inspires you to want to learn more?

Think beyond your immediate environment as you search for your passion. One of my most impactful reads was Jacob Riis's *How the Other Half Lives*. Riis published his research in 1890 and caught America by storm. He genuinely wanted to see another America, and that's what you need to think about as you begin your search. What do you want to do and learn? You truly have to see this. As you try to determine what drives you and what your passion is, you have to look beyond your neighborhood and see how your other half lives. What will you find? What within these other worlds will captivate you and sustain your attention? Your first half is family, school, and friends. What is your other half?

From there, think about how you can take your passion to the next level. You need to know one topic through and through. Years ago, I watched an interview with Condoleezza Rice. She noted that one should concentrate on a subject and be the best at it. She specialized in Soviet and Eastern European affairs, which served as her stepping-stone from education to government to secretary of state.

Weed out the poor choices. I was awful at foreign languages, so that would have been a worse choice for me than sales. I was more blinded by science than Thomas Dolby. So, hone your focus, be Jeffersonian, and figure out your top three interests for your life, liberty, and pursuit of happiness.

2. **Be nice.** People will be more willing to help you if you ask for their time pleasantly. As a young, brash sales rep, it took me a while to learn this—but please believe that you catch more flies with honey than vinegar.

I hope this book inspires you to ask people in careers you're interested in questions, even if those careers aren't represented in this book. Figure out what you want to do and inquire, inquire, inquire—but do it kindly. For example: "Mr. Dooley, you're a civil engineer. Might you be able to spare fifteen minutes to talk to me about a day in the life of a civil engineer? What? I can spend a day with you? I'll take it! And I'd like to buy you lunch."

Be professional in your interactions with everyone, as you never know where their road may lead or how they might influence your future. Several of the more laconic associates I worked with turned out to be influential leaders in technology. Treat everyone fairly and with respect, as you never know who is connected to whom—or what their story is.

Don't disregard the elderly. Many have been through hell and back and will have a better understanding of the world than your college buddies or older siblings.

3. **Don't fear failure.** Oddly, I embrace it. One can learn a great deal from failure.

One person who always comes to mind is Abe Lincoln. Even if you only do a quick read about his failures, you'll find that the man's life was incredible. He went through the wringer and, per the majority of scholar surveys, is the gold standard of presidents. I once heard that he had a horrifically shrill voice—this, on top of his other obstacles. Model yourself after him. Have a forehead of steel. Know that you will be rejected, that you will not win at everything, that you will be passed over for weaker and more egotistical candidates. Don't get addicted to failure, but also don't care about half of it. When you play a board game, you don't really need to care if you win. It won't be in the record books; it won't be anywhere. We all know people who are hyper-competitive; sometimes that level of drive helps, and other times these people blow gaskets when they lose, which is awful for their health and the health of those around them. Do you really need to win at every social event, video game, or sporting activity? Don't cry over spilled milk, and keep in mind that failures make you stronger. As Henry Rollins bellowed, "Rise above!"

My issues, or, as one could say, "career ambitions" or goal to acquire a clear strategy, reemerged around the age of twenty-six. I was selling software in Massachusetts and getting no career satisfaction other than a short commute and some fun people to work with. We had a few different types of sales teams (large accounts, government, advertising, etc.) plus other divisions of the company, such as newsletter, catalog, etc. During talks with my manager, she asked me how I wanted my career to grow in the company. I built a career plan over the next few days comprising all my strengths and how I could team with the variety of divisions at the company, such as being a part of the sales team but also writing articles for the newsletter. Then I offered the plan to my manager, and she blissfully shot me down in minutes. She still ranks as one of my worst sales managers of all time. Looking back, I wonder if she was using some odd power play to keep me in line or let me know, as Tony Danza would say, "Who's the boss?" You got me, but sometimes people send you down a rat hole for their own personal enjoyment. Be aware of toxic places and anyone who uses the word "boss" to describe themselves. It's a word for little people who just acquired a little power. So, I jumped ship and grabbed a gig in a telemarketer company selling "800" numbers for easy cash. It was awful and depressing. Within three months, I was Double Live Gonzo. I wanted to make something of myself but had dug myself so deep into a hole it seemed impossible to get out. During this time, I took any job to pay the bills with the hope of finding some joy. This never occurred. To gain some semblance of stability, I acquired a simple temp gig at a bank in Boston. I thought it would help me determine what I needed to do to figure out what I wanted to do. Until I hit twenty-six, I wasn't that worried, but it was apparent I was failing. At the bank, I pushed around a mail cart, which required almost no skill. In social settings, I was the butt of many jokes, because in prior years I had boasted about my future value and net worth, only to see it all dwindle on a daily basis. This wasn't how life was supposed to go. I got the fancy degree, so where was the money? Where was the easy life? The only thing holding me back was me, so why wasn't it working? Why was I such a failure?

I concocted a theory that when men hit age twenty-six, they gain some insight as their career clock starts ticking. Mine was on overdrive. So this was my "thinking time," the stint that would allow me to figure it all out. I told my theory to my gym friend, Forrest. He laughed it off as he was a few years younger and of course had life's answers. As time passed, I stayed focused on my quest. One day, Forrest came into the gym totally distraught. "What's up, Forrest?" I asked. "I turned twenty-six last week, and you were right," he replied. "I'm a mess." At this point I was planning my future. I was talking to anyone I thought had a clue about ideas of what to do, where to do it, and how to find an exciting career. Maybe this book was in the making years before I realized it. One advisor told me to check out New Mexico and go where the growth was. I began carrying notebooks so I could record ideas, angles, and ways to get out of my rut. I took a part-time job to learn bartending and tried to live cheaply and save a few bucks. My choice was this—make it out of my slump or be another failed loser.

"Get busy living or get busy dying." —"Red" Redding, *The Shawshank Redemption*

The Bonus Round: Risk and Reward

The only reason I thought teaching might be fun was so I could add bonus questions to quizzes. In middle school, I always got a kick out of quizzes with bonus questions. So consider this your bonus round.

As I was talking about this book and careers in general with a very knowledgeable friend, he mentioned that a lot of career success has to do with "serendipity"—aka, being in the right place at the right time. You have to get out there and meet the right people, yes, but finding the best profession also comes down to trusting your decisions, challenging yourself, testing your boundaries, not always taking the easy road, and listening to new ideas. The potential is out there. You have to have the chutzpah to grab it. You have to believe in yourself and understand that you will take some beatings but that you will also get up and dust yourself off.

"Take risks: if you win, you will be happy; if you lose, you will be wise." —Anonymous

"This is Boston, not LA." —The Freeze

Consider my own story. In 1992, the Los Angeles riots devastated the city and had a ripple effect throughout the nation. My life in Boston felt like it paralleled LA. There was no hope or potential; I was going nowhere slowly. To help me out of my mental rut, I picked up the menial temp gig at the bank so I could hardly work and only think about my future. The temp gig was great as everyone I worked with was also at their lowest point in life, and it was a melting pot of ethnicities and sexual orientations. There were no rules, no caste system. No one was better than the other; we were all failures. Basically, it was the organized chaos Riis saw on the Lower East Side a hundred years earlier. To add to the social debasement, we were literally in the basement. It was that pathetic. Moreover, they were redoing the bank, so the place was a disaster.

I was still interviewing around Boston in case an excellent opportunity arose, even if it might have halted my plans to move west. One did—the opportunity with the state. In Massachusetts, working with the state is a dream for many as there's tons of growth—or, if you prefer to do nothing, that's acceptable too. For some reason, mooching off the state is a badge of pride.

The opportunity that was offered was exactly what I was looking for. I was dumbfounded that my dream job was actually available. Sadly, as noted earlier, I came in second and it was awarded to another—someone with fewer qualifications but better connections. By this time, I was fed up with Massachusetts and believed the "unspoken theory" that they used social profiling when hiring. I hope and pray this philosophy has been thwarted. This is/was known as the Masshole Life, and its hierarchy goes something like this:

One: "Did you go to Harvard or MIT?"

Two: "Who are you connected to?"

Three: "Let's hire from outside of local . . . "

So, in my mind, I didn't make the Masshole cut. On my twenty-eighth birthday, in 1993, I said farewell to Massachusetts and headed to LA, the land of millionaires and movie stars. I thought, what's there to lose? Many I knew disregarded it and said to go elsewhere or to give Boston another chance. I was done, though. I said, "I'm trusting my gut on this." I had a dumpy car packed and fueled up. The riots had ceased and TV was boring, so why not sell television scripts in warm weather? It made sense to me.

Let's just say that my first year in LA didn't go all that well. And yet, I persevered. I went back into technology sales and began moving my way up the ladder. Twenty-plus years passed, and no matter how much bashing LA gets, it was good to me.

"I'll figure it out" was the first line of this book. That was my younger, arrogant, impetuous, obnoxious self. At twenty-two, we all think we know more than anyone, that we will make history. It took me more than three decades to figure many things out. I hope you don't have to learn the hard way. Is hindsight twenty-twenty? I suppose, but I also didn't do the homework. I heard "easy money" and took it. My father told me he did the same thing. He was training to become an accountant but painting paid more, so he painted the same hospital over and over for more than thirty years. Begin at room 1, end at room 300, start all over again. Same with me in sales—constant repetition.

We read about 101 others and their paths—some good, some bad, and some just plain nutty. If I could go back and speak to that twenty-two-year-old self—or, better yet, that eighteen-year-old self—I would encourage him to study professions, look into internships, and meet with organizations and associations. I would tell my younger self to take the time to determine my best career path.

Listen to the ones who have walked the road before you and get their thoughts and insights. The surveys in *Careers By the People* offer some intriguing questions, ideas, and angles. Remember the Rule of Three. Find your passion. Be nice and professional to everyone. Don't fear failure; learn from it. Lastly, take some risks, as they often arrive with rewards. Maybe over the next thirty or forty years, you'll look forward not only to Mondays but also to every day of the week, as each one will offer joy, challenge, and a sense of self-worth. After all, Confucius was right when he said, "Choose a job you love, and you will never have to work a day in your life."

Aloha.

TALKING POINTS

Here are a few questions you can ask people that are in an occupation that interest you.

1. Mr. Murphy, might you have a few minutes to talk about your occupation?

2. How long have you been in your line of work?

3. On a scale of 1 to 10, what would you rate your satisfaction? 10 being the best.

4. How did you get your start?

5. What is a typical day like?

With those 5 questions you will know if you want to move forward with learning more or not. If you want to learn more, ask if you can shadow them for a day or if they offer internships. If not, thank them for their time.

For a field you are very interested in.

1. Ms. Dugan, I hear that you are in [field of your interest], is that correct?

2. Might you have a few minutes to talk about your occupation?

3. I am thinking of that as a career; do you have any suggestions?

4. What is a typical day like?

5. Does your firm offer internships or shadowing opportunities with associates? (If not, maybe she knows others that offer it or you could check with an association in that field.)

To learn about any occupation, you have to talk to and get to know the people in that field. Then, work with them via internships, volunteering or professional associations. LinkedIn is a great resource to find the people. Also, calling the company and asking for a meeting. Family and friends want to be helpful, but often they will sugarcoat it for you so you feel better and they feel better about themselves. Uncle Louie won't tell you that he's hated being a litigator for thirty years—it just won't happen. Most don't want to admit failure and defeat.

Prior to a meeting with someone in a career that interest you, reread the career questions within the book. Also, do as much reading on the profession as possible. Be prepared for the meeting. Learn as much about the person as possible via LinkedIn or the bio on their website. Arrive on time, prepared with questions, looking sharp, and ready to listen.

Welcome to the real world!